Lightning Components Developer Guide

Create Lightning components for Salesforce1 and Lightning Experience with JavaScript and Apex. Components can be used in standalone apps, Visualforce, Lightning App Builder, and Community Builder.

Lightning Components Developer Guide

CONTENTS

Chapter 1: What is the Lightning Component Framework? 1

What is Salesforce Lightning? 2
Why Use the Lightning Component Framework? 2
Open Source Aura Framework 3
Components 3
Events 4
Using the Developer Console 4
Online Version of this Guide 6

Chapter 2: Quick Start 7

Before You Begin 8
Create a Standalone Lightning App 9
    Optional: Install the Expense Tracker App 11
    Create an Expense Object 13
    Step 1: Create A Static Mockup 16
    Step 2: Create A Component for User Input 19
    Step 3: Load the Expense Data 25
    Step 4: Create a Nested Component 29
    Step 5: Enable Input for New Expenses 31
    Step 6: Make the App Interactive With Events 35
    Summary 39
Create a Component for Salesforce1 and Lightning Experience 41
    Load the Contacts 43
    Fire the Events 47

Chapter 3: Creating Components 51

Component Markup 52
Component Namespace 54
    Using the Default Namespace in Organizations with No Namespace Set 54
    Using Your Organization's Namespace 55
    Using a Namespace in or from a Managed Package 55
    Creating a Namespace in Your Organization 56
    Namespace Usage Examples and Reference 56

Contents

Component Bundles 60

Component IDs 61

HTML in Components 63

CSS in Components 63

Component Attributes 65

Component Composition 67

Component Body 70

Component Facets 72

Best Practices for Conditional Markup 73

Component Versioning 74

Using Expressions 76

    Dynamic Output in Expressions 77

    Conditional Expressions 78

    Value Providers 79

        $Browser 81

        $Locale 82

        $Resource 85

    Expression Evaluation 87

    Expression Operators Reference 88

    Expression Functions Reference 92

Using Labels 97

    Using Custom Labels 97

    Input Component Labels 98

    Dynamically Populating Label Parameters 99

    Setting Label Values via a Parent Attribute 100

Localization 101

Providing Component Documentation 103

Working with UI Components 106

    UI Events 109

    Using the UI Components 110

        Date and Time Fields 111

        Number Fields 113

        Text Fields 116

        Rich Text Fields 118

        Checkboxes 119

Radio Buttons 121
Buttons 123
Drop-down Lists 125
Field-level Errors 130
Menus 130
Supporting Accessibility 132
Button Labels 133
Help and Error Messages 133
Audio Messages 134
Forms, Fields, and Labels 134
Events 135
Menus 135

Chapter 4: Using Components 137
Adding Components to Apps 138
Add Lightning Components to Salesforce1 139
Add Lightning Components to Lightning Experience 140
Use Lightning Components in Visualforce Pages 141
Add Lightning Components to Any App with Lightning Out (Beta) 143
Lightning Out Requirements 145
Lightning Out Dependencies 145
Lightning Out Markup 146
Authentication from Lightning Out 149
Lightning Out Considerations and Limitations 149
Configure Components for Communities 150
Create Custom Page Layout Components for Communities 151
Configure Components for Lightning Pages and the Lightning App Builder 153
Configure Components for Lightning Experience Record Home Pages 156
Tips and Considerations for Configuring Components for Lightning App Builder . . 158

Chapter 5: Communicating with Events 161
Handling Events with Client-Side Controllers 162
Actions and Events 164
Component Events 166
Handling Component Events 168
Component Handling Its Own Event 168

Contents

Component Event Bubbling 168
Handling Component Events Dynamically 173
Component Event Example 173
Application Events 176
Handling Application Events 178
Application Event Example 178
Event Handling Lifecycle 181
Advanced Events Example 183
Firing Lightning Events from Non-Lightning Code 189
Events Best Practices 190
Events Anti-Patterns 191
Events Fired During the Rendering Lifecycle 192
Salesforce1 Events 197
System Events 198

Chapter 6: Creating Apps 201
App Overview 202
Designing App UI 202
Creating App Templates 202
Developing Secure Code 203
Content Security Policy Overview 204
LockerService Rules for Writing Secure Code 205
Salesforce Lightning CLI 206
Install Salesforce Lightning CLI 207
Use Salesforce Lightning CLI 207
Review and Resolve Problems 208
Salesforce Lightning CLI Rules 209
Salesforce Lightning CLI Options 220
Styling Apps 221
More Readable Styling Markup with the join Expression 222
Using External CSS 223
Tips for CSS in Components 225
Vendor Prefixes 226
Styling with Design Tokens 227
Tokens Bundles 227

Create a Tokens Bundle 228
Defining and Using Tokens 229
Using Expressions in Tokens 229
Extending Tokens Bundles 231
Using Standard Design Tokens 232
Using JavaScript 248
Accessing the DOM 250
Using External JavaScript Libraries 251
Working with Attribute Values in JavaScript 253
Working with a Component Body in JavaScript 254
Sharing JavaScript Code in a Component Bundle 256
Client-Side Rendering to the DOM 258
Invoking Actions on Component Initialization 262
Modifying Components Outside the Framework Lifecycle 263
Validating Fields 264
Throwing and Handling Errors 266
Calling Component Methods 269
Making API Calls 270
JavaScript Cookbook 271
Dynamically Creating Components 271
Detecting Data Changes 275
Finding Components by ID 276
Dynamically Adding Event Handlers 276
Dynamically Showing or Hiding Markup 277
Adding and Removing Styles 278
Which Button Was Pressed? 279
Using Apex 280
Creating Server-Side Logic with Controllers 281
Apex Server-Side Controller Overview 282
Creating an Apex Server-Side Controller 283
Returning Errors from an Apex Server-Side Controller 284
Calling a Server-Side Action 285
Queueing of Server-Side Actions 288
Abortable Actions 289
Storable Actions 290

Contents

Creating Components 292
Working with Salesforce Records 293
    CRUD and Field-Level Security (FLS) 296
    Saving Records 298
    Deleting Records 300
Testing Your Apex Code 303
Making API Calls from Apex 304
Controlling Access 304
Application Access Control 307
Interface Access Control 308
Component Access Control 308
Attribute Access Control 308
Event Access Control 309
Using Object-Oriented Development 309
What is Inherited? 310
Inherited Component Attributes 311
Abstract Components 313
Interfaces 314
    Marker Interfaces 315
Inheritance Rules 315
Caching with Storage Service 315
Initializing Storage Service 316
Using the AppCache 317
Enabling the AppCache 318
Loading Resources with AppCache 318
Distributing Applications and Components 319

Chapter 7: Debugging 321
Enable Debug Mode for Lightning Components 322
Salesforce Lightning Inspector Chrome Extension 322
Install Salesforce Lightning Inspector 323
Use Salesforce Lightning Inspector 323
    Component Tree Tab 324
    Performance Tab 327
    Transactions Tab 329

Event Log Tab 330

Actions Tab 332

Storage Tab 339

Log Messages 340

Warning Messages 342

Chapter 8: Reference 343

Reference Doc App 344

Supported aura:attribute Types 344

Basic Types 345

Object Types 347

Standard and Custom Object Types 348

Collection Types 349

Custom Apex Class Types 351

Framework-Specific Types 351

aura:application 352

aura:dependency 354

aura:event 355

aura:interface 356

aura:method 356

aura:set 358

Setting Attributes Inherited from a Super Component 358

Setting Attributes on a Component Reference 360

Setting Attributes Inherited from an Interface 360

INDEX 363

CHAPTER 1 What is the Lightning Component Framework?

In this chapter ...

- What is Salesforce Lightning?
- Why Use the Lightning Component Framework?
- Open Source Aura Framework
- Components
- Events
- Using the Developer Console
- Online Version of this Guide

The Lightning Component framework is a UI framework for developing dynamic web apps for mobile and desktop devices. It's a modern framework for building single-page applications engineered for growth.

The framework supports partitioned multi-tier component development that bridges the client and server. It uses JavaScript on the client side and Apex on the server side.

What is Salesforce Lightning?

Lightning includes the Lightning Component Framework and some exciting tools for developers. Lightning makes it easier to build responsive applications for any device.

Lightning includes these technologies:

- Lightning components give you a client-server framework that accelerates development, as well as app performance, and is ideal for use with the Salesforce1 mobile app and Salesforce Lightning Experience.

- The Lightning App Builder empowers you to build apps visually, without code, quicker than ever before using off-the-shelf and custom-built Lightning components. You can make your Lightning components available in the Lightning App Builder so administrators can build custom user interfaces without code.

Using these technologies, you can seamlessly customize and easily deploy new apps to mobile devices running Salesforce1. In fact, the Salesforce1 mobile app and Salesforce Lightning Experience are built with Lightning components.

This guide provides you with an in-depth resource to help you create your own standalone Lightning apps, as well as custom Lightning components that can be used in the Salesforce1 mobile app. You will also learn how to package applications and components and distribute them in the AppExchange.

Why Use the Lightning Component Framework?

The benefits include an out-of-the-box set of components, event-driven architecture, and a framework optimized for performance.

Out-of-the-Box Component Set

Comes with an out-of-the-box set of components to kick start building apps. You don't have to spend your time optimizing your apps for different devices as the components take care of that for you.

Rich component ecosystem

Create business-ready components and make them available in Salesforce1, Lightning Experience, and Communities. Salesforce1 users access your components via the navigation menu. Customize Lightning Experience or Communities using drag-and-drop components on a Lightning Page in the Lightning App Builder or using Community Builder. Additional components are available for your org in the AppExchange. Similarly, you can publish your components and share them with other users.

Performance

Uses a stateful client and stateless server architecture that relies on JavaScript on the client side to manage UI component metadata and application data. The client calls the server only when absolutely necessary; for example to get more metadata or data. The server only sends data that is needed by the user to maximize efficiency. The framework uses JSON to exchange data between the server and the client. It intelligently utilizes your server, browser, devices, and network so you can focus on the logic and interactions of your apps.

Event-driven architecture

Uses an event-driven architecture for better decoupling between components. Any component can subscribe to an application event, or to a component event they can see.

Faster development

Empowers teams to work faster with out-of-the-box components that function seamlessly with desktop and mobile devices. Building an app with components facilitates parallel design, improving overall development efficiency.

Components are encapsulated and their internals stay private, while their public shape is visible to consumers of the component. This strong separation gives component authors freedom to change the internal implementation details and insulates component consumers from those changes.

Device-aware and cross browser compatibility

Apps use responsive design and provide an enjoyable user experience. The Lightning Component framework supports the latest in browser technology such as HTML5, CSS3, and touch events.

Open Source Aura Framework

The Lightning Component framework is built on the open source Aura framework. The Aura framework enables you to build apps completely independent of your data in Salesforce.

The Aura framework is available at `https://github.com/forcedotcom/aura`. Note that the open source Aura framework has features and components that are not currently available in the Lightning Component framework. We are working to surface more of these features and components for Salesforce developers.

The sample code in this guide uses out-of-the-box components from the Aura framework, such as `aura:iteration` and `ui:button`. The `aura` namespace contains components to simplify your app logic, and the `ui` namespace contains components for user interface elements like buttons and input fields. The `force` namespace contains components specific to Salesforce.

Components

Components are the self-contained and reusable units of an app. They represent a reusable section of the UI, and can range in granularity from a single line of text to an entire app.

The framework includes a set of prebuilt components. You can assemble and configure components to form new components in an app. Components are rendered to produce HTML DOM elements within the browser.

A component can contain other components, as well as HTML, CSS, JavaScript, or any other Web-enabled code. This enables you to build apps with sophisticated UIs.

The details of a component's implementation are encapsulated. This allows the consumer of a component to focus on building their app, while the component author can innovate and make changes without breaking consumers. You configure components by setting the named attributes that they expose in their definition. Components interact with their environment by listening to or publishing events.

SEE ALSO:

Creating Components

Events

Event-driven programming is used in many languages and frameworks, such as JavaScript and Java Swing. The idea is that you write handlers that respond to interface events as they occur.

A component registers that it may fire an event in its markup. Events are fired from JavaScript controller actions that are typically triggered by a user interacting with the user interface.

There are two types of events in the framework:

- **Component events** are handled by the component itself or a component that instantiates or contains the component.
- **Application events** are handled by all components that are listening to the event. These events are essentially a traditional publish-subscribe model.

You write the handlers in JavaScript controller actions.

SEE ALSO:

Communicating with Events

Handling Events with Client-Side Controllers

Using the Developer Console

The Developer Console provides tools for developing your components and applications.

```
File ▾   Edit ▾   Debug ▾   Test ▾   Workspace ▾   Help ▾   <   >          ┌─────┐
                                                                          │  1  │
ExpenseTracker.app ×   formController.js ×   form.cmp ×   formHelper.js ×   form.css ×  └─────┘

 1  ▾ ({                                                          form                              ⏩
 2  ▾     getExpenses : function(component) {                     Ctrl + Shift + 1   COMPONENT
 3            var action = component.get("c.getExpenses");        Ctrl + Shift + 2   CONTROLLER
 4            var self = this;                           ┌─────┐  Ctrl + Shift + 3   HELPER
 5  ▾         action.setCallback(this, function(a) {     │  2  │  Ctrl + Shift + 4   STYLE
 6                component.set("v.expenses", a.getReturnValue()); Ctrl + Shift + 5   DOCUMENTATION   Create
 7                self.updateTotal(component);           └─────┘  Ctrl + Shift + 6   RENDERER        Create
 8            });                                                 Ctrl + Shift + 7   DESIGN          Create
 9            $A.enqueueAction(action);                           Ctrl + Shift + 8   SVG             Create
10        },
11                                                                       Bundle Version Settings
12  ▾     updateTotal : function(component) {
13            var expenses = component.get("v.expenses");                  ┌─────┐
14            var total = 0;                                               │  3  │
15  ▾         for(var i = 0 ; i < expenses.length ; i++){                  └─────┘
16                var e = expenses[i];
17                total += e.Amount__c;
18            }
```

The Developer Console enables you to perform these functions.

- Use the menu bar (1) to create or open these Lightning resources.

  - Application
  - Component
  - Interface
  - Event
  - Tokens

- Use the workspace (2) to work on your Lightning resources.
- Use the sidebar (3) to create or open client-side resources that are part of a specific component bundle.

  - Controller
  - Helper
  - Style
  - Documentation
  - Renderer
  - Design
  - SVG

For more information on the Developer Console, see Developer Console User Interface Overview.

SEE ALSO:

Salesforce Help: Open the Developer Console

Component Bundles

Online Version of this Guide

This guide is available online. To view the latest version, go to:

`https://developer.salesforce.com/docs/atlas.en-us.lightning.meta/lightning/`

CHAPTER 2   Quick Start

In this chapter ...

- Before You Begin
- Create a Standalone Lightning App
- Create a Component for Salesforce1 and Lightning Experience

The quick start steps you through building and running two simple apps: a standalone Lightning app for tracking expenses and a Lightning component to manage selected contacts in Salesforce1. You'll create all components from the Developer Console. A standalone app is directly accessible by going to the URL:

`https://<myDomain>.lightning.force.com/<namespace>/<appName>.app`
where `<myDomain>` is the name of your custom Salesforce domain

The standalone app you're creating accesses a custom object and displays its records. It enables you to edit a field on the records, capturing changes in a client-side controller and passing that information using a component event to an Apex controller, which then persists the data.

The Lightning component you're creating accesses the contact object and displays its records in Salesforce1. You'll use built-in Salesforce1 events to create or edit contact records, and view related cases.

Before You Begin

To work with Lightning apps and components , follow these prerequisites.

1. Create a Developer Edition organization
2. Define a Custom Salesforce Domain Name

Note: For this quick start tutorial, you don't need to create a Developer Edition organization or register a namespace prefix. But you want to do so if you're planning to offer managed packages. You can create Lightning components using the UI in **Enterprise**, **Performance**, **Unlimited**, **Developer** Editions or a sandbox. If you don't plan to use a Developer Edition organization, you can go directly to Define a Custom Salesforce Domain Name.

Create a Developer Edition Organization

You need an org to do this quick start tutorial, and we recommend you don't use your production org. You only need to create a Developer Edition org if you don't already have one.

1. In your browser, go to `http://bit.ly/lightningguide`.
2. Fill in the fields about you and your company.
3. In the `Email` field, make sure to use a public address you can easily check from a Web browser.
4. Type a unique `Username`. Note that this field is also in the *form* of an email address, but it does not have to be the same as your email address, and in fact, it's usually better if they aren't the same. Your username is your login and your identity on `developer.salesforce.com`, so you're often better served by choosing a username such as `firstname@lastname.com`.
5. Read and then select the checkbox for the `Master Subscription Agreement` and then click **Submit Registration**.
6. In a moment you'll receive an email with a login link. Click the link and change your password.

Define a Custom Salesforce Domain Name

A custom domain name helps you enhance access security and better manage login and authentication for your organization. If your custom domain is *universalcontainers*, then your login URL would be `https://universalcontainers.lightning.force.com`. For more information, see My Domain in the Salesforce Help.

Create a Standalone Lightning App

This tutorial walks you through creating a simple expense tracker app using the Developer Console.

The goal of the app is to take advantage of many of the out-of-the-box Lightning components, and to demonstrate the client and server interactions using JavaScript and Apex. As you build the app, you'll learn how to use expressions to interact with data dynamically and use events to communicate data between components.

Make sure you've created the expense custom object shown in Create an Expense Object on page 13. Using a custom object to store your expense data, you'll learn how an app interacts with records, how to handle user interactions using client-side controller actions, and how to persist data updates using an Apex controller.

After you create a component, you can include it in Salesforce1 by following the steps in Add Lightning Components to Salesforce1 on page 139. For packaging and distributing your components and apps on AppExchange, see Distributing Applications and Components on page 319.

 Note: Lightning components can be added to the Salesforce1 navigation menu, the App Launcher in Lightning Experience, as well as a standalone app. To create components that utilize Salesforce1-specific components and events that can be used only in Salesforce1 and Lightning Experience, see Create a Component for Salesforce1 and Lightning Experience on page 41.

The following image shows the expense tracker as a standalone app.

1. The form contains Lightning input components (1) that update the view and expense records when the **Submit** button is pressed.

2. Counters are initialized (2) with total amount of expenses and number of expenses, and updated on record creation or deletion. The counter turns red when the sum exceeds $100.

3. Display of expense list (3) uses Lightning output components and are updated as more expenses are added.

4. User interaction on the expense list (4) triggers an update event that saves the record changes.

These are the resources you are creating for the expense tracker app.

Resources	Description
expenseTracker Bundle	
`expenseTracker.app`	The top-level component that contains all other components
Form Bundle	

Resources	Description
form.cmp	A collection of Lightning input components to collect user input
formController.js	A client-side controller containing actions to handle user interactions on the form
formHelper.js	A client-side helper functions called by the controller actions
form.css	The styles for the form component
expenseList Bundle	
expenseList.cmp	A collection of Lightning output components to display data from expense records
expenseListController.js	A client-side controller containing actions to handle user interactions on the display of the expense list
Apex Class	
ExpenseController.apxc	Apex controller that loads data, inserts, or updates an expense record
Event	
updateExpenseItem.evt	The event fired when an expense item is updated from the display of the expense list

Optional: Install the Expense Tracker App

If you want to skip over the quick start tutorial, you can install the Expense Tracker app as an unmanaged package. Make sure that you have a custom domain enabled in your organization.

A package is a bundle of components that you can install in your org. This packaged app is useful if you want to learn about the Lightning app without going through the quick start tutorial. If you're new to Lightning components, we recommend that you go through the quick start tutorial. This package can be installed in an org without a namespace prefix. If your org has a registered namespace, follow the inline comments in the code to customize the app with your namespace.

 Note: Make sure that you have a custom domain enabled. Install the package in an org that doesn't have any of the objects with the same API name as the quick start objects.

To install the Expense Tracker app:

1. Click the installation URL link:
   https://login.salesforce.com/packaging/installPackage.apexp?p0=04t1a000000EbZp

2. Log in to your organization by entering your username and password.

3. On the Package Installation Details page, click **Continue**.

4. Click **Next**, and on the Security Level page click **Next**.

5. Click **Install**.

6. Click **Deploy Now** and then **Deploy**.

When the installation completes, you can select the **Expenses** tab on the user interface to add new expense records.

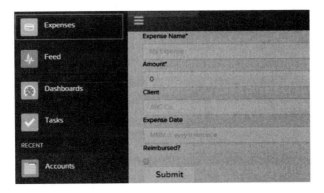

The Expenses menu item on the Salesforce1 navigation menu. If you don't see the menu item in Salesforce1, you must create a Lightning Components tab for expenses and include it in the Salesforce1 navigation menu. See Add Lightning Components to Salesforce1 for more information.

 Note: The Lightning component tab isn't available if you don't have a custom domain enabled in your org. Verify that you have a custom domain and that the Expenses tab is available in the Lightning Components Tabs section of the Tabs page.

Salesforce1 Navigation.

For Lightning Experience, the Expenses tab is available via the App Launcher in the custom app titled "Lightning".

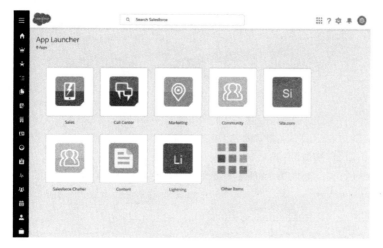

Next, you can modify the code in the Developer Console or explore the standalone app at `https://<myDomain>.lightning.force.com/<namespace>/expenseTracker.app`, where `<myDomain>` is the name of your custom Salesforce domain.

 Note: To delete the package, from Setup, enter `Installed Package` in the `Quick Find` box, select **Installed Package**, and then delete the package.

Create an Expense Object

Create an expense object to store your expense records and data for the app.

You'll need to create this object if you're following the tutorial at Create a Standalone Lightning App on page 9.

1. From your management settings for custom objects, if you're using Salesforce Classic, click **New Custom Object**, or if you're using Lightning Experience, select **Create > Custom Object**.

2. Define the custom object.
   - For the `Label`, enter `Expense`.
   - For the `Plural Label`, enter `Expenses`.

3. Click **Save** to finish creating your new object. The Expense detail page is displayed.

    Note: If you're using a namespace prefix, you might see `namespace__Expense__c` instead of `Expense__c`.

4. On the Expense detail page, add the following custom fields.

Field Type	Field Label
Number(16, 2)	Amount
Text (20)	Client
Date/Time	Date
Checkbox	Reimbursed?

When you finish creating the custom object, your Expense definition detail page should look similar to this.

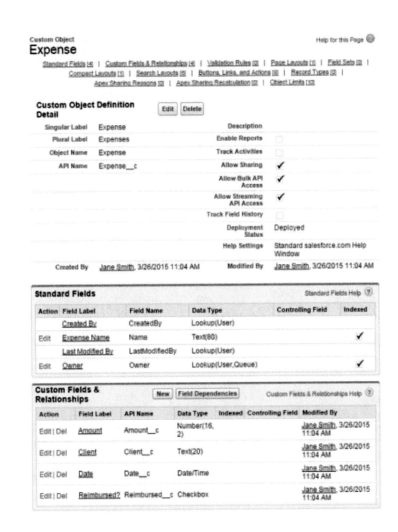

5. Create a custom object tab to display your expense records.

   a. From Setup, enter `Tabs` in the `Quick Find` box, then select **Tabs**.

   b. In the Custom Object Tabs related list, click **New** to launch the New Custom Tab wizard.

      • For the `Object`, select `Expense`.

      • For the `Tab Style`, click the lookup icon and select the `Credit Card` icon.

   c. Accept the remaining defaults and click **Next**.

   d. Click **Next** and **Save** to finish creating the tab.

In Salesforce Classic, you should now see a tab for your Expenses at the top of the screen. In Lightning Experience, click the App Launcher icon (▦) and then the `Other Items` icon. You should see `Expenses` in the Items list.

6. Create a few expense records.

   a. Click the Expenses tab and click **New**.

   b. Enter the values for these fields and repeat for the second record.

Expense Name	Amount	Client	Date	Reimbursed?
Lunch	21		4/1/2015 12:00 PM	Unchecked
Dinner	70	ABC Co.	3/30/2015 7:00 PM	Checked

Step 1: Create A Static Mockup

Create a static mockup in a `.app` file, which is the entry point for your app. It can contain other components and HTML markup.

The following flowchart summarizes the data flow in the app. The app retrieves data from the records through a combination of client-side controller and helper functions, and an Apex controller, which you'll create later in this quick start.

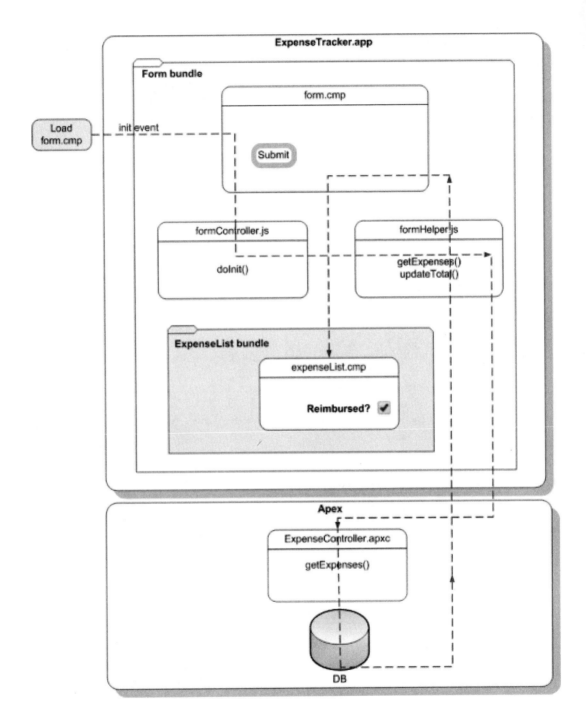

This tutorial uses the Lightning Design System CSS framework, which provides a look and feel that's consistent with Lightning Experience.

1. Go to `https://www.lightningdesignsystem.com/resources/downloads` and download the latest version of the Design System Unmanaged Package. At the prompt, install the unmanaged package in your organization. Your installation is successful when you see the SLDS package on the Installed Packages page.

2. Open the Developer Console.

   a. In Salesforce Classic, click `Your Name` > **Developer Console**.

   b. In Lightning Experience, click the quick access menu (⚙), and then **Developer Console**.

3. Create a new Lightning app. In the Developer Console, click **File** > **New** > **Lightning Application**.

4. Enter `expenseTracker` for the `Name` field in the New Lightning Bundle popup window. This creates a new app, `expenseTracker.app`.

5. In the source code editor, enter this code.

```
<aura:application>
    <!-- Include the SLDS static resource (adjust to match package
version) -->
    <ltng:require styles="{!$Resource.SLDSv1 +

'/assets/styles/salesforce-lightning-design-system-ltng.css'}"/>


    <div class="slds">
        <div class="slds-page-header">
          <div class="slds-grid">
            <div class="slds-col slds-has-flexi-truncate">
              <p class="slds-text-heading--label">Expenses</p>
              <div class="slds-grid">
                <div class="slds-grid slds-type-focus
slds-no-space">
                  <h1 class="slds-text-heading--medium
slds-truncate" title="My Expenses">My Expenses</h1>
                </div>
              </div>
            </div>
          </div>
        </div>
    </div>
</aura:application>
```

An application is a top-level component and the main entry point to your components. It can include components and HTML markup, such as `<div>` and `<header>` tags. The CSS classes are provided by the Lightning Design System CSS framework.

6. Save your changes and click **Preview** in the sidebar to preview your app. Alternatively, navigate to
   `https://<myDomain>.lightning.force.com/<namespace>/expenseTracker.app`, where `<myDomain>` is the name of your custom Salesforce domain. If you're not using a namespace, your app is available at `/c/expenseTracker.app`.
   You should see the header `My Expenses`.

SEE ALSO:

Salesforce Help: Open the Developer Console

aura:application

Step 2: Create A Component for User Input

Components are the building blocks of an app. They can be wired up to an Apex controller class to load your data. The component you create in this step provides a form that takes in user input about an expense, such as expense amount and date.

1. Click **File** > **New** > **Lightning Component**.

2. Enter `form` for the `Name` field in the New Lightning Bundle popup window. This creates a new component, `form.cmp`.

3. In the source code editor, enter this code.

    Note: The following code creates an input form that takes in user input to create an expense, which works in both a standalone app, and in Salesforce1 and Lightning Experience. For apps specific to Salesforce1 and Lightning Experience, you can use `force:createRecord` to open the create record page.

```
<aura:component implements="force:appHostable">
  <ltng:require styles="{!$Resource.SLDSv1 +

'/assets/styles/salesforce-lightning-design-system-ltng.css'}"/>

  <aura:attribute name="expenses" type="Expense__c[]"/>
  <aura:attribute name="newExpense" type="Expense__c"
       default="{ 'sobjectType': 'Expense__c',
                    'Name': '',
```

```
                                'Amount__c': 0,
                                'Client__c': '',
                                'Date__c': '',
                                'Reimbursed__c': false
                        }"/>
    <!-- If you registered a namespace, replace the previous
aura:attribute tags with the following -->
    <!-- <aura:attribute name="expenses"
type="myNamespace.Expense__c[]"/>
    <aura:attribute name="newExpense" type="myNamespace__Expense__c"

                default="{ 'sobjectType':
'myNamespace__Expense__c',
                            'Name': '',
                            'myNamespace__Amount__c': 0,
                            'myNamespace__Client__c': '',
                            'myNamespace__Date__c': '',
                            'myNamespace__Reimbursed__c': false
                        }"/> -->
    <!-- Attributes for Expense Counters -->
    <aura:attribute name="total" type="Double" default="0.00" />
    <aura:attribute name="exp" type="Double" default="0" />


    <!-- Input Form using components -->
    <div class="container">
      <form class="slds-form--stacked">
        <div class="slds-form-element slds-is-required">
          <div class="slds-form-element__control">


          <!-- If you registered a namespace,
                the attributes include your namespace.
                For example,
value="{!v.newExpense.myNamespace__Amount__c}" -->

            <ui:inputText aura:id="expname" label="Expense Name"
                        class="slds-input"
                        labelClass="slds-form-element__label"
                        value="{!v.newExpense.Name}"
                        required="true"/>
          </div>
        </div>
        <div class="slds-form-element slds-is-required">
          <div class="slds-form-element__control">
            <ui:inputNumber aura:id="amount" label="Amount"
```

```
                        class="slds-input"
                        labelClass="slds-form-element__label"

                        value="{!v.newExpense.Amount__c}"
                        placeholder="20.80" required="true"/>

        </div>
      </div>
      <div class="slds-form-element">
        <div class="slds-form-element__control">
          <ui:inputText aura:id="client" label="Client"
                        class="slds-input"
                        labelClass="slds-form-element__label"
                        value="{!v.newExpense.Client__c}"
                        placeholder="ABC Co."/>
        </div>
      </div>
      <div class="slds-form-element">
        <div class="slds-form-element__control">
          <ui:inputDateTime aura:id="expdate" label="Expense
Date"
                            class="slds-input"
labelClass="slds-form-element__label"
                            value="{!v.newExpense.Date__c}"
                            displayDatePicker="true"/>
        </div>
      </div>
      <div class="slds-form-element">
        <ui:inputCheckbox aura:id="reimbursed"
label="Reimbursed?"
                            class="slds-checkbox"

labelClass="slds-form-element__label"

value="{!v.newExpense.Reimbursed__c}"/>
        <ui:button label="Submit"
                    class="slds-button slds-button--neutral"
                    labelClass="label"
                    press="{!c.createExpense}"/>
      </div>
    </form>
  </div><!-- ./container-->
```

```
<!-- Expense Counters -->
<div class="container slds-p-top--medium">
      <div class="row">
          <div class="slds-tile ">
              <!-- Make the counter red if total amount is more
than 100 -->
              <div class="{!v.total >= 100
                    ? 'slds-notify slds-notify--toast
slds-theme--error slds-theme--alert-texture'
                    : 'slds-notify slds-notify--toast
slds-theme--alert-texture'}">
                  <p class="slds-tile__title
slds-truncate">Total Expenses</p>
                  $<ui:outputNumber class="slds-truncate"
value="{!v.total}" format=".00"/>
              </div>
          </div>
          <div class="slds-tile ">
              <div class="slds-notify slds-notify--toast
slds-theme--alert-texture">
                  <p class="slds-tile__title
slds-truncate">No. of Expenses</p>
                  <ui:outputNumber class="slds-truncate"
value="{!v.exp}"/>
              </div>
          </div>
      </div>
   </div>
       <!-- Display expense records -->
       <div class="container slds-p-top--medium">
          <div id="list" class="row">
              <aura:iteration items="{!v.expenses}"
var="expense">

                  <!-- If you're using a namespace,
                     use the format
                     {!expense.myNamespace__myField__c}
instead. -->

                  <p>{!expense.Name}, {!expense.Client__c},
                     {!expense.Amount__c}, {!expense.Date__c},

                     {!expense.Reimbursed__c}</p>
```

```
                    </aura:iteration>
                </div>
            </div>
</aura:component>
```

Components provide a rich set of attributes and browser event support. Attributes are typed fields that are set on a specific instance of a component, and can be referenced using an expression syntax. All `aura:attribute` tags have name and type values. For more information, see Supported aura:attribute Types on page 344.

The attributes and expressions here will become clearer as you build the app. `{!v.exp}` evaluates the number of expenses records and `{!v.total}` evaluates the total amount. `{!c.createExpense}` represents the client-side controller action that runs when the **Submit** button (1) is clicked, which creates a new expense. The `press` event in `ui:button` enables you to wire up the action when the button is pressed.

EXPENSES

My Expenses

Expense Name*

Amount*

0

Client

ABC Co.

Expense Date

📅   📅

Reimbursed? ☐

| Submit | | 1 |

The expression `{!v.expenses}` wires up the component to the expenses object. `var="expense"` denotes the name of the variable to use for each item inside the iteration. `{!expense.Client__c}` represents data binding to the client field in the expense object.

> ✅ Note: The default value for `newExpense` of type `Expense__c` must be initialized with the correct fields, including `sobjectType`. Initializing the default value ensures that the expense is saved in the correct format.

4. Click **STYLE** in the sidebar to create a new resource named `form.css`. Enter these CSS rule sets.

```
.THIS .uiInputDateTime .datePicker-openIcon {
    position: absolute;
     left: 45%;
     top: 45%;
}


.THIS .uiInputDateTime .timePicker-openIcon {
    position: absolute;
     left: 95%;
     top: 70%;
}


.THIS .uiInputDefaultError li {
   list-style: none;
}
```

> Note: `THIS` is a keyword that adds namespacing to CSS to prevent any conflicts with another component's styling. The `.uiInputDefaultError` selector styles the default error component when you add field validation in Step 5: Enable Input for New Expenses on page 31.

5. Add the component to the app. In `expenseTracker.app`, add the new component to the markup.

   This step adds `<c:form />` to the markup. If you're using a namespace, you can use `<myNamespace:form />` instead. If you haven't set a namespace prefix for your organization, use the default namespace `c` when referencing components that you've created.

```
<aura:application>
    <ltng:require styles="{!$Resource.SLDSv1 +

'/assets/styles/salesforce-lightning-design-system-ltng.css'}"/>


    <div class="slds">
        <div class="slds-page-header">
          <div class="slds-grid">
            <div class="slds-col slds-has-flexi-truncate">
              <p class="slds-text-heading--label">Expenses</p>
              <div class="slds-grid">
                <div class="slds-grid slds-type-focus
slds-no-space">
```

```
                    <h1 class="slds-text-heading--medium
        slds-truncate" title="My Expenses">My Expenses</h1>
                    </div>
                </div>
            </div>
        </div>
    </div>

        <div class="slds-col--padded slds-p-top--large">
            <c:form />
        </div>
    </div>
    </aura:application>
```

6. Save your changes and click **Update Preview** in the sidebar to preview your app. Alternatively, reload your browser.

     Note: In this step, the component you created doesn't display any data since you haven't created the Apex controller class yet.

Good job! You created a component that provides an input form and view of your expenses. Next, you'll create the logic to display your expenses.

SEE ALSO:

Component Markup

Component Body

Step 3: Load the Expense Data

Load expense data using an Apex controller class. Display this data via component attributes and update the counters dynamically.

Create the expense controller class.

1. Click **File** > **New** > **Apex Class** and enter *ExpenseController* in the **New Class** window. This creates a new Apex class, ExpenseController.apxc.

2. Enter this code.

```
public with sharing class ExpenseController {
    @AuraEnabled
    public static List<Expense__c> getExpenses() {
```

```
      // Perform isAccessible() check here
      return [SELECT Id, Name, Amount__c, Client__c, Date__c,
      Reimbursed__c, CreatedDate FROM Expense__c];
   }
}
```

The `getExpenses()` method contains a SOQL query to return all expense records. Recall the syntax `{!v.expenses}` in `form.cmp`, which displays the result of the `getExpenses()` method in the component markup.

 Note: For more information on using SOQL, see the *Force.com SOQL and SOSL Reference*.

`@AuraEnabled` enables client- and server-side access to the controller method. Server-side controllers must be static and all instances of a given component share one static controller. They can return or take in any types, such as a List or Map.

 Note: For more information on server-side controllers, see Apex Server-Side Controller Overview on page 282.

3. In `form.cmp`, update the `aura:component` tag to include the `controller` attribute.

```
<aura:component controller="ExpenseController">
```

 Note: If your org has a namespace, use `controller="myNamespace.ExpenseController"` instead.

4. Add an `init` handler to load your data on component initialization.

```
<aura:component controller="ExpenseController">
  <aura:handler name="init" value="{!this}" action="{!c.doInit}"
 />
  <!-- Other aura:attribute tags here -->
  <!-- Other code here -->
</aura:component>
```

On initialization, this event handler runs the `doInit` action that you're creating next. This `init` event is fired before component rendering.

5. Add the client-side controller action for the `init` handler. In the sidebar, click **CONTROLLER** to create a new resource, `formController.js`. Enter this code.

```
({
    doInit : function(component, event, helper) {
       //Update expense counters
       helper.getExpenses(component);
```

```
      },//Delimiter for future code
})
```

During component initialization, the expense counters should reflect the latest sum and total number of expenses, which you're adding next using a helper function, `getExpenses(component)`.

> Note: A client-side controller handles events within a component and can take in three parameters: the component to which the controller belongs, the event that the action is handling, and the helper if it's used. A helper is a resource for storing code that you want to reuse in your component bundle, providing better code reusability and specialization. For more information about using client-side controllers and helpers, see Handling Events with Client-Side Controllers on page 162 and Sharing JavaScript Code in a Component Bundle on page 256.

6. Create the helper function to display the expense records and dynamically update the counters. Click **HELPER** to create a new resource, `formHelper.js` and enter this code.

```
({
  getExpenses: function(component) {
        var action = component.get("c.getExpenses");
        action.setCallback(this, function(response) {
            var state = response.getState();
            if (component.isValid() && state === "SUCCESS") {
                component.set("v.expenses",
response.getReturnValue());
                this.updateTotal(component);
            }
        });
        $A.enqueueAction(action);
  },
  updateTotal : function(component) {
      var expenses = component.get("v.expenses");
      var total = 0;
      for(var i=0; i<expenses.length; i++){
          var e = expenses[i];

          //If you're using a namespace, use
e.myNamespace__Amount__c instead
          total += e.Amount__c;
      }
      //Update counters
      component.set("v.total", total);
```

```
        component.set("v.exp", expenses.length);
    },//Delimiter for future code

})
```

`component.get("c.getExpenses")` returns an instance of the server-side action.
`action.setCallback()` passes in a function to be called after the server responds. In
`updateTotal`, you are retrieving the expenses and summing up their amount values and
length of expenses, setting those values on the `total` and `exp` attributes.

 Note: `$A.enqueueAction(action)` adds the action to the queue. All the action
calls are asynchronous and run in batches. For more information about server-side actions,
see Calling a Server-Side Action on page 285.

7. Save your changes and reload your browser.

   You should see the expense records created in Create an Expense Object on page 13. The counters
   aren't working at this point as you'll be adding the programmatic logic later.

Your app now retrieves the expense object and displays its records as a list, iterated over by
`aura:iteration`. The counters now reflect the total sum and number of expenses.

In this step, you created an Apex controller class to load expense data. `getExpenses()` returns the
list of expense records. By default, the framework doesn't call any getters. To access a method, annotate
the method with `@AuraEnabled`, which exposes the data in that method. Only methods that are
annotated with `@AuraEnabled` in the controller class are accessible to the components.

Component markup that uses the `ExpenseController` class can display the expense name or id
with the `{!expense.name}` or `{!expense.id}` expression, as shown in Step 2: Create A
Component for User Input on page 19.

▪▪ **Beyond the Basics**

Client-side controller definitions are surrounded by brackets and curly braces. The curly braces
denotes a JSON object, and everything inside the object is a map of name-value pairs. For example,
`updateTotal` is a name that corresponds to a client-side action, and the value is a function.
The function is passed around in JavaScript like any other object.

SEE ALSO:
   CRUD and Field-Level Security (FLS)

Step 4: Create a Nested Component

As your component grows, you want to break it down to maintain granularity and encapsulation. This step walks you through creating a component with repeating data and whose attributes are passed to its parent component. You'll also add a client-side controller action to load your data on component initialization.

1. Click **File** > **New** > **Lightning Component**.

2. Enter *expenseList* in the New Lightning Bundle window. This creates a new component, `expenseList.cmp`.

3. In `expenseList.cmp`, enter this code.

    Note: Use the API name of the fields to bind the field values. For example, if you're using a namespace, you must use `{!v.expense.myNamespace__Amount__c}` instead of `{!v.expense.Amount__c}`.

```
<aura:component>
    <aura:attribute name="expense" type="Expense__c"/>
    <!-- Color the item blue if the expense is reimbursed -->
    <div class="slds-card">
    <!-- If you registered a namespace,
            use v.expense.myNamespace__Reimbursed__c == true
 instead. -->
    <div class="{!v.expense.Reimbursed__c == true
                    ? 'slds-theme--success' :
'slds-theme--warning'}">
        <header class="slds-card__header slds-grid
grid--flex-spread">
            <a aura:id="expense" href="{!'/' + v.expense.Id}">

                <h3>{!v.expense.Name}</h3>
            </a>
        </header>

      <section class="slds-card__body">
        <!-- If you registered a namespace,
            use v.expense.myNamespace__Reimbursed__c instead.
 -->

        <div class="slds-tile slds-hint-parent">
            <p class="slds-tile__title slds-truncate">Amount:

            <ui:outputNumber value="{!v.expense.Amount__c}"
```

```
    format=".00"/>
                </p>
        <p class="slds-truncate">Client:
            <ui:outputText value="{!v.expense.Client__c}"/>
        </p>
        <p class="slds-truncate">Date:
            <ui:outputDateTime value="{!v.expense.Date__c}" />
        </p>
        <p class="slds-truncate">Reimbursed?
            <ui:inputCheckbox value="{!v.expense.Reimbursed__c}"
 click="{!c.update}"/>
        </p>
    </div>
        </section>
    </div>
    </div>
</aura:component>
```

Instead of using `{!expense.Amount__c}`, you're now using
`{!v.expense.Amount__c}`. This expression accesses the `expense` object and the
`amount` values on it.

Additionally, `href="{!'/' + v.expense.Id}"` uses the expense ID to set the link to
the detail page of each expense record.

4. In `form.cmp`, update the `aura:iteration` tag to use the new nested component,
   `expenseList`. Locate the existing `aura:iteration` tag.

```
<aura:iteration items="{!v.expenses}" var="expense">
    <p>{!expense.Name}, {!expense.Client__c},
{!expense.Amount__c}, {!expense.Date__c},
{!expense.Reimbursed__c}</p>
</aura:iteration>
```

Replace it with an `aura:iteration` tag that uses the `expenseList` component.

```
<aura:iteration items="{!v.expenses}" var="expense">
    <!--If you're using a namespace, use myNamespace:expenseList
 instead-->
    <c:expenseList expense="{!expense}"/>
</aura:iteration>
```

Notice how the markup is simpler as you're just passing each `expense` record to the
`expenseList` component, which handles the display of the expense details.

5. Save your changes and reload your browser.

You created a nested component and passed its attributes to a parent component. Next, you'll learn how to process user input and update the expense object.

▚ Beyond the Basics

When you create a component, you are providing the definition of that component. When you put the component in another component, you are create a reference to that component. This means that you can add multiple instances of the same component with different attributes. For more information about component attributes, see Component Composition on page 67.

SEE ALSO:

Component Attributes

Step 5: Enable Input for New Expenses

When you enter text into the form and press Submit, you want to insert a new expense record. This action is wired up to the button component via the `press` attribute.

The following flowchart shows the flow of data in your app when you create a new expense. The data is captured when you click the **Submit** button in the component `form.cmp`, processed by your JavaScript code and sent to the server-side controller to be saved as a record. Data from the records is displayed in the nested component you created in the previous step.

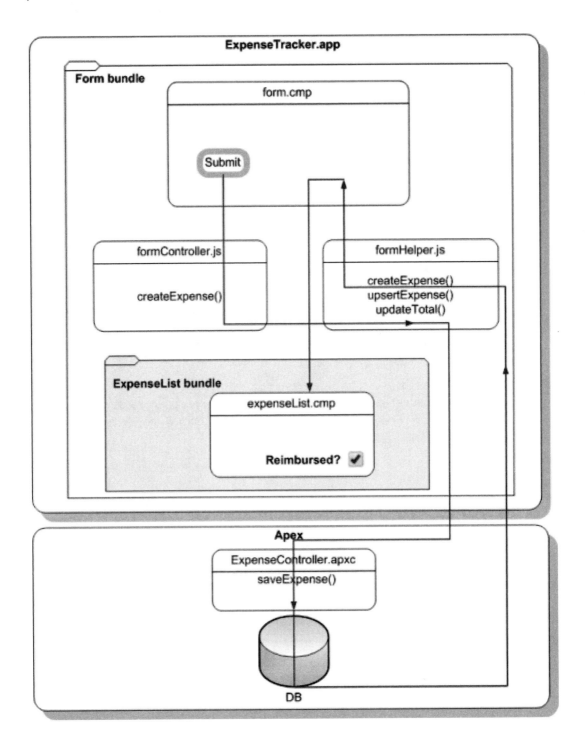

First, update the Apex controller with a new method that inserts or updates the records.

1. In the `ExpenseController` class, enter this code below the `getExpenses()` method.

```
@AuraEnabled
public static Expense__c saveExpense(Expense__c expense) {

    // Perform isUpdateable() check here
    upsert expense;
    return expense;
}
```

The `saveExpense()` method enables you to insert or update an expense record using the `upsert` operation.

📝 Note: Fore more information about the `upsert` operation, see the *Apex Developer Guide*.

2. Create the client-side controller action to create a new expense record when the **Submit** button is pressed. In `formController.js`, add this code after the `doInit` action.

```
createExpense : function(component, event, helper) {
    var amtField = component.find("amount");
    var amt = amtField.get("v.value");
    if (isNaN(amt)||amt==''){
        amtField.set("v.errors", [{message:"Enter an expense
amount."}]);
    }
    else {
        amtField.set("v.errors", null);
        var newExpense = component.get("v.newExpense");
        helper.createExpense(component, newExpense);
    }
},//Delimiter for future code
```

`createExpense` validates the amount field using the default error handling of input components. If the validation fails, we set an error message in the `errors` attribute of the input component. For more information on field validation, see Validating Fields on page 264.

Notice that you're passing in the arguments to a helper function `helper.createExpense()`, which then triggers the Apex class `saveExpense`.

📝 Note: Recall that you specified the `aura:id` attributes in Step 2: Create A Component for User Input on page 19. `aura:id` enables you to find the component by name using the syntax `component.find("amount")` within the scope of this component and its controller.

3. Create the helper function to handle the record creation. In `formHelper.js`, add these helper functions after the `updateTotal` function.

```
createExpense: function(component, expense) {
    this.upsertExpense(component, expense, function(a) {
        var expenses = component.get("v.expenses");
        expenses.push(a.getReturnValue());
        component.set("v.expenses", expenses);
        this.updateTotal(component);
    });
},
upsertExpense : function(component, expense, callback) {
    var action = component.get("c.saveExpense");
    action.setParams({
        "expense": expense
    });
    if (callback) {
      action.setCallback(this, callback);
    }
    $A.enqueueAction(action);
}
```

`createExpense` calls `upsertExpense`, which defines an instance of the `saveExpense` server-side action and sets the `expense` object as a parameter. The callback is executed after the server-side action returns, which updates the records, view, and counters. `$A.enqueueAction(action)` adds the server-side action to the queue of actions to be executed.

 Note: Different possible action states are available and you can customize their behaviors in your callback. For more information on action callbacks, see Calling a Server-Side Action.

4. Save your changes and reload your browser.

5. Test your app by entering a new expense record with field values: `Breakfast, 10, ABC Co., Apr 30, 2014 9:00:00` AM. For the date field, you can also use the date picker to set a date and time value. Click the Submit button. The record is added to both your component view and records, and the counters are updated.

 Note: To debug your Apex code, use the Logs tab in the Developer Console. For example, if you don't have input validation for the date time field and entered an invalid date time format, you might get an INVALID_TYPE_ON_FIELD_IN_RECORD exception, which is listed both on the Logs tab in the Developer Console and in the response header on your browser. Otherwise, you might see an Apex error displayed in your browser. For more information on debugging your JavaScript code, see Enable Debug Mode for Lightning Components on page 322.

Congratulations! You have successfully created a simple expense tracker app that includes several components, client- and server-side controllers, and helper functions. Your app now accepts user input, which updates the view and database. The counters are also dynamically updated as you enter new user input. The next step shows you how to add a layer of interactivity using events.

SEE ALSO:

Handling Events with Client-Side Controllers

Calling a Server-Side Action

CRUD and Field-Level Security (FLS)

Step 6: Make the App Interactive With Events

Events add an interactive layer to your app by enabling you to share data between components. When the checkbox is checked or unchecked in the expense list view, you want to fire an event that updates both the view and records based on the relevant component data.

This flowchart shows the data flow in the app when a data change is captured by the selecting and deselecting of a checkbox on the `expenseList` component. When the **Reimbursed?** checkbox is selected or deselected, this browser click event fires the component event you're creating here. This event communicates the expense object to the handler component, and its controller calls the Apex controller method to update the relevant expense record, after which the response is ignored by the client since we won't be handling this server response here.

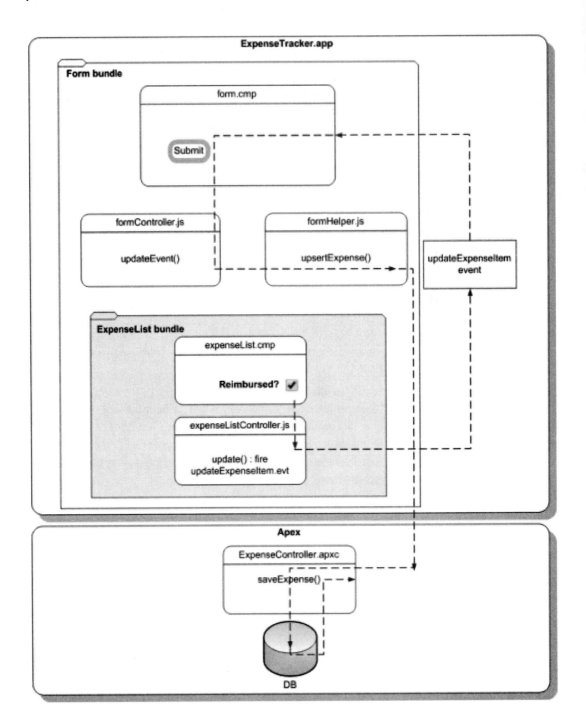

Let's start by creating the event and its handler before firing it and handling the event in the parent component.

1. Click **File** > **New** > **Lightning Event**.

2. Enter `updateExpenseItem` in the New Event window. This creates a new event, `updateExpenseItem.evt`.

3. In `updateExpenseItem.evt`, enter this code.

    The attribute you're defining in the event is passed from the firing component to the handlers.

    ```
    <aura:event type="COMPONENT">
        <!-- If you're using a namespace, use myNamespace.Expense__c
     instead. -->
        <aura:attribute name="expense" type="Expense__c"/>
    </aura:event>
    ```

    The framework has two types of events: component events and application events.

     Note: Always try to use a component event instead of an application event, if possible. Component events can only be handled by components above them in the containment hierarchy so their usage is more localized to the components that need to know about them. Application events are best used for something that should be handled at the application level, such as navigating to a specific record.

    We'll use a component event. Recall that `expenseList.cmp` contains the **Reimbursed?** checkbox.

4. Update `expenseList.cmp` to register that it fires the event. Add this tag after the `<aura:attribute>` tag.

    ```
    <aura:registerEvent name="updateExpense"
    type="c:updateExpenseItem"/>
    ```

    The **Reimbursed?** checkbox is wired up to a client-side controller action, denoted by `change="{!c.update}"`. You'll set up the `update` action next.

5. In the `expenseList` sidebar, click **CONTROLLER**. This creates a new resource, `expenseListController.js`. Enter this code.

    ```
    ({
        update: function(component, evt, helper) {
          var expense = component.get("v.expense");
          // Note that updateExpense matches the name attribute in
    <aura:registerEvent>
          var updateEvent = component.getEvent("updateExpense");
    ```

```
        updateEvent.setParams({ "expense": expense }).fire();
    }
})
```

When the checkbox is checked or unchecked, the `update` action runs, setting the `reimbursed` parameter value to `true` or `false`. The `updateExpenseItem.evt` event is fired with the updated `expense` object.

6. In the handler component, `form.cmp`, add this handler code before the `<aura:attribute>` tags.

```
<aura:handler name="updateExpense" event="c:updateExpenseItem"
action="{!c.updateEvent}" />
```

This event handler runs the `updateEvent` action when the component event you created is fired. The `<aura:handler>` tag uses the same value of the `name` attribute, `updateExpense`, from the `<aura:registerEvent>` tag in `c:expenseList`

7. Wire up the `updateEvent` action to handle the event. In `formController.js`, enter this code after the `createExpense` controller action.

```
updateEvent : function(component, event, helper) {
    helper.upsertExpense(component, event.getParam("expense"));
}
```

This action calls a helper function and passes in `event.getParam("expense")`, which contains the expense object with its parameters and values in this format: { `Name` : `"Lunch"` , `Client__c` : `"ABC Co."` , `Reimbursed__c` : `true` , `CreatedDate` : `"2014-08-12T20:53:09.000Z"` , `Amount__c` : `20`}.

8. Save your changes and reload your browser.

9. Click the **Reimbursed?** checkbox for one of the records.

   Note that the background color for the record changes. When you change the reimbursed status on the view, the `update` event is fired, handled by the parent component, which then updates the expense record by running the server-side controller action `saveExpense`.

That's it! You have successfully added a layer of interaction in your expense tracker app using a component event.

▪▪ Beyond the Basics

The framework fires several events during the rendering lifecycle, such as the `init` event you used in this tutorial. For example, you can also customize the app behavior during the `waiting` event when the client is waiting for a server response and when the `doneWaiting` event is fired to signal that the response has been received. This example shows how you can add text in the app during the `waiting` event, and remove it when the `doneWaiting` event is fired.

```
<!-- form.cmp markup -->
<aura:handler event="aura:waiting" action="{!c.waiting}"/>
<aura:handler event="aura:doneWaiting" action="{!c.doneWaiting}"/>
<aura:attribute name="wait" type="String"/>

<div class="wait">
    {!v.wait}
</div>
```

```
/** formController.js **/
waiting : function(component, event, helper) {
    component.set("v.wait", "updating...");
},
doneWaiting : function(component, event, helper) {
    component.set("v.wait", "");
}
```

The app displays this text when you click the **Submit** button to create a new record or when you click the checkbox on an expense item. For more information, see Events Fired During the Rendering Lifecycle on page 192.

The app you just created is currently accessible as a standalone app by accessing `https://<myDomain>.lightning.force.com/<namespace>/expenseTracker.app`, where `<myDomain>` is the name of your custom Salesforce domain. To make it accessible in Salesforce1, see Add Lightning Components to Salesforce1 on page 139. To package and distribute your app on AppExchange, see Distributing Applications and Components on page 319.

SEE ALSO:

Component Events

Event Handling Lifecycle

Summary

You created several components with controllers and events that interact with your expense records. The expense tracker app performs three distinct tasks: load the expense data and counters on app initialization, take in user input to create a new record and update the view, and handle user interactions by communicating relevant component data via events.

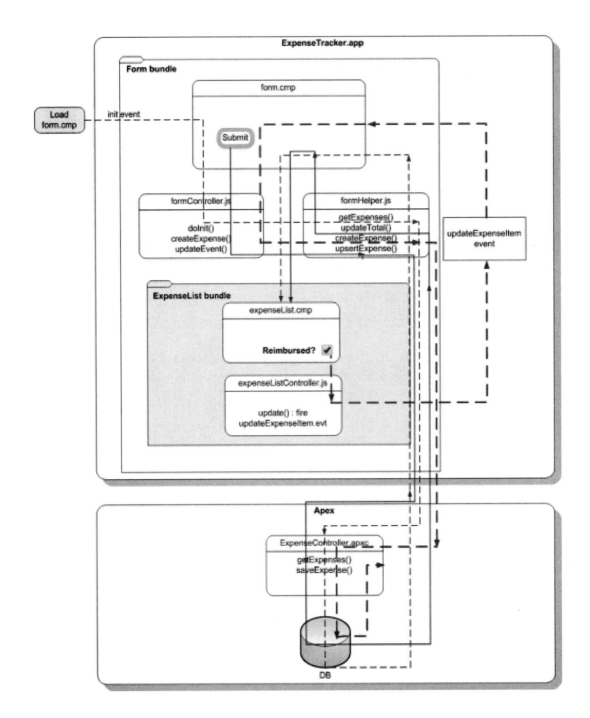

When `form.cmp` is initialized, the `init` handler triggers the `doInit` client-side controller, which calls the `getExpenses` helper function. `getExpenses` calls the `getExpenses` server-side controller to load the expenses. The callback sets the expenses data on the `v.expenses` attribute and calls `updateTotal` to update the counters.

Clicking the **Submit** button triggers the `createExpense` client-side controller. After field validation, the `createExpense` helper function is run, in which the `upsertExpense` helper function calls the `saveExpense` server-side controller to save the record. The callback pushes the new expense to the list of expenses and updates the attribute `v.expenses` in `form.cmp`, which in turn updates the expenses in `expenseList.cmp`. Finally, the helper calls `updateTotal` to update the counters represented by the `v.total` and `v.exp` attributes.

`expenseList.cmp` displays the list of expenses. When the **Reimbursed?** checkbox is selected or deselected, the `click` event triggers the `update` client-side controller. The `updateExpenseItem` event is fired with the relevant expense passed in as a parameter. `form.cmp` handles the event, triggering the `updateEvent` client-side controller. This controller action then calls the `upsertExpense` helper function, which calls the `saveExpense` server-side controller to save the relevant record.

Create a Component for Salesforce1 and Lightning Experience

Create a component that loads contacts data and interacts with Salesforce1 and Lightning Experience. Some of the events that are used in this tutorial are not supported for standalone apps.

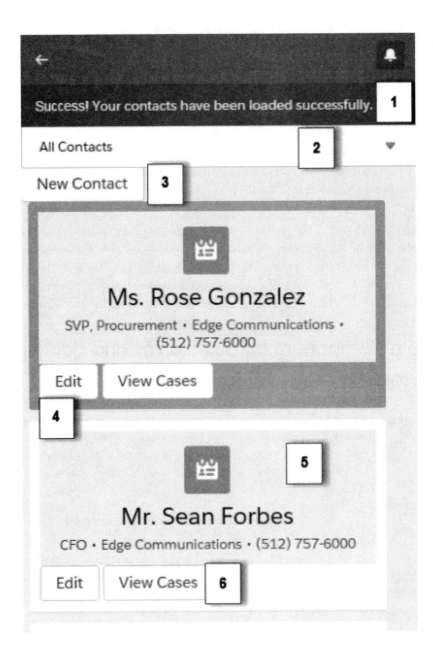

The component has these features.

- Displays a toast message (1) when all contacts are loaded successfully

- Use a nested component that displays all contacts or displays all primary contacts that are colored green when the input select value (2) is changed
- Opens the create record page to create a new contact when the New Contact button (3) is clicked
- Opens the edit record page to update the selected contact when the Edit button (4) is clicked
- Navigates to the record when the contact (5) is clicked
- Navigates to related cases when the View Cases button (6) is clicked

You'll create the following resources.

Resource	Description
Contacts Bundle	
`contacts.cmp`	The component that loads contact data
`contactsController.js`	The client-side controller actions that loads contact data, handles input select change event, and opens the create record page
`contactsHelper.js`	The helper function that retrieves contact data and display toast messages based on the loading status
contactList Bundle	
`contactList.cmp`	The contact list component
`contactListController.js`	The client-side controller actions that opens the edit record page, and navigates to a contact record, related cases, and map of contact address
`contactList.css`	The styles for the component
Apex Controller	
`ContactController.apxc`	The Apex controller that queries the contact records

Load the Contacts

Create an Apex controller and load your contacts.

Your organization must have existing contact records for this tutorial. This tutorial uses a custom picklist field, `Level`, which is represented by the API name `Level__c`. This field contains three picklist values: `Primary`, `Secondary`, and `Tertiary`.

1. Click **File** > **New** > **Apex Class**, and then enter *ContactController* in the **New Class** window. This creates a new Apex class, `ContactController.apxc`. Enter this code and then save.

   If you're using a namespace in your organization, replace `Level__c` with `myNamespace__Level__c`.

   ```
   public with sharing class ContactController {
   @AuraEnabled
       public static List<Contact> getContacts() {
           List<Contact> contacts =
                   [SELECT Id, Name, MailingStreet, Phone, Email,
   Level__c FROM Contact];

           //Add isAccessible() check
           return contacts;
       }


       @AuraEnabled
       // Retrieve all primary contacts
       public static List<Contact> getPrimary() {
           List<Contact> primaryContacts =
                   [SELECT Id, Name, MailingStreet, Phone, Email,
   Level__c FROM Contact WHERE Level__c = 'Primary'];

           //Add isAccessible() check
           return primaryContacts;
       }
   }
   ```

   `getPrimary()` returns all contacts whose `Level__c` field is set to `Primary`.

2. Click **File** > **New** > **Lightning Component**, and then enter *contactList* for the Name field in the New Lightning Bundle popup window. This creates a new component, `contactList.cmp`. Enter this code and then save.

   ```
   <aura:component>
       <aura:attribute name="contact" type="Contact"/>
       <!-- If you're using a namespace,
            use {!v.contact.myNamespace__Level__c} instead -->
       <div class="{!v.contact.Level__c == 'Primary'
                   ? 'row primary' : 'row '}" >

           <div onclick="{!c.gotoRecord}">
               <force:recordView recordId="{!v.contact.Id}"
   ```

```
type="MINI"/>
        </div>

        <!-- Open the record edit page when the button is clicked
 -->
        <ui:button label="Edit" press="{!c.editRecord}"/>
        <!-- Navigate to the related list when the button is
clicked -->
        <ui:button label="View Cases" press="{!c.relatedList}"/>

    </div>
</aura:component>
```

3. In the **contactList** sidebar, click **STYLE** to create a new resource named `contactList.css`. Replace the placeholder code with the following code and then save.

```
.THIS.primary{
    background: #4ECDC4   !important;
}

.THIS.row {
    background: #fff;
    max-width:90%;
    border-bottom: 2px solid #f0f1f2;
    padding: 10px;
    margin-left: 2%;
    margin-bottom: 10px;
    min-height: 70px;
    border-radius: 4px;
}
```

4. Click **File** > **New** > **Lightning Component**, and then enter *contacts* for the Name field in the New Lightning Bundle popup window. This creates a new component, `contacts.cmp`. Enter this code and then save. If you're using a namespace in your organization, replace `ContactController` with `myNamespace.ContactController`.

```
<aura:component controller="ContactController"
implements="force:appHostable">
    <!-- Handle component initialization in a client-side
controller -->
    <aura:handler name="init" value="{!this}"
action="{!c.doInit}"/>
```

```
    <!-- Dynamically load the list of contacts -->
    <aura:attribute name="contacts" type="Contact[]"/>

    <!-- Create a drop-down list with two options -->
    <ui:inputSelect aura:id="selection" change="{!c.select}">
        <ui:inputSelectOption text="All Contacts" label="All
Contacts"/>
        <ui:inputSelectOption text="All Primary" label="All
Primary"/>
    </ui:inputSelect>

    <!-- Display record create page when button is clicked -->
    <ui:button label="New Contact" press="{!c.createRecord}"/>

    <!-- Iterate over the list of contacts and display them -->
    <aura:iteration var="contact" items="{!v.contacts}">
        <!-- If you're using a namespace, replace with
myNamespace:contactList -->
        <c:contactList contact="{!contact}"/>
    </aura:iteration>
</aura:component>
```

5. In the **contacts** sidebar, click **CONTROLLER** to create a new resource named
   `contactsController.js`. Replace the placeholder code with the following code and then
   save.

```
({
    doInit : function(component, event, helper) {
        // Retrieve contacts during component initialization
        helper.getContacts(component);
    },//Delimiter for future code
})
```

6. In the **contacts** sidebar, click **HELPER** to create a new resource named `contactsHelper.js`.
   Replace the placeholder code with the following code and then save.

```
({
    getContacts : function(cmp) {
        // Load all contact data
        var action = cmp.get("c.getContacts");
        action.setCallback(this, function(response) {
            var state = response.getState();
            if (cmp.isValid() && state === "SUCCESS") {
```

46

```
        cmp.set("v.contacts", response.getReturnValue());

    }

    // Display toast message to indicate load status
    var toastEvent = $A.get("e.force:showToast");
    if (state === 'SUCCESS'){
        toastEvent.setParams({
            "title": "Success!",
            "message": " Your contacts have been loaded
successfully."
        });
    }
    else {
        toastEvent.setParams({
                "title": "Error!",
                "message": " Something has gone wrong."
        });
    }
    toastEvent.fire();
    });
    $A.enqueueAction(action);
    }
})
```

7. Create a new Lightning Component tab by following the steps on Add Lightning Components to Salesforce1 on page 139. Make sure you include the component in the Salesforce1 navigation menu.

Finally, you can go to the Salesforce1 mobile browser app to check your output. When your component is loaded, you should see a toast message that indicates your contacts are loaded successfully.

Next, we'll wire up the other events so that your input select displays either all contacts or only primary contacts that are colored green. We'll also wire up events for opening the create record and edit record pages, and events for navigating to a record and a URL.

Fire the Events

Fire the events in your client-side controller or helper functions. The `force` events are handled by Salesforce1.

This demo builds on the contacts component you created in Load the Contacts on page 43.

1. In the **contactList** sidebar, click **CONTROLLER** to create a new resource named
   `contactListController.js`. Replace the placeholder code with the following code and
   then save.

```
({
    gotoRecord : function(component, event, helper) {
        // Fire the event to navigate to the contact record
        var sObjectEvent = $A.get("e.force:navigateToSObject");
        sObjectEvent.setParams({
            "recordId": component.get("v.contact.Id"),
            "slideDevName": 'related'
        })
        sObjectEvent.fire();
    },

    editRecord : function(component, event, helper) {
        // Fire the event to navigate to the edit contact page
        var editRecordEvent = $A.get("e.force:editRecord");
        editRecordEvent.setParams({
            "recordId": component.get("v.contact.Id")
        });
        editRecordEvent.fire();
    },

    relatedList : function (component, event, helper) {
        // Navigate to the related cases
        var relatedListEvent =
$A.get("e.force:navigateToRelatedList");
        relatedListEvent.setParams({
            "relatedListId": "Cases",
            "parentRecordId": component.get("v.contact.Id")
        });
        relatedListEvent.fire();
    }
})
```

2. Refresh the Salesforce1 mobile browser app, and click these elements to test the events.

   - Contact: `force:navigateToSObject` is fired, which updates the view with the contact
     record page. The contact name corresponds to the following component.

```
<div onclick="{!c.gotoRecord}">
    <force:recordView recordId="{!v.contact.Id}" type="MINI"/>
</div>
```

- Edit Contact button: `force:editRecord` is fired, which opens the edit record page. The Edit Contact icon corresponds to the following component.

```
<ui:button label="Edit" press="{!c.editRecord}"/>
```

3. Open `contactsController.js`. After the `doInit` controller, enter this code and then save.

```
createRecord : function (component, event, helper) {
    // Open the create record page
    var createRecordEvent = $A.get("e.force:createRecord");
    createRecordEvent.setParams({
        "entityApiName": "Contact"
    });
    createRecordEvent.fire();
},

select : function(component, event, helper){
    // Get the selected value of the ui:inputSelect component
    var selectCmp = component.find("selection");
    var selectVal = selectCmp.get("v.value");

    // Display all primary contacts or all contacts
    if (selectVal==="All Primary"){
        var action = component.get("c.getPrimary");
        action.setCallback(this, function(response){
            var state = response.getState();
            if (component.isValid() && state === "SUCCESS") {
                component.set("v.contacts",
response.getReturnValue());
            }
        });
        $A.enqueueAction(action);
    }
    else {
        // Return all contacts
        helper.getContacts(component);
    }
}
```

Notice that if you pull down the page and release it, the page refreshes all data in the view. Now you can test your components by clicking on the areas highlighted in Create a Component for Salesforce1 and Lightning Experience on page 41.

For an example on creating a standalone app that can be used independent of Salesforce1, see Create a Standalone Lightning App on page 9.

CHAPTER 3   Creating Components

In this chapter ...

- Component Markup
- Component Namespace
- Component Bundles
- Component IDs
- HTML in Components
- CSS in Components
- Component Attributes
- Component Composition
- Component Body
- Component Facets
- Best Practices for Conditional Markup
- Component Versioning
- Using Expressions
- Using Labels
- Localization
- Providing Component Documentation
- Working with UI Components
- Supporting Accessibility

Components are the functional units of the Lightning Component framework.

A component encapsulates a modular and potentially reusable section of UI, and can range in granularity from a single line of text to an entire application.

Use the Developer Console to create components.

Component Markup

Component resources contain markup and have a `.cmp` suffix. The markup can contain text or references to other components, and also declares metadata about the component.

Let's start with a simple "Hello, world!" example in a `helloWorld.cmp` component.

```
<aura:component>
    Hello, world!
</aura:component>
```

This is about as simple as a component can get. The "Hello, world!" text is wrapped in the `<aura:component>` tags, which appear at the beginning and end of every component definition.

Components can contain most HTML tags so you can use markup, such as `<div>` and `<span>`. HTML5 tags are also supported.

```
<aura:component>
    <div class="container">
        <!--Other HTML tags or components here-->
    </div>
</aura:component>
```

Note: Case sensitivity should be respected as your markup interacts with JavaScript, CSS, and Apex.

Use the Developer Console to create components.

`aura:component` has the following optional attributes.

Attribute	Type	Description
access	String	Indicates whether the component can be used outside of its own namespace. Possible values are `public` (default), and `global`.
controller	String	The server-side controller class for the component. The format is `namespace.myController`.
description	String	A description of the component.
extends	Component	The component to be extended, if applicable. For example, `extends="ui:input"`.
extensible	Boolean	Set to `true` if the component can be extended. The default is `false`.

Attribute	Type	Description
`implements`	String	A comma-separated list of interfaces that the component implements.
`isTemplate`	Boolean	Set to `true` if the component is a template. The default is `false`. A template must have `isTemplate="true"` set in its `<aura:component>` tag. `<aura:component isTemplate="true" extends="aura:template">`
`template`	Component	The template for this component. A template bootstraps loading of the framework and app. The default template is `aura:template`. You can customize the template by creating your own component that extends the default template. For example: `<aura:component extends="aura:template" ... >`

`aura:component` also includes a `body` attribute defined in a `<aura:attribute>` tag. Attributes usually control the output or behavior of a component, but not the configuration information in system attributes.

Attribute	Type	Description
`body`	`Component[]`	The body of the component. In markup, this is everything in the body of the tag.

SEE ALSO:

   Using the Developer Console

   Component Access Control

   Client-Side Rendering to the DOM

   Dynamically Creating Components

Component Namespace

Every component is part of a namespace, which is used to group related components together. If your organization has a namespace prefix set, use that namespace to access your components. Otherwise, use the default namespace to access your components.

Another component or application can reference a component by adding `<myNamespace:myComponent>` in its markup. For example, the `helloWorld` component is in the `docsample` namespace. Another component can reference it by adding `<docsample:helloWorld />` in its markup.

Lightning components that Salesforce provides are grouped into several namespaces, such as `aura`, `ui`, and `force`. Components from third-party managed packages have namespaces from the providing organizations.

In your organization, you can choose to set a namespace prefix. If you do, that namespace is used for all of your Lightning components. A namespace prefix is required if you plan to offer managed packages on the AppExchange.

If you haven't set a namespace prefix for your organization, use the default namespace `c` when referencing components that you've created.

Namespaces in Code Samples

The code samples throughout this guide use the default `c` namespace. Replace `c` with your namespace if you've set a namespace prefix.

Using the Default Namespace in Organizations with No Namespace Set

If your organization hasn't set a namespace prefix, use the default namespace `c` when referencing Lightning components that you've created.

The following items must use the `c` namespace when your organization doesn't have a namespace prefix set.

- References to components that you've created
- References to events that you've defined

The following items use an implicit namespace for your organization and don't require you to specify a namespace.

- References to custom objects

- References to custom fields on standard and custom objects
- References to Apex controllers

See Namespace Usage Examples and Reference on page 56 for examples of all of the preceding items.

Using Your Organization's Namespace

If your organization has set a namespace prefix, use that namespace to reference Lightning components, events, custom objects and fields, and other items in your Lightning markup.

The following items use your organization's namespace when your organization has a namespace prefix set.

- References to components that you've created
- References to events that you've defined
- References to custom objects
- References to custom fields on standard and custom objects
- References to Apex controllers
- References to static resources

 Note: Support for the c namespace in organizations that have set a namespace prefix is incomplete. The following items can use the c namespace if you prefer to use the shortcut, but it's not currently a recommended practice.

- References to components that you've created when used in Lightning markup, but not in expressions or JavaScript
- References to events that you've defined when used in Lightning markup, but not in expressions or JavaScript
- References to custom objects when used in component and event type and default system attributes, but not in expressions or JavaScript

See Namespace Usage Examples and Reference on page 56 for examples of the preceding items.

Using a Namespace in or from a Managed Package

Always use the complete namespace when referencing items from a managed package, or when creating code that you intend to distribute in your own managed packages.

Creating a Namespace in Your Organization

Create a namespace for your organization by registering a namespace prefix.

If you're not creating managed packages for distribution then registering a namespace prefix isn't required, but it's a best practice for all but the smallest organizations.

Your namespace prefix must:

- Begin with a letter
- Contain one to 15 alphanumeric characters
- Not contain two consecutive underscores

For example, `myNp123` and `my_np` are valid namespaces, but `123Company` and `my__np` are not.

To register a namespace prefix:

1. From Setup, enter `Packages` in the `Quick Find` box, then select **Packages**.
2. Click **Edit**.

   > Note: This button doesn't appear if you've already configured your developer settings.

3. Review the selections that are required for configuring developer settings, and then click **Continue**.
4. Enter the namespace prefix you want to register.
5. Click **Check Availability** to determine if the namespace prefix is already in use.
6. If the namespace prefix that you entered isn't available, repeat the previous two steps.
7. Click **Review My Selections**.
8. Click **Save**.

Namespace Usage Examples and Reference

This topic provides examples of referencing components, objects, fields, and so on in Lightning components code.

Examples are provided for the following.

- Components, events, and interfaces in your organization
- Custom objects in your organization
- Custom fields on standard and custom objects in your organization
- Server-side Apex controllers in your organization
- Dynamic creation of components in JavaScript

- Static resources in your organization

Organizations with No Namespace Prefix Set

The following illustrates references to elements in your organization when your organization doesn't have a namespace prefix set. References use the default namespace, c, where necessary.

Referenced Item	Example
Component used in markup	`<c:myComponent />`
Component used in a system attribute	`<aura:component extends="c:myComponent">` `<aura:component  implements="c:myInterface">`
Apex controller	`<aura:component  controller="ExpenseController">`
Custom object in attribute data type	`<aura:attribute name="expense"` `type="Expense__c" />`

Custom object or custom field in attribute defaults	`<aura:attribute name="newExpense"`
	`type="Expense__c"`
	`    default="{ 'sobjectType': 'Expense__c',`
	`                'Name': '',`
	`                'Amount__c': 0,`
	`                ...`
	`        }" />`

Custom field in an expression	`<ui:inputNumber` `value="{!v.newExpense.Amount__c}" label=... />`

Custom field in a JavaScript function	`updateTotal: function(component) {`
	`    ...`
	`    for(var i = 0 ; i < expenses.length ; i++){`
	`        var exp = expenses[i];`
	`        total += exp.Amount__c;`
	`    }`
	`    ...`
	`}`

Referenced Item	Example
Component created dynamically in a JavaScript function	```var myCmp = $A.createComponent("c:myComponent", {}, function(myCmp) { });```
Interface comparison in a JavaScript function	`aCmp.isInstanceOf("c:myInterface")`
Event registration	`<aura:registerEvent type="c:updateExpenseItem" name=... />`
Event handler	`<aura:handler event="c:updateExpenseItem" action=... />`
Explicit dependency	`<aura:dependency resource="markup://c:myComponent" />`
Application event in a JavaScript function	`var updateEvent = $A.get("e.c:updateExpenseItem");`
Static resources	`<ltng:require scripts="{!$Resource.resourceName}" styles="{!$Resource.resourceName}" />`

Organizations with a Namespace Prefix

The following illustrates references to elements in your organization when your organization has set a namespace prefix. References use an example namespace `yournamespace`.

Referenced Item	Example
Component used in markup	`<yournamespace:myComponent />`
Component used in a system attribute	`<aura:component extends="yournamespace:myComponent">` `<aura:component implements="yournamespace:myInterface">`

Referenced Item	Example
Apex controller	```<aura:component``` ```controller="`**`yournamespace.ExpenseController`**`">```
Custom object in attribute data type	```<aura:attribute name="expenses"``` ```type="`**`yournamespace__Expense__c[]`**`" />```

Custom object or custom field in attribute defaults	```<aura:attribute name="newExpense"```
	```type="yournamespace__Expense__c"```
	``` default="{ 'sobjectType':```
	`'yournamespace__Expense__c'``,`
	``` 'Name': '',```
	``` `**`'yournamespace__Amount__c'`**`: 0,`
	``` ...```
	``` }" />```

Custom field in an expression	```<ui:inputNumber```
	```value="{!v.newExpense.`**`yournamespace__Amount__c`**`}"`
	```label=... />```

Custom field in a JavaScript function	```updateTotal: function(component) {```
	``` ...```
	``` for(var i = 0 ; i < expenses.length ; i++){```
	``` var exp = expenses[i];```
	``` total += exp.`**`yournamespace__Amount__c`**`;`
	``` }```
	``` ...```
	```}```

Component created dynamically in a JavaScript function	```var myCmp =```
	```$A.createComponent("`**`yournamespace:myComponent`**`",`
	``` {},```
	``` function(myCmp) { }```
	```);```

Interface comparison in a JavaScript function	```aCmp.isInstanceOf("`**`yournamespace:myInterface`**`")```

Referenced Item	Example

Event registration	`<aura:registerEvent`
	`type="`**`yournamespace:updateExpenseItem`**`" name=…`
	`/>`

Event handler	`<aura:handler`
	`event="`**`yournamespace:updateExpenseItem`**`" action=…`
	`/>`

Explicit dependency	`<aura:dependency`
	`resource="markup://`**`yournamespace:myComponent`**`"`
	`/>`

Application event in a JavaScript function	`var updateEvent =` `$A.get("e.`**`yournamespace:updateExpenseItem`**`");`

Static resources	`<ltng:require`
	`scripts="{!$Resource.`**`yournamespace__resourceName`**`}"`
	`styles="{!$Resource.`**`yournamespace__resourceName`**`}"`
	`/>`

Component Bundles

A component bundle contains a component or an app and all its related resources.

Resource	Resource Name	Usage	See Also
Component or Application	`sample.cmp` or `sample.app`	The only required resource in a bundle. Contains markup for the component or app. Each bundle contains only one component or app resource.	Creating Components on page 51 aura:application on page 352
CSS Styles	`sample.css`	Styles for the component.	CSS in Components on page 63

Resource	Resource Name	Usage	See Also
Controller	`sampleController.js`	Client-side controller methods to handle events in the component.	Handling Events with Client-Side Controllers on page 162
Design	`sample.design`	Required for components used in the Lightning App Builder, Lightning Pages, or Community Builder.	Configure Components for Lightning Pages and the Lightning App Builder
Documentation	`sample.auradoc`	A description, sample code, and one or multiple references to example components	Providing Component Documentation on page 103
Renderer	`sampleRenderer.js`	Client-side renderer to override default rendering for a component.	Client-Side Rendering to the DOM on page 258
Helper	`sampleHelper.js`	JavaScript functions that can be called from any JavaScript code in a component's bundle	Sharing JavaScript Code in a Component Bundle on page 256
SVG File	`sample.svg`	Custom icon resource for components used in the Lightning App Builder or Community Builder.	Configure Components for Lightning Pages and the Lightning App Builder on page 153

All resources in the component bundle follow the naming convention and are auto-wired. For example, a controller `<componentName>Controller.js` is auto-wired to its component, which means that you can use the controller within the scope of that component.

Component IDs

A component has two types of IDs: a local ID and a global ID.

Local IDs

A local ID is an ID that is only scoped to the component. A local ID enables you to retrieve a component by its ID in JavaScript code. A local ID is often unique but it's not required to be unique.

Create a local ID by using the `aura:id` attribute. For example:

```
<ui:button aura:id="button1" label="button1"/>
```

📝 Note: `aura:id` doesn't support expressions. You can only assign literal string values to `aura:id`.

Find the button component by calling `cmp.find("button1")` in your client-side controller, where `cmp` is a reference to the component containing the button.

`find()` returns different types depending on the result.

- If the local ID is unique, `find()` returns the component.
- If there are multiple components with the same local ID, `find()` returns an array of the components.
- If there is no matching local ID, `find()` returns `undefined`.

To find the local ID for a component in JavaScript, use `cmp.getLocalId()`.

Global IDs

Every component has a unique `globalId`, which is the generated runtime-unique ID of the component instance. A global ID is not guaranteed to be the same beyond the lifetime of a component, so it should never be relied on.

To create a unique ID for an HTML element, you can use the `globalId` as a prefix or suffix for your element. For example:

```
<div id="{!globalId + '_footer'}"></div>
```

You can use the `getGlobalId()` function in JavaScript to get a component's global ID.

```
var globalId = cmp.getGlobalId();
```

SEE ALSO:
Finding Components by ID
Which Button Was Pressed?

HTML in Components

An HTML tag is treated as a first-class component by the framework. Each HTML tag is translated into a component, allowing it to enjoy the same rights and privileges as any other component.

You can add HTML markup in components. Note that you must use strict XHTML. For example, use `<br/>` instead of `<br>`. You can also use HTML attributes and DOM events, such as `onclick`.

 Warning: Some tags, like `<applet>` and `<font>`, aren't supported. For a full list of unsupported tags, see Supported HTML Tags.

Unescaping HTML

To output pre-formatted HTML, use `aura:unescapedHTML`. For example, this is useful if you want to display HTML that is generated on the server and add it to the DOM. You must escape any HTML if necessary or your app might be exposed to security vulnerabilities.

You can pass in values from an expression, such as in `<aura:unescapedHtml value="{!v.note.body}"/>`.

`{!expression}` is the framework's expression syntax. For more information, see Using Expressions on page 76.

SEE ALSO:

CSS in Components

CSS in Components

Style your components with CSS.

Add CSS to a component bundle by clicking the **STYLE** button in the Developer Console sidebar.

For external CSS resources, see Styling Apps on page 221.

All top-level elements in a component have a special `THIS` CSS class added to them. This, effectively, adds namespacing to CSS and helps prevent one component's CSS from blowing away another component's styling. The framework throws an error if a CSS file doesn't follow this convention.

Let's look at a sample `helloHTML.cmp` component. The CSS is in `helloHTML.css`.

Component source

```
<aura:component>
  <div class="white">
     Hello, HTML!
  </div>

  <h2>Check out the style in this list.</h2>

  <ul>
    <li class="red">I'm red.</li>
    <li class="blue">I'm blue.</li>
    <li class="green">I'm green.</li>
  </ul>
</aura:component>
```

CSS source

```
.THIS {
    background-color: grey;
}

.THIS.white {
    background-color: white;
}

.THIS .red {
    background-color: red;
}

.THIS .blue {
    background-color: blue;
}

.THIS .green {
    background-color: green;
}
```

Output

Hello, HTML!
Check out the style in this list.

- I'm red
-
- I'm green

The top-level elements, h2 and ul, match the THIS class and render with a grey background. Top-level elements are tags wrapped by the HTML body tag and not by any other tags. In this example, the li tags are not top-level because they are nested in a ul tag.

The <div class="white"> element matches the .THIS.white selector and renders with a white background. Note that there is no space in the selector as this rule is for top-level elements.

The <li class="red"> element matches the .THIS .red selector and renders with a red background. Note that this is a descendant selector and it contains a space as the <li> element is not a top-level element.

SEE ALSO:

Adding and Removing Styles

HTML in Components

Component Attributes

Component attributes are like member variables on a class in Apex. They are typed fields that are set on a specific instance of a component, and can be referenced from within the component's markup using an expression syntax. Attributes enable you to make components more dynamic.

Use the <aura:attribute> tag to add an attribute to the component or app. Let's look at the following sample, helloAttributes.app:

```
<aura:application>
    <aura:attribute name="whom" type="String" default="world"/>
    Hello {!v.whom}!
</aura:application>
```

All attributes have a name and a type. Attributes may be marked as required by specifying required="true", and may also specify a default value.

In this case we've got an attribute named whom of type String. If no value is specified, it defaults to "world".

Though not a strict requirement, <aura:attribute> tags are usually the first things listed in a component's markup, as it provides an easy way to read the component's shape at a glance.

Attribute names must start with a letter or underscore. They can also contain numbers or hyphens after the first character.

Note: You can't use attributes with hyphens in expressions. For example, `cmp.get("v.name-withHyphen")` is supported, but not `<ui:button label="{!v.name-withHyphen}"/>`.

Now, append `?whom=you` to the URL and reload the page. The value in the query string sets the value of the `whom` attribute. Supplying attribute values via the query string when requesting a component is one way to set the attributes on that component.

 Warning: This only works for attributes of type String.

Expressions

`helloAttributes.app` contains an expression, `{!v.whom}`, which is responsible for the component's dynamic output.

`{!expression}` is the framework's expression syntax. In this case, the expression we are evaluating is `v.whom`. The name of the attribute we defined is `whom`, while `v` is the value provider for a component's attribute set, which represents the view.

 Note: Expressions are case sensitive. For example, if you have a custom field `myNamespace__Amount__c`, you must refer to it as `{!v.myObject.myNamespace__Amount__c}`.

Attribute Validation

We defined the set of valid attributes in `helloAttributes.app`, so the framework automatically validates that only valid attributes are passed to that component.

Try requesting `helloAttributes.app` with the query string `?fakeAttribute=fakeValue`. You should receive an error that `helloAttributes.app` doesn't have a `fakeAttribute` attribute.

SEE ALSO:
   Supported aura:attribute Types
   Using Expressions

Component Composition

Composing fine-grained components in a larger component enables you to build more interesting components and applications.

Let's see how we can fit components together. We will first create a few simple components: `c:helloHTML` and `c:helloAttributes`. Then, we'll create a wrapper component, `c:nestedComponents`, that contains the simple components.

Here is the source for `helloHTML.cmp`.

```
<!--c:helloHTML-->
<aura:component>
  <div class="white">
    Hello, HTML!
  </div>

  <h2>Check out the style in this list.</h2>

  <ul>
    <li class="red">I'm red.</li>
    <li class="blue">I'm blue.</li>
    <li class="green">I'm green.</li>
  </ul>
</aura:component>
```

CSS source

```
.THIS {
    background-color: grey;
}

.THIS.white {
    background-color: white;
}

.THIS .red {
    background-color: red;
}

.THIS .blue {
    background-color: blue;
}
```

```
.THIS .green {
    background-color: green;
}
```

Output

Here is the source for `helloAttributes.cmp`.

```
<!--c:helloAttributes-->
<aura:component>
    <aura:attribute name="whom" type="String" default="world"/>
    Hello {!v.whom}!
</aura:component>
```

`nestedComponents.cmp` uses composition to include other components in its markup.

```
<!--c:nestedComponents-->
<aura:component>
    Observe!  Components within components!

    <c:helloHTML/>

    <c:helloAttributes whom="component composition"/>
</aura:component>
```

Output

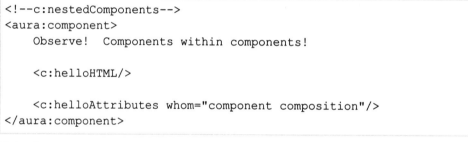

Hello component composition!

Including an existing component is similar to including an HTML tag. Reference the component by its "descriptor", which is of the form *namespace:component*. `nestedComponents.cmp` references the `helloHTML.cmp` component, which lives in the `c` namespace. Hence, its descriptor is `c:helloHTML`.

Note how `nestedComponents.cmp` also references `c:helloAttributes`. Just like adding attributes to an HTML tag, you can set attribute values in a component as part of the component tag. `nestedComponents.cmp` sets the `whom` attribute of `helloAttributes.cmp` to "component composition".

Attribute Passing

You can also pass attributes to nested components. `nestedComponents2.cmp` is similar to `nestedComponents.cmp`, except that it includes an extra `passthrough` attribute. This value is passed through as the attribute value for `c:helloAttributes`.

```
<!--c:nestedComponents2-->
<aura:component>
    <aura:attribute name="passthrough" type="String" default="passed
attribute"/>
    Observe!  Components within components!

    <c:helloHTML/>

    <c:helloAttributes whom="{!v.passthrough}"/>
</aura:component>
```

Output

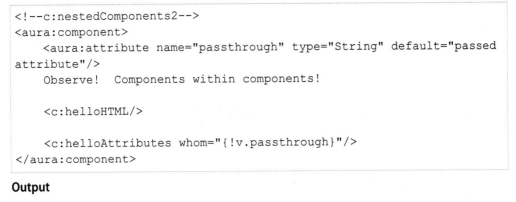

`helloAttributes` is now using the passed through attribute value.

Definitions versus Instances

In object-oriented programming, there's a difference between a class and an instance of that class. Components have a similar concept. When you create a `.cmp` resource, you are providing the definition (class) of that component. When you put a component tag in a `.cmp`, you are creating a reference to (instance of) that component.

It shouldn't be surprising that we can add multiple instances of the same component with different attributes. `nestedComponents3.cmp` adds another instance of `c:helloAttributes` with a different attribute value. The two instances of the `c:helloAttributes` component have different values for their `whom` attribute .

```
<!--c:nestedComponents3-->
<aura:component>
    <aura:attribute name="passthrough" type="String" default="passed
attribute"/>
    Observe!  Components within components!
```

```
    <c:helloHTML/>

    <c:helloAttributes whom="{!v.passthrough}"/>

    <c:helloAttributes whom="separate instance"/>
</aura:component>
```

Output

Observe! Components within components!
Hello, HTML!
Check out the style in this list

- I'm red.
-
- I'm green.

Hello passed attribute! Hello separate instance!

Component Body

The root-level tag of every component is `<aura:component>`. Every component inherits the `body` attribute from `<aura:component>`.

The `<aura:component>` tag can contain tags, such as `<aura:attribute>`, `<aura:registerEvent>`, `<aura:handler>`, `<aura:set>`, and so on. Any free markup that is not enclosed in one of the tags allowed in a component is assumed to be part of the body and is set in the `body` attribute.

The `body` attribute has type `Aura.Component[]`. It can be an array of one component, or an empty array, but it's always an array.

In a component, use "v" to access the collection of attributes. For example, `{!v.body}` outputs the body of the component.

Setting the Body Content

To set the `body` attribute in a component, add free markup within the `<aura:component>` tag. For example:

```
<aura:component>
    <!--START BODY-->
    <div>Body part</div>
    <ui:button label="Push Me"/>
```

```
        <!--END BODY-->
</aura:component>
```

To set the value of an inherited attribute, use the `<aura:set>` tag. Setting the body content is equivalent to wrapping that free markup inside `<aura:set attribute="body">`. Since the `body` attribute has this special behavior, you can omit `<aura:set attribute="body">`.

The previous sample is a shortcut for this markup. We recommend the less verbose syntax in the previous sample.

```
<aura:component>
    <aura:set attribute="body">
        <!--START BODY-->
        <div>Body part</div>
        <ui:button label="Push Me/>
        <!--END BODY-->
    </aura:set>
</aura:component>
```

The same logic applies when you use any component that has a `body` attribute, not just `<aura:component>`. For example:

```
<ui:panel>
    Hello world!
</ui:panel>
```

This is a shortcut for:

```
<ui:panel>
    <aura:set attribute="body">
        Hello World!
    </aura:set>
</ui:panel>
```

Accessing the Component Body

To access a component body in JavaScript, use `component.get("v.body")`.

SEE ALSO:

aura:set

Working with a Component Body in JavaScript

Component Facets

A facet is any attribute of type `Aura.Component[]`. The `body` attribute is an example of a facet.

To define your own facet, add an `aura:attribute` tag of type `Aura.Component[]` to your component. For example, let's create a new component called `facetHeader.cmp`.

```
<!--c:facetHeader-->
<aura:component>
    <aura:attribute name="header" type="Aura.Component[]"/>

    <div>
        <span class="header">{!v.header}</span><br/>
        <span class="body">{!v.body}</span>
    </div>
</aura:component>
```

This component has a header facet. Note how we position the output of the header using the `v.header` expression.

The component doesn't have any output when you access it directly as the `header` and `body` attributes aren't set. Let's create another component, `helloFacets.cmp`, that sets these attributes.

```
<!--c:helloFacets-->
<aura:component>
    See how we set the header facet.<br/>

    <auradocs:facetHeader>

        Nice body!

        <aura:set attribute="header">
            Hello Header!
        </aura:set>
    </auradocs:facetHeader>

</aura:component>
```

Note that `aura:set` sets the value of the `header` attribute of `facetHeader.cmp`, but you don't need to use `aura:set` if you're setting the `body` attribute.

SEE ALSO:

Component Body

Best Practices for Conditional Markup

Use the `<aura:if>` or `<aura:renderIf>` tags to conditionally display markup. Alternatively, you can conditionally set markup in JavaScript logic. Consider the performance cost as well as code maintainability when you design components. The best design choice depends on your use case.

`<aura:if>` versus `<aura:renderIf>`

`<aura:if>` is more lightweight than `<aura:renderIf>` as it only creates and renders the markup in its body or in the `else` attribute. Always try `<aura:if>` first when you want conditional markup.

Only consider using `<aura:renderIf>` if you expect to show the markup for both the true and false states, and it would require a server round trip to create the components that aren't initially rendered.

Here's a quick comparison of `<aura:if>` versus `<aura:renderIf>`.

	`<aura:if>`	`<aura:renderIf>`
Displaying	Creates and displays only one branch	Creates both branches but only displays one
Switching condition	Unrenders and destroys the current branch. Creates and displays the other branch.	Unrenders the current branch and renders the other branch
Empty branch	Creates a DOM placeholder	Creates a DOM placeholder

Consider Alternatives to Conditional Markup

Here are some use cases where you should consider alternatives to `<aura:if>` or `<aura:renderIf>`.

You want to toggle visibility

Don't use `<aura:if>` or `<aura:renderIf>` tags to toggle markup visibility. Use CSS instead. See Dynamically Showing or Hiding Markup on page 277.

You need to nest conditional logic or use conditional logic in an iteration

Using `<aura:if>` or `<aura:renderIf>` tags can hurt performance by creating a large number of components. Excessive use of conditional logic in markup can also lead to cluttered markup that is harder to maintain.

Consider alternatives, such as using JavaScript logic in an `init` event handler instead. See Invoking Actions on Component Initialization on page 262.

SEE ALSO:

Conditional Expressions

Component Versioning

Component versioning enables you to declare dependencies against specific revisions of an installed managed package.

By assigning a version to your component, you have granular control over how the component functions when new versions of a managed package are released. For example, imagine that a **`<packageNamespace>`**`:button` is pinned to version 2.0 of a package. Upon installing version 3.0, the button retains its version 2.0 functionality.

 Note: The package developer is responsible for inserting versioning logic into the markup when updating a component. If the component wasn't changed in the update or if the markup doesn't account for version, the component behaves in the context of the most recent version.

Versions are assigned declaratively in the Developer Console. When you're working on a component, click **Bundle Version Settings** in the right panel to define the version. You can only version a component if you've installed a package, and the valid versions for the component are the available versions of that package. Versions are in the format `<major>.<minor>`. So if you assign a component version 1.4, its behavior depends on the first major release and fourth minor release of the associated package.

Bundle Version Settings [X]

API Version	35
jsh2	1.4

Save Cancel

When working with components, you can version:

- Apex controllers
- JavaScript controllers
- JavaScript helpers
- JavaScript renderers
- Bundle markup
    - Applications (.app)
    - Components (.cmp)
    - Interfaces (.intf)
    - Events (.evt)

You can't version any other types of resources in bundles. Unsupported types include:

- Styles (.css)
- Documentation (.doc)
- Design (.design)
- SVG (.svg)

Once you've assigned versions to components, or if you're developing components for a package, you can retrieve the version in several contexts.

Resource	Return Type	Expression
Apex	Version	System.requestVersion()

75

Resource	Return Type	Expression
JavaScript	String	`cmp.getVersion()`
Lightning component markup	String	`{!Version}`

You can use the retrieved version to add logic to your code or markup to assign different functionality to different versions. Here's an example of using versioning in an `<aura:if>` statement.

```
<aura:component>
 <aura:if isTrue="{!Version > 1.0}">
  <c:newVersionFunctionality/>
 </aura:if>
 <c:oldVersionFunctionality/>
 ...
</aura:component>
```

Using Expressions

Expressions allow you to make calculations and access property values and other data within component markup. Use expressions for dynamic output or passing values into components by assigning them to attributes.

An expression is any set of literal values, variables, sub-expressions, or operators that can be resolved to a single value. Method calls are not allowed in expressions.

The expression syntax is: `{!`***expression***`}`

expression is a placeholder for the expression.

Anything inside the `{!  }` delimiters is evaluated and dynamically replaced when the component is rendered or when the value is used by the component. Whitespace is ignored.

The resulting value can be a primitive, such as an integer, string, or boolean. It can also be a JavaScript object, a component or collection, a controller method such as an action method, and other useful results.

 Note: If you're familiar with other languages, you may be tempted to read the `!` as the "bang" operator, which negates boolean values in many programming languages. In the Lightning Component framework, `{!` is simply the delimiter used to begin an expression.

If you're familiar with Visualforce, this syntax will look familiar.

Identifiers in an expression, such as attribute names accessed through the view, controller values, or labels, must start with a letter or underscore. They can also contain numbers or hyphens after the first character. For example, `{!v.2count}` is not valid, but `{!v.count}` is.

 Important: Only use the `{! }` syntax in markup in `.app` or `.cmp` files. In JavaScript, use string syntax to evaluate an expression. For example:

```
var theLabel = cmp.get("v.label");
```

If you want to escape `{!`, use this syntax:

```
<aura:text value="{!"/>
```

This renders `{!` in plain text because the `aura:text` component never interprets `{!` as the start of an expression.

IN THIS SECTION:

Dynamic Output in Expressions
The simplest way to use expressions is to output dynamic values.

Conditional Expressions
Here are examples of conditional expressions using the ternary operator and the `<aura:if>` tag.

Value Providers
Value providers are a way to access data. Value providers encapsulate related values together, similar to how an object encapsulates properties and methods.

Expression Evaluation
Expressions are evaluated much the same way that expressions in JavaScript or other programming languages are evaluated.

Expression Operators Reference
The expression language supports operators to enable you to create more complex expressions.

Expression Functions Reference
The expression language contains math, string, array, comparison, boolean, and conditional functions. All functions are case-sensitive.

Dynamic Output in Expressions

The simplest way to use expressions is to output dynamic values.

Values used in the expression can be from component attributes, literal values, booleans, and so on. For example:

```
{!v.desc}
```

In this expression, `v` represents the view, which is the set of component attributes, and `desc` is an attribute of the component. The expression is simply outputting the `desc` attribute value for the component that contains this markup.

If you're including literal values in expressions, enclose text values within single quotes, such as `{!'Some text'}`.

Include numbers without quotes, for example, `{!123}`.

For booleans, use `{!true}` for `true` and `{!false}` for `false`.

SEE ALSO:

Component Attributes

Value Providers

Conditional Expressions

Here are examples of conditional expressions using the ternary operator and the `<aura:if>` tag.

Ternary Operator

This expression uses the ternary operator to conditionally output one of two values dependent on a condition.

```
<a class="{!v.location == '/active' ? 'selected' : ''}"
href="#/active">Active</a>
```

The `{!v.location == '/active' ? 'selected' : ''}` expression conditionally sets the `class` attribute of an HTML `<a>` tag, by checking whether the `location` attribute is set to `/active`. If true, the expression sets `class` to `selected`.

Using `<aura:if>` for Conditional Markup

This snippet of markup uses the `<aura:if>` tag to conditionally display an edit button.

```
<aura:attribute name="edit" type="Boolean" default="true"/>
<aura:if isTrue="{!v.edit}">
```

```
    <ui:button label="Edit"/>
    <aura:set attribute="else">
        You can't edit this.
    </aura:set>
</aura:if>
```

If the `edit` attribute is set to `true`, a `ui:button` displays. Otherwise, the text in the `else` attribute displays.

SEE ALSO:

Best Practices for Conditional Markup

Value Providers

Value providers are a way to access data. Value providers encapsulate related values together, similar to how an object encapsulates properties and methods.

The value providers for a component are `v` (view) and `c` (controller).

Value Provider	Description	See Also
v	A component's attribute set. This value provider enables you to access the value of a component's attribute in the component's markup.	Component Attributes
c	A component's controller, which enables you to wire up event handlers and actions for the component	Handling Events with Client-Side Controllers

All components have a `v` value provider, but aren't required to have a controller. Both value providers are created automatically when defined for a component.

 Note: Expressions are bound to the specific component that contains them. That component is also known as the attribute value provider, and is used to resolve any expressions that are passed to attributes of its contained components.

Global Value Providers

Global value providers are global values and methods that a component can use in expressions.

Global Value Provider	Description	See Also
globalID	The `globalId` global value provider returns the global ID for a component. Every component has a unique `globalId`, which is the generated runtime-unique ID of the component instance.	Component IDs
$Browser	The `$Browser` global value provider returns information about the hardware and operating system of the browser accessing the application.	$Browser
$Label	The `$Label` global value provider enables you to access labels stored outside your code.	Using Custom Labels
$Locale	The `$Locale` global value provider returns information about the current user's preferred locale.	$Locale
$Resource	The `$Resource` global value provider lets you reference images, style sheets, and JavaScript code you've uploaded in static resources.	$Resource

Accessing Fields and Related Objects

Values in a value provider are accessed as named properties. To use a value, separate the value provider and the property name with a dot (period). For example, `v.body`. You can access value providers in markup or in JavaScript code.

When an attribute of a component is an object or other structured data (not a primitive value), access the values on that attribute using the same dot notation.

For example, `{!v.accounts.id}` accesses the id field in the accounts record.

For deeply nested objects and attributes, continue adding dots to traverse the structure and access the nested values.

SEE ALSO:

Dynamic Output in Expressions

$Browser

The $Browser global value provider returns information about the hardware and operating system of the browser accessing the application.

Attribute	Description
formFactor	Returns a `FormFactor` enum value based on the type of hardware the browser is running on. • DESKTOP for a desktop client • PHONE for a phone including a mobile phone with a browser and a smartphone • TABLET for a tablet client (for which `isTablet` returns `true`)
isAndroid	Indicates whether the browser is running on an Android device (`true`) or not (`false`).
isIOS	Not available in all implementations. Indicates whether the browser is running on an iOS device (`true`) or not (`false`).
isIPad	Not available in all implementations. Indicates whether the browser is running on an iPad (`true`) or not (`false`).
isIPhone	Not available in all implementations. Indicates whether the browser is running on an iPhone (`true`) or not (`false`).
isPhone	Indicates whether the browser is running on a phone including a mobile phone with a browser and a smartphone (`true`), or not (`false`).
isTablet	Indicates whether the browser is running on an iPad or a tablet with Android 2.2 or later (`true`) or not (`false`).
isWindowsPhone	Indicates whether the browser is running on a Windows phone (`true`) or not (`false`). Note that this only detects Windows phones and does not detect tablets or other touch-enabled Windows 8 devices.

Example: This example shows usage of the `$Browser` global value provider.

```
<aura:component>
    {!$Browser.isTablet}
    {!$Browser.isPhone}
    {!$Browser.isAndroid}
    {!$Browser.formFactor}
</aura:component>
```

Similarly, you can check browser information in a client-side controller using `$A.get()`.

```
({
    checkBrowser: function(component) {
        var device = $A.get("$Browser.formFactor");
        alert("You are using a " + device);
    }
})
```

$Locale

The `$Locale` global value provider returns information about the current user's preferred locale.

These attributes are based on Java's `Calendar`, `Locale` and `TimeZone` classes.

Attribute	Description	Sample Value
country	The ISO 3166 representation of the country code based on the language locale.	"US", "DE", "GB"
currency	The currency symbol.	"$"
currencyCode	The ISO 4217 representation of the currency code.	"USD"
decimal	The decimal separator.	"."
firstDayOfWeek	The first day of the week, where 1 is Sunday.	1
grouping	The grouping separator.	","
isEasternNameStyle	Specifies if a name is based on eastern style, for example, `last name`	false

Attribute	Description	Sample Value
	first name [middle] [suffix].	
labelForToday	The label for the Today link on the date picker.	"Today"
language	The language code based on the language locale.	"en", "de", "zh"
langLocale	The locale ID.	"en_US", "en_GB"
nameOfMonths	The full and short names of the calendar months	{ fullName: "January", shortName: "Jan" }
nameOfWeekdays	The full and short names of the calendar weeks	{ fullName: "Sunday", shortName: "SUN" }
timezone	The time zone ID.	"America/Los_Angeles"
userLocaleCountry	The country based on the current user's locale	"US"
userLocaleLang	The language based on the current user's locale	"en"
variant	The vendor and browser-specific code.	"WIN", "MAC", "POSIX"

Number and Date Formatting

The framework's number and date formatting are based on Java's `DecimalFormat` and `DateFormat` classes.

Attribute	Description	Sample Value
currencyformat	The currency format.	"¤#,##0.00;(¤#,##0.00)" ¤ represents the currency sign, which is replaced by the currency symbol.
dateFormat	The date format.	"MMM d, yyyy"
datetimeFormat	The date time format.	"MMM d, yyyy h:mm:ss a"

Attribute	Description	Sample Value
numberformat	The number format.	"#,##0.###" # represents a digit, the comma is a placeholder for the grouping separator, and the period is a placeholder for the decimal separator. Zero (0) replaces # to represent trailing zeros.
percentformat	The percentage format.	"#,##0%"
timeFormat	The time format.	"h:mm:ss a"
zero	The character for the zero digit.	"0"

Example: This example shows how to retrieve different $Locale attributes.

Component source

```
<aura:component>
    {!$Locale.language}
    {!$Locale.timezone}
    {!$Locale.numberFormat}
    {!$Locale.currencyFormat}
</aura:component>
```

Similarly, you can check locale information in a client-side controller using $A.get().

```
({
    checkDevice: function(component) {
        var locale = $A.get("$Locale.language");
        alert("You are using " + locale);
    }
})
```

SEE ALSO:

Localization

$Resource

The $Resource global value provider lets you reference images, style sheets, and JavaScript code you've uploaded in static resources.

Using $Resource lets you reference assets by name, without worrying about the gory details of URLs or file paths. You can use $Resource in Lightning components markup and within JavaScript controller and helper code.

Using $Resource in Component Markup

To reference a specific resource in component markup, use $Resource.*resourceName* within an expression. *resourceName* is the Name of the static resource. In a managed packaged, the resource name must include the package namespace prefix, such as $Resource.yourNamespace__resourceName. For a stand-alone static resource, such as an individual graphic or script, that's all you need. To reference an item within an archive static resource, add the rest of the path to the item using string concatenation. Here are a few examples.

```
<aura:component>
    <!-- Stand-alone static resources -->
    <img src="{!$Resource.generic_profile_svg}"/>
    <img src="{!$Resource.yourNamespace__generic_profile_svg}"/>

    <!-- Asset from an archive static resource -->
    <img src="{!$Resource.SLDSv1 + '/assets/images/avatar1.jpg'}"/>
    <img src="{!$Resource.yourNamespace__SLDSv1 +
'/assets/images/avatar1.jpg'}"/>
</aura:component>
```

Include CSS style sheets or JavaScript libraries into a component using the <ltng:require> tag. For example:

```
<aura:component>
  <ltng:require
    styles="{!$Resource.SLDSv1 +
'/assets/styles/lightning-design-system-ltng.css'}"
    scripts="{!$Resource.jsLibraries + '/jsLibOne.js'}"
    afterScriptsLoaded="{!c.scriptsLoaded}" />
</aura:component>
```

Note: Due to a quirk in the way $Resource is parsed in expressions, use the join operator to include multiple $Resource references in a single attribute. For example, if you have more than one JavaScript library to include into a component the `scripts` attribute should be something like the following.

```
scripts="{!join(',',
    $Resource.jsLibraries + '/jsLibOne.js',
    $Resource.jsLibraries + '/jsLibTwo.js')}"
```

Using `$Resource` in JavaScript

To obtain a reference to a static resource in JavaScript code, use `$A.get('$Resource.`***resourceName***`')`.

resourceName is the `Name` of the static resource. In a managed packaged, the resource name must include the package namespace prefix, such as `$Resource.yourNamespace__resourceName`. For a stand-alone static resource, such as an individual graphic or script, that's all you need. To reference an item within an archive static resource, add the rest of the path to the item using string concatenation. For example:

```
({
    profileUrl: function(component) {
        var profUrl = $A.get('$Resource.SLDSv1') +
'/assets/images/avatar1.jpg';
        alert("Profile URL: " + profUrl);
    }
})
```

> **Note:** Static resources referenced in JavaScript aren't automatically added to packages. If your JavaScript depends on a resource that isn't referenced in component markup, add it manually to any packages the JavaScript code is included in.

`$Resource` Considerations

Global value providers in the Lightning Component framework are, behind the scenes, implemented quite differently from global variables in Salesforce. Although `$Resource` looks like the global variable with the same name available in Visualforce, formula fields, and elsewhere, there are important differences. Don't use other documentation as a guideline for its use or behavior.

Here are two specific things to keep in mind about `$Resource` in the Lightning Component framework.

First, `$Resource` isn't available until the Lightning Component framework is loaded on the client. Some very simple components that are composed of only markup can be rendered server-side, where `$Resource` isn't available. To avoid this, when you create a new app, stub out a client-side controller to force components to be rendered on the client.

Second, if you've worked with the `$Resource` global variable, in Visualforce or elsewhere, you've also used the `URLFOR()` formula function to construct complete URLs to specific resources. There's nothing similar to `URLFOR()` in the Lightning Component framework. Instead, use simple string concatenation, as illustrated in the preceding examples.

SEE ALSO:

Salesforce Help: Static Resources

Expression Evaluation

Expressions are evaluated much the same way that expressions in JavaScript or other programming languages are evaluated.

Operators are a subset of those available in JavaScript, and evaluation order and precedence are generally the same as JavaScript. Parentheses enable you to ensure a specific evaluation order. What you may find surprising about expressions is how often they are evaluated. The framework notices when things change, and trigger re-rendering of any components that are affected. Dependencies are handled automatically. This is one of the fundamental benefits of the framework. It knows when to re-render something on the page. When a component is re-rendered, any expressions it uses will be re-evaluated.

Action Methods

Expressions are also used to provide action methods for user interface events: `onclick, onhover`, and any other component attributes beginning with "`on`". Some components simplify assigning actions to user interface events using other attributes, such as the `press` attribute on `<ui:button>`.

Action methods must be assigned to attributes using an expression, for example `{!c.theAction}`. This assigns an `Aura.Action`, which is a reference to the controller function that handles the action.

Assigning action methods via expressions allows you to assign them conditionally, based on the state of the application or user interface. For more information, see Conditional Expressions on page 78.

```
<ui:button aura:id="likeBtn"
     label="{!(v.likeId == null) ? 'Like It' : 'Unlike It'}"
     press="{!(v.likeId == null) ? c.likeIt  : c.unlikeIt}"
/>
```

This button will show "Like It" for items that have not yet been liked, and clicking it will call the `likeIt` action method. Then the component will re-render, and the opposite user interface display and method assignment will be in place. Clicking a second time will unlike the item, and so on.

Expression Operators Reference

The expression language supports operators to enable you to create more complex expressions.

Arithmetic Operators

Expressions based on arithmetic operators result in numerical values.

Operator	Usage	Description
+	1 + 1	Add two numbers.
−	2 - 1	Subtract one number from the other.
*	2 * 2	Multiply two numbers.
/	4 / 2	Divide one number by the other.
%	5 % 2	Return the integer remainder of dividing the first number by the second.
−	-v.exp	Unary operator. Reverses the sign of the succeeding number. For example if the value of `expenses` is `100`, then `-expenses` is `-100`.

Numeric Literals

Literal	Usage	Description
Integer	2	Integers are numbers without a decimal point or exponent.
Float	3.14 -1.1e10	Numbers with a decimal point, or numbers with an exponent.
Null	null	A literal null number. Matches the explicit null value **and** numbers with an undefined value.

String Operators

Expressions based on string operators result in string values.

Operator	Usage	Description
+	`'Title: ' + v.note.title`	Concatenates two strings together.

String Literals

String literals must be enclosed in single quotation marks `'like this'`.

Literal	Usage	Description
string	`'hello world'`	Literal strings must be enclosed in single quotation marks. Double quotation marks are reserved for enclosing attribute values, and must be escaped in strings.
\<escape>	`'\n'`	Whitespace characters: • \t (tab) • \n (newline) • \r (carriage return) Escaped characters: • \" (literal ") • \' (literal ') • \\ (literal \)
Unicode	`'\u####'`	A Unicode code point. The # symbols are hexadecimal digits. A Unicode literal requires four digits.
null	`null`	A literal null string. Matches the explicit null value and strings with an undefined value.

Comparison Operators

Expressions based on comparison operators result in a `true` or `false` value. For comparison purposes, numbers are treated as the same type. In all other cases, comparisons check both value and type.

Operator	Alternative	Usage	Description

==	eq	`1 == 1`
		
		`1 == 1.0`
		
		`1 eq 1`
		
		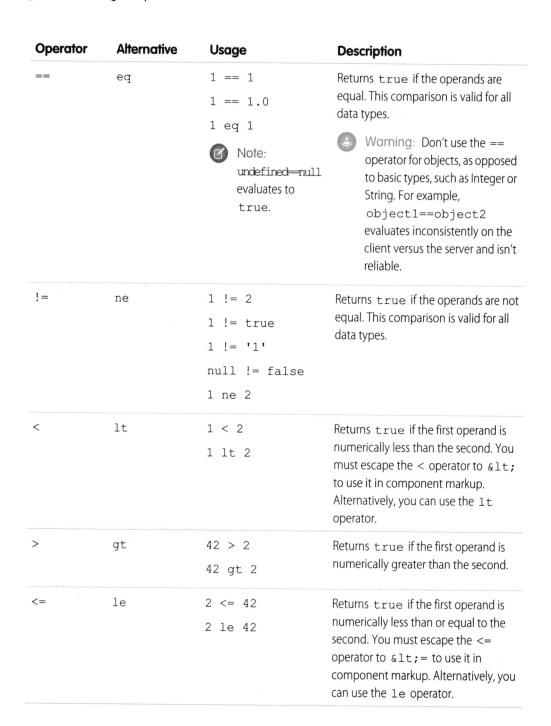 Note:
		~~undefined~~=null
		evaluates to
		true.
			Returns `true` if the operands are equal. This comparison is valid for all data types.
			
			Warning: Don't use the `==` operator for objects, as opposed to basic types, such as Integer or String. For example, `object1==object2` evaluates inconsistently on the client versus the server and isn't reliable.

!=	ne	`1 != 2`
		
		`1 != true`
		
		`1 != '1'`
		
		`null != false`
		
		`1 ne 2`
			Returns `true` if the operands are not equal. This comparison is valid for all data types.

<	lt	`1 < 2`
		
		`1 lt 2`
			Returns `true` if the first operand is numerically less than the second. You must escape the < operator to `&lt;` to use it in component markup. Alternatively, you can use the `lt` operator.

>	gt	`42 > 2`
		
		`42 gt 2`
			Returns `true` if the first operand is numerically greater than the second.

<=	le	`2 <= 42`
		
		`2 le 42`
			Returns `true` if the first operand is numerically less than or equal to the second. You must escape the <= operator to `&lt;=` to use it in component markup. Alternatively, you can use the `le` operator.

Operator	Alternative	Usage	Description
>=	ge	42 >= 42 42 ge 42	Returns `true` if the first operand is numerically greater than or equal to the second.

Logical Operators

Expressions based on logical operators result in a `true` or `false` value.

Operator	Usage	Description
&&	isEnabled && hasPermission	Returns `true` if both operands are individually true. You must escape the `&&` operator to `&amp;&amp;` to use it in component markup. Alternatively, you can use the `and()` function and pass it two arguments. For example, `and(isEnabled, hasPermission)`.
||	hasPermission || isRequired	Returns `true` if either operand is individually true.
!	!isRequired	Unary operator. Returns `true` if the operand is false. This operator should not be confused with the `!` delimiter used to start an expression in `{!`. You can combine the expression delimiter with this negation operator to return the logical negation of a value, for example, `{!!true}` returns `false`.

Logical Literals

Logical values are never equivalent to non-logical values. That is, only `true == true`, and only `false == false`; `1 != true`, and `0 != false`, and `null != false`.

Literal	Usage	Description
true	true	A boolean `true` value.
false	false	A boolean `false` value.

Conditional Operator

There is only one conditional operator, the traditional ternary operator.

Operator	Usage	Description
? :	(1 != 2) ? "Obviously" : "Black is White"	The operand before the ? operator is evaluated as a boolean. If true, the second operand is returned. If false, the third operand is returned.

SEE ALSO:

Expression Functions Reference

Expression Functions Reference

The expression language contains math, string, array, comparison, boolean, and conditional functions. All functions are case-sensitive.

Math Functions

The math functions perform math operations on numbers. They take numerical arguments. The Corresponding Operator column lists equivalent operators, if any.

Function	Alternative	Usage	Description	Corresponding Operator
add	concat	add(1,2)	Adds the first argument to the second.	+
sub	subtract	sub(10,2)	Subtracts the second argument from the first.	−
mult	multiply	mult(2,10)	Multiplies the first argument by the second.	*

Function	Alternative	Usage	Description	Corresponding Operator
div	divide	div(4,2)	Divides the first argument by the second.	/
mod	modulus	mod(5,2)	Returns the integer remainder resulting from dividing the first argument by the second.	%
abs		abs(-5)	Returns the absolute value of the argument: the same number if the argument is positive, and the number without its negative sign if the number is negative. For example, abs(-5) is 5.	None
neg	negate	neg(100)	Reverses the sign of the argument. For example, neg(100) is -100.	- (unary)

String Functions

Function	Alternative	Usage	Description	Corresponding Operator
concat	add	concat('Hello ', 'world') add('Walk ', 'the dog')	Concatenates the two arguments.	+
format		format($Label.ns.labelName, v.myVal) 📝 Note: This function works for arguments of type String, Decimal, Double, Integer, Long, Array, String[], List, and Set.	Replaces any parameter placeholders with comma-separated attribute values.	
join		join(separator, subStr1, subStr2, subStrN) join(' ','class1', 'class2', v.class)	Joins the substrings adding the separator String (first argument) between each subsequent argument.	

Label Functions

Function	Usage	Description
format	format($Label.np.labelName, v.attribute1 , v.attribute2) format($Label.np.hello, v.name)	Outputs a label and updates it. Replaces any parameter placeholders with comma-separated attribute values. Supports

Function	Usage	Description
		ternary operators in labels and attributes.

Informational Functions

Function	Usage	Description
length	`myArray.length`	Returns the length of an array or a string.
empty	`empty(v.attributeName)` Note: This function works for arguments of type `String`, `Array`, `Object`, `List`, `Map`, or `Set`.	Returns `true` if the argument is empty. An empty argument is `undefined`, `null`, an empty array, or an empty string. An object with no properties is not considered empty. Tip: `{! !empty(v.myArray)}` evaluates faster than `{!v.myArray && v.myArray.length > 0}` so we recommend `empty()` to improve performance. The `$A.util.isEmpty()` method in JavaScript is equivalent to the `empty()` expression in markup.

Comparison Functions

Comparison functions take two number arguments and return `true` or `false` depending on the comparison result. The `eq` and `ne` functions can also take other data types for their arguments, such as strings.

Function	Usage	Description	Corresponding Operator
equals	`equals(1,1)`	Returns `true` if the specified arguments are equal. The arguments can be any data type.	`==` or `eq`

Function	Usage	Description	Corresponding Operator
notequals	notequals(1,2)	Returns true if the specified arguments are not equal. The arguments can be any data type.	!= or ne
lessthan	lessthan(1,5)	Returns true if the first argument is numerically less than the second argument.	< or lt
greaterthan	greaterthan(5,1)	Returns true if the first argument is numerically greater than the second argument.	> or gt
lessthanorequal	lessthanorequal(1,2)	Returns true if the first argument is numerically less than or equal to the second argument.	<= or le
greaterthanorequal	greaterthanorequal(2,1)	Returns true if the first argument is numerically greather than or equal to the second argument.	>= or ge

Boolean Functions

Boolean functions operate on Boolean arguments. They are equivalent to logical operators.

Function	Usage	Description	Corresponding Operator
and	and(isEnabled, hasPermission)	Returns true if both arguments are true.	&&
or	or(hasPermission, hasVIPPass)	Returns true if either one of the arguments is true.	||
not	not(isNew)	Returns true if the argument is false.	!

Conditional Function

Function	Usage	Description	Corresponding Operator
if	if(isEnabled, 'Enabled', 'Not enabled')	Evaluates the first argument as a boolean. If true, returns the second argument. Otherwise, returns the third argument.	?: (ternary)

Using Labels

The framework supports various methods to provide labels in your code using the $Label global value provider, which accesses labels stored outside your code.

This section discusses how to use the $Label global value provider with these methods:

- The label attribute in input components
- The format() expression function for dynamically populating placeholder values in labels

IN THIS SECTION:

Using Custom Labels
Use custom labels in Lightning components with the $Label global value provider.

Input Component Labels
A label describes the purpose of an input component. To set a label on an input component, use the label attribute.

Dynamically Populating Label Parameters
Output and update labels using the format() expression function.

Setting Label Values via a Parent Attribute
Setting label values via a parent attribute is useful if you want control over labels in child components.

Using Custom Labels

Use custom labels in Lightning components with the $Label global value provider.

Custom labels are custom text values that can be translated into any language Salesforce supports. Custom labels enable developers to create multilingual applications by automatically presenting information (for example, help text or error messages) in a user's native language.

To create custom labels, from Setup, enter `Custom Labels` in the `Quick Find` box, then select **Custom Labels**.

Use this syntax to access custom labels in Lightning components:

- `$Label.c.`***labelName*** for the default namespace
- `$Label.`***namespace***`.`***labelName*** if your org has a namespace

Here are some examples.

Label in a markup expression using the default namespace

`{!$Label.c.`***labelName***`}`

Label in JavaScript code if your org has a namespace

`$A.get("$Label.`***namespace***`.`***labelName***`")`

 Note: Custom labels referenced in a Lightning component are not automatically added when you create a package containing the Lightning component. To include a custom label in a package, another member of the package, such as a Visualforce page, must reference the custom label.

SEE ALSO:

Value Providers

Input Component Labels

A label describes the purpose of an input component. To set a label on an input component, use the `label` attribute.

This example shows how to use labels using the `label` attribute on an input component.

```
<ui:inputNumber label="Pick a Number:" value="54" />
```

The label is placed on the left of the input field and can be hidden by setting `labelClass="assistiveText"`. `assistiveText` is a global style class used to support accessibility.

Using `$Label`

Use the `$Label` global value provider to access labels stored in an external source. For example:

```
<ui:inputNumber label="{!$Label.Number.PickOne}" />
```

To output a label and dynamically update it, use the `format()` expression function. For example, if you have `np.labelName` set to `Hello {0}`, the following expression returns `Hello World` if `v.name` is set to `World`.

```
{!format($Label.np.labelName, v.name)}
```

SEE ALSO:

Supporting Accessibility

Dynamically Populating Label Parameters

Output and update labels using the `format()` expression function.

You can provide a string with placeholders, which are replaced by the substitution values at runtime.

Add as many parameters as you need. The parameters are numbered and are zero-based. For example, if you have three parameters, they will be named `{0}`, `{1}`, and `{2}`, and they will be substituted in the order they're specified.

Let's look at a custom label, `$Label.mySection.myLabel`, with a value of `Hello {0} and {1}`, where `$Label` is the global value provider that accesses your labels.

This expression dynamically populates the placeholder parameters with the values of the supplied attributes.

```
{!format($Label.mySection.myLabel, v.attribute1, v.attribute2)}
```

The label is automatically refreshed if one of the attribute values changes.

 Note: Always use the `$Label` global value provider to reference a label with placeholder parameters. You can't set a string with placeholder parameters as the first argument for `format()`. For example, this syntax doesn't work:

```
{!format('Hello {0}', v.name)}
```

Use this expression instead.

```
{!format($Label.mySection.salutation, v.name)}
```

where `$Label.mySection.salutation` is set to `Hello {0}`.

Setting Label Values via a Parent Attribute

Setting label values via a parent attribute is useful if you want control over labels in child components.

Let's say that you have a container component, which contains another component, `inner.cmp`. You want to set a label value in `inner.cmp` via an attribute on the container component. This can be done by specifying the attribute type and default value. You must set a default value in the parent attribute if you are setting a label on an inner component, as shown in the following example.

This is the container component, which contains a default value `My Label` for the `_label` attribute
.

```
<aura:component>
    <aura:attribute name="_label"
                    type="String"
                    default="My Label"/>
    <ui:button label="Set Label" aura:id="button1"
press="{!c.setLabel}"/>
    <auradocs:inner aura:id="inner" label="{!v._label}"/>
</aura:component>
```

This `inner` component contains a text area component and a `label` attribute that's set by the container component.

```
<aura:component>
    <aura:attribute name="label" type="String"/>
    <ui:inputTextarea aura:id="textarea"
                    label="{!v.label}"/>
</aura:component>
```

This client-side controller action updates the label value.

```
({
    setLabel:function(cmp) {
        cmp.set("v._label", 'new label');
    }
})
```

When the component is initialized, you'll see a button and a text area with the label `My Label`. When the button in the container component is clicked, the `setLabel` action updates the label value in the `inner` component. This action finds the `label` attribute and sets its value to `new label`.

SEE ALSO:

  Input Component Labels

  Component Attributes

Localization

The framework provides client-side localization support on input and output components.

The following example shows how you can override the default `langLocale` and `timezone` attributes. The output displays the time in the format `hh:mm` by default.

 Note: For more information on supported attributes, see the Reference Doc App.

Component source

```
<aura:component>
    <ui:outputDateTime value="2013-10-07T00:17:08.997Z"
timezone="Europe/Berlin" langLocale="de"/>
</aura:component>
```

The component renders as `Okt. 7, 2015 2:17:08 AM`.

Additionally, you can use the global value provider, `$Locale`, to obtain the locale information. The locale settings in your organization overrides the browser's locale information.

Working with Locale Information

The Salesforce settings for language, locale, time zone, and currency can affect how objects (Accounts, Leads, Opportunities, etc.) are displayed. In a single currency organization, the Salesforce administrators set the currency locale, default language, default locale, and default time zone for their organizations and the users can set their individual language, locale, and time zone on their personal settings pages. In a multiple currency organization, the Salesforce administrators set the corporate currency, default language, default locale, and default time zone for their organizations and the users can set their individual currency, language, locale, and time zone on their personal settings pages.

 Note: Single language organizations cannot change their language, although they can change their locale.

For example, setting the time zone on the Language & Time Zone page to `(GMT+02:00)` returns `28.09.2015 09:00:00` when you run the following code.

```
<ui:outputDateTime value="09/28/2015" />
```

Running `$A.get("$Locale.timezone")` returns the time zone name, for example, `Europe/Paris`. For more information, see "Supported Time Zones" in the Salesforce Help.

Setting the currency locale on the Company Information page to `Japanese (Japan) - JPY` returns ¥`100,000` when you run the following code.

```
<ui:outputCurrency value="100000" />
```

Similarly, running `$A.get("$Locale.currency")` returns `"¥"` when your org's currency locale is set to `Japanese (Japan) - JPY`. For more information, see "Supported Currencies" in the Salesforce Help.

Using the Localization Service

The framework's localization service enables you to manage the localization of date, time, numbers, and currencies. These methods are available in the `AuraLocalizationService` JavaScript API.

This example sets the formatted date time using `$Locale` and the localization service.

```
var dateFormat = $A.get("$Locale.dateFormat");
var dateString = $A.localizationService.formatDateTime(new Date(),
dateFormat);
```

If you're not retrieving the browser's date information, you can specify the date format on your own. This example specifies the date format and uses the browser's language locale information.

```
var dateFormat = "MMMM d, yyyy h:mm a";
var userLocaleLang = $A.get("$Locale.langLocale");
return $A.localizationService.formatDate(date, dateFormat,
userLocaleLang);
```

The `AuraLocalizationService` JavaScript API provides methods for working with localization. For example, you can compare two dates to check that one is later than the other.

```
var startDateTime = new Date();
//return the date time at end of the day
var endDateTime = $A.localizationService.endOf(d, 'day');
if( $A.localizationService.isAfter(startDateTime,endDateTime)) {
    //throw an error if startDateTime is after endDateTime
}
```

> Note: For more information on the localization service, see the JavaScript API in the Reference Doc App.

SEE ALSO:

Value Providers

Providing Component Documentation

Component documentation helps others understand and use your components.

You can provide two types of component reference documentation:

- Documentation definition (DocDef): Full documentation on a component, including a description, sample code, and a reference to an example. DocDef supports extensive HTML markup and is useful for describing what a component is and what it does.
- Inline descriptions: Text-only descriptions, typically one or two sentences, set via the `description` attribute in a tag.

To provide a DocDef, click **DOCUMENTATION** in the component sidebar of the Developer Console. The following example shows the DocDef for `np:myComponent`.

> Note: DocDef is currently supported for components and applications. Events and interfaces support inline descriptions only.

```
<aura:documentation>
    <aura:description>
        <p>An <code>np:myComponent</code> component represents an
element that executes an action defined by a controller.</p>
        <!--More markup here, such as <pre> for code samples-->
    </aura:description>
    <aura:example name="myComponentExample" ref="np:myComponentExample"
 label="Using the np:myComponent Component">
 <p>This example shows a simple setup of <code>myComponent</code>.</p>

    </aura:example>
    <aura:example name="mySecondExample" ref="np:mySecondExample"
label="Customizing the np:myComponent Component">
        <p>This example shows how you can customize
<code>myComponent</code>.</p>
    </aura:example>
</aura:documentation>
```

A documentation definition contains these tags.

Tag	Description
`<aura:documentation>`	The top-level definition of the DocDef
`<aura:description>`	Describes the component using extensive HTML markup. To include code samples in the description, use the `<pre>` tag, which renders as a code block. Code entered in the `<pre>` tag must be escaped. For example, escape `<aura:component>` by entering `&lt;aura:component&gt;`.
`<aura:example>`	References an example that demonstrates how the component is used. Supports extensive HTML markup, which displays as text preceding the visual output and example component source. The example is displayed as interactive output. Multiple examples are supported and should be wrapped in individual `<aura:example>` tags. • `name`: The API name of the example • `ref`: The reference to the example component in the format `<namespace:exampleComponent>` • `label`: The label of the title

Providing an Example Component

Recall that the DocDef includes a reference to an example component. The example component is rendered as an interactive demo in the component reference documentation when it's wired up using `aura:example`.

```
<aura:example name="myComponentExample" ref="np:myComponentExample"
label="Using the np:myComponent Component">
```

The following is an example component that demonstrates how `np:myComponent` can be used.

```
<!--The np:myComponentExample example component-->
<aura:component>
    <np:myComponent>
        <aura:set attribute="myAttribute">This sets the attribute on
the np:myComponent component.</aura:set>
        <!--More markup that demonstrates the usage of np:myComponent-->
```

```
    </np:myComponent>
</aura:component>
```

Providing Inline Descriptions

Inline descriptions provide a brief overview of what an element is about. HTML markup is not supported in inline descriptions. These tags support inline descriptions via the `description` attribute.

Tag	Example
`<aura:component>`	`<aura:component description="Represents a button element">`
`<aura:attribute>`	`<aura:attribute name="langLocale" type="String" description="The language locale used to format date value."/>`
`<aura:event>`	`<aura:event type="COMPONENT" description="Indicates that a keyboard key has been pressed and released"/>`
`<aura:interface>`	`<aura:interface description="A common interface for date components"/>`
`<aura:registerEvent>`	`<aura:registerEvent name="keydown" type="ui:keydown" description="Indicates that a key is pressed"/>`

Viewing the Documentation

The documentation you create will be available at `https://<myDomain>.lightning.force.com/auradocs/reference.app`, where `<myDomain>` is the name of your custom Salesforce domain.

SEE ALSO:

Reference

Working with UI Components

The framework provides common user interface components in the `ui` namespace. All of these components extend either `aura:component` or a child component of `aura:component`. `aura:component` is an abstract component that provides a default rendering implementation. User interface components such as `ui:input` and `ui:output` provide easy handling of common user interface events like keyboard and mouse interactions. Each component can be styled and extended accordingly.

For all the components available, see the component reference at `https://<myDomain>.lightning.force.com/auradocs/reference.app`, where `<myDomain>` is the name of your custom Salesforce domain.

Complex, Interactive Components

The following components contain one or more sub-components and are interactive.

Type	Key Components	Description
Message	`ui:message`	A message notification of varying severity levels
Menu	`ui:menu`	A drop-down list with a trigger that controls its visibility
	`ui:menuList`	A list of menu items
	`ui:actionMenuItem`	A menu item that triggers an action
	`ui:checkboxMenuItem`	A menu item that supports multiple selection and can be used to trigger an action
	`ui:radioMenuItem`	A menu item that supports single selection and can be used to trigger an action
	`ui:menuItemSeparator`	A visual separator for menu items
	`ui:menuItem`	An abstract and extensible component for menu items in a `ui:menuList` component
	`ui:menuTrigger`	A trigger that expands and collapses a menu
	`ui:menuTriggerLink`	A link that triggers a dropdown menu. This component extends `ui:menuTrigger`

Input Control Components

The following components are interactive, for example, like buttons and checkboxes.

Type	Key Components	Description
Button	`ui:button`	An actionable button that can be pressed or clicked
Checkbox	`ui:inputCheckbox`	A selectable option that supports multiple selections
	`ui:outputCheckbox`	Displays a read-only value of the checkbox
Radio button	`ui:inputRadio`	A selectable option that supports only a single selection
Drop-down List	`ui:inputSelect`	A drop-down list with options
	`ui:inputSelectOption`	An option in a `ui:inputSelect` component

Visual Components

The following components provides informative cues, for example, like error messages and loading spinners.

Type	Key Components	Description
Field-level error	`ui:inputDefaultError`	An error message that is displayed when an error occurs
Spinner	`ui:spinner`	A loading spinner

Field Components

The following components enables you to enter or display values.

Type	Key Components	Description
Currency	`ui:inputCurrency`	An input field for entering currency
	`ui:outputCurrency`	Displays currency in a default or specified format
Email	`ui:inputEmail`	An input field for entering an email address
	`ui:outputEmail`	Displays a clickable email address

Type	Key Components	Description
Date and time	ui:inputDate	An input field for entering a date
	ui:inputDateTime	An input field for entering a date and time
	ui:outputDate	Displays a date in the default or specified format
	ui:outputDateTime	Displays a date and time in the default or specified format
Password	ui:inputSecret	An input field for entering secret text
Phone Number	ui:inputPhone	An input field for entering a telephone number
	ui:outputPhone	Displays a phone number
Number	ui:inputNumber	An input field for entering a numerical value
	ui:outputNumber	Displays a number
Range	ui:inputRange	An input field for entering a value within a range
Rich Text	ui:inputRichText	An input field for entering rich text
	ui:outputRichText	Displays rich text
Text	ui:inputText	An input field for entering a single line of text
	ui:outputText	Displays text
Text Area	ui:inputTextArea	An input field for entering multiple lines of text
	ui:outputTextArea	Displays a read-only text area
URL	ui:inputURL	An input field for entering a URL
	ui:outputURL	Displays a clickable URL

SEE ALSO:

Using the UI Components

Creating Components

Component Bundles

UI Events

UI components provide easy handling of user interface events such as keyboard and mouse interactions. By listening to these events, you can also bind values on UI input components using the `updateon` attribute, such that the values update when those events are fired.

Capture a UI event by defining its handler on the component. For example, you want to listen to the HTML DOM event, `onblur`, on a `ui:inputTextArea` component.

```
<ui:inputTextArea aura:id="textarea" value="My text area" label="Type
  something"
      blur="{!c.handleBlur}" />
```

The `blur="{!c.handleBlur}"` listens to the `onblur` event and wires it to your client-side controller. When you trigger the event, the following client-side controller handles the event.

```
handleBlur : function(cmp, event, helper){
    var elem = cmp.find("textarea").getElement();
    //do something else
}
```

For all available events on all components, see the #aura_compref.

Value Binding for Browser Events

Any changes to the UI are reflected in the component attribute, and any change in that attribute is propagated to the UI. When you load the component, the value of the input elements are initialized to those of the component attributes. Any changes to the user input causes the value of the component variable to be updated. For example, a `ui:inputText` component can contain a value that's bound to a component attribute, and the `ui:outputText` component is bound to the same component attribute. The `ui:inputText` component listens to the `onkeyup` browser event and updates the corresponding component attribute values.

```
<aura:attribute name="first" type="String" default="John"/>
<aura:attribute name="last" type="String" default="Doe"/>

<ui:inputText label="First Name" value="{!v.first}" updateOn="keyup"/>
<ui:inputText label="Last Name" value="{!v.last}" updateOn="keyup"/>

<!-- Returns "John Doe" -->
<ui:outputText value="{!v.first +' '+ v.last}"/>
```

The next example takes in numerical inputs and returns the sum of those numbers. The `ui:inputNumber` component listens to the `onkeyup` browser event. When the value in this component changes on the keyup event, the value in the `ui:outputNumber` component is updated as well, and returns the sum of the two values.

```
<aura:attribute name="number1" type="integer" default="1"/>
<aura:attribute name="number2" type="integer" default="2"/>

<ui:inputNumber label="Number 1" value="{!v.number1}" updateOn="keyup"
 />
<ui:inputNumber label="Number 2" value="{!v.number2}"  updateOn="keyup"
 />

<!-- Adds the numbers and returns the sum -->
<ui:outputNumber  value="{!(v.number1 * 1) + (v.number2 * 1)}"/>
```

 Note: The input fields return a string value and must be properly handled to accommodate numerical values. In this example, both values are multiplied by 1 to obtain their numerical equivalents.

Using the UI Components

Users interact with your app through input elements to select or enter values. Components such as `ui:inputText` and `ui:inputCheckbox` correspond to common input elements. These components simplify event handling for user interface events.

 Note: For all available component attributes and events, see the component reference at `https://<myDomain>.lightning.force.com/auradocs/reference.app`, where `<myDomain>` is the name of your custom Salesforce domain .

To use input components in your own custom component, add them to your `.cmp` or `.app` resource. This example is a basic set up of a text field and button. The `aura:id` attribute defines a unique ID that enables you to reference the component from your JavaScript code using `cmp.find("myID");`.

```
<ui:inputText label="Name" aura:id="name" placeholder="First, Last"/>
<ui:outputText aura:id="nameOutput" value=""/>
<ui:button aura:id="outputButton" label="Submit" press="{!c.getInput}"/>
```

 Note: All text fields must specify the `label` attribute to provide a textual label of the field. If you must hide the label from view, set `labelClass="assitiveText"` to make the label available to assistive technologies.

The `ui:outputText` component acts as a placeholder for the output value of its corresponding `ui:inputText` component. The value in the `ui:outputText` component can be set with the following client-side controller action.

```
getInput : function(cmp, event) {
    var fullName = cmp.find("name").get("v.value");
    var outName = cmp.find("nameOutput");
    outName.set("v.value", fullName);
}
```

The following example is similar to the previous, but uses value binding without a client-side controller. The `ui:outputText` component reflects the latest value on the `ui:inputText` component when the `onkeyup` browser event is fired.

```
<aura:attribute name="first" type="String" default="John"/>
<aura:attribute name="last" type="String" default="Doe"/>

<ui:inputText label="First Name" value="{!v.first}" updateOn="keyup"/>
<ui:inputText label="Last Name" value="{!v.last}" updateOn="keyup"/>

<!-- Returns "John Doe" -->
<ui:outputText value="{!v.first +' '+ v.last}"/>
```

> **Tip:** To create and edit records in Salesforce1, use the `force:createRecord` and `force:recordEdit` events to utilize the built-in record create and edit pages.

Date and Time Fields

Date and time fields provide client-side localization, date picker support, and support for common keyboard and mouse events. If you want to render the output from these field components, use the respective `ui:output` components. For example, to render the output for the `ui:inputDate` component, use `ui:outputDate`.

Date and Time fields are represented by the following components.

Field Type	Description	Related Components
Date	An input field for entering a date of type `text`. Provide a date picker by setting `displayDatePicker="true"`. Web apps running on mobiles	`ui:inputDate` `ui:outputDate`

Field Type	Description	Related Components
	and tablets use an input field of type `date`.	
Date and Time	An input field for entering a date and time of type `text`. Provide a date picker and time picker by setting `displayDatePicker="true"`. On desktop, the date and time fields display as two separate fields. The time picker displays a list of time in 30-minute increments. Web apps running on mobiles and tablets use an input field of type `datetime-local`.	`ui:inputDateTime` `ui:outputDateTime`

Using the Date and Time Fields

This is a basic set up of a date field with a date picker.

```
<ui:inputDate aura:id="dateField" label="Birthday" value="2000-01-01"
  displayDatePicker="true"/>
```

This example results in the following HTML.

```
<div class="uiInput uiInputDate uiInput--default uiInput--input
uiInput--datetime">
  <label class="uiLabel-left form-element__label uiLabel">
    <span>Birthday</span>
  </label>
  <form class="form--stacked form-element">
      <input placeholder="MMM d, yyyy" type="text">
      <a class="datePicker-openIcon display" aria-haspopup="true">
         <span class="assistiveText">Date Picker</span>
      </a>
  <a class="clearIcon hide">
    <span class="assistiveText">Clear Button</span>
  </a>
  </form>
```

```
</div>
<div class="DESKTOP uiDatePicker--default uiDatePicker">
    <!--Date picker set to visible when icon is clicked-->
</div>
```

Binding Field Values

You can bind field values to a field in an object using expressions such as `{!v.myAttribute.Name}` or `{!v.myAttribute.namespace__MyField__c}`, and saving an input value via an Apex controller. For an example, see Create a Standalone Lightning App on page 9.

Styling Your Date and Time Fields

You can style the appearance of your date and time field and output in the CSS resource of your component.

The following example provides styles to a `ui:inputDateTime` component with the `myStyle` selector.

```
<!-- Component markup -->
<ui:inputDateTime class="myStyle" label="Date"
displayDatePicker="true"/>

/* CSS */
.THIS .myStyle {
  border: 1px solid #dce4ec;
  border-radius: 4px;
}
```

SEE ALSO:

Input Component Labels

Handling Events with Client-Side Controllers

Localization

CSS in Components

Number Fields

Number fields can contain a numerical value. They support client-side formatting, localization, and common keyboard and mouse events.

If you want to render the output from these field components, use the respective `ui:output` components. For example, to render the output for the `ui:inputNumber` component, use `ui:outputNumber`.

Number fields are represented by the following components.

Type	Related Components	Description
Number	`ui:inputNumber`	An input field for entering a numerical value
	`ui:outputNumber`	Displays a number
Currency	`ui:inputCurrency`	An input field for entering currency
	`ui:outputCurrency`	Displays currency

Using the Number Fields

This example shows a number field, which displays a value of `10`.

```
<aura:attribute name="num" type="integer" default="10"/>
<ui:inputNumber aura:id="num" label="Age" value="{!v.num}"/>
```

The previous example results in the following HTML.

```
<div class="uiInput uiInputText uiInputNumber">
  <label class="uiLabel-left uiLabel">
    <span>Enter age</span>
  </label>
  <input aria-describedby placeholder type="text"
         class="uiInput uiInputText uiInputNumber">
</div>
```

Binding Field Values

You can bind field values to a field in an object using expressions such as `{!v.myAttribute.Name}` or `{!v.myAttribute.namespace__MyField__c}`, and saving an input value via an Apex controller. For an example, see Create a Standalone Lightning App on page 9.

Returning a Valid Number

The value of the `ui:inputNumber` component expects a valid number and won't work with commas. If you want to include commas, use `type="Integer"` instead of `type="String"`.

This example returns `100,000`.

```
<aura:attribute name="number" type="Integer" default="100,000"/>
<ui:inputNumber label="Number" value="{!v.number}"/>
```

This example also returns `100,000`.

```
<aura:attribute name="number" type="String" default="100000"/>
<ui:inputNumber label="Number" value="{!v.number}"/>
```

Formatting and Localizing the Number Fields

The `format` attribute determines the format of the number input. The Locale default format is used if none is provided. The following code is a basic set up of a number field, which displays `10,000.00` based on the provided `format` attribute.

```
<ui:inputNumber label="Cost" aura:id="costField" format="#,##0,000.00#"
  value="10000"/>
```

Styling Your Number Fields

You can style the appearance of your number field and output. In the CSS file of your component, add the corresponding class selectors. The following class selectors provide styles to the string rendering of the numbers. For example, to style the `ui:inputCurrency` component, use `.THIS .uiInputCurrency`, or `.THIS.uiInputCurrency` if it's a top-level element.

The following example provides styles to a `ui:inputNumber` component with the `myStyle` selector.

```
<!-- Component markup -->
<ui:inputNumber class="myStyle" label="Amount" placeholder="0" />

/* CSS */
.THIS .myStyle {
  border: 1px solid #dce4ec;
```

```
    border-radius: 4px;
}
```

SEE ALSO:

Input Component Labels

Handling Events with Client-Side Controllers

Localization

CSS in Components

Text Fields

A text field can contain alphanumerical characters and special characters. They provide common keyboard and mouse events. If you want to render the output from these field components, use the respective `ui:output` components. For example, to render the output for the `ui:inputPhone` component, use `ui:outputPhone`.

Text fields are represented by the following components.

Type	Related Components	Description
Email	`ui:inputEmail`	An input field for entering an email address
	`ui:outputEmail`	Displays a clickable email address
Password	`ui:inputSecret`	An input field for entering secret text
Phone Number	`ui:inputPhone`	An input field for entering a telephone number
	`ui:outputPhone`	Displays a clickable phone number
Rich Text	`ui:inputRichText`	An input field for entering rich text
	`ui:outputRichText`	Displays rich text
Text	`ui:inputText`	An input field for entering single line of text

Type	Related Components	Description
	`ui:outputText`	Displays text
Text Area	`ui:inputTextArea`	An input field for entering multiple lines of text
	`ui:outputTextArea`	Displays a read-only text area
URL	`ui:inputURL`	An input field for entering a URL
	`ui:outputURL`	Displays a clickable URL

Using the Text Fields

Text fields are typically used in a form. For example, this is a basic set up of an email field.

```
<ui:inputEmail aura:id="email" label="Email"
placeholder="abc@email.com"/>
```

This example results in the following HTML.

```
<div class="uiInput uiInputEmail uiInput--default uiInput--input">
  <label class="uiLabel-left form-element__label uiLabel">
    <span>Email</span>
  </label>
  <input placeholder="abc@email.com" type="email" class="input">
</div>
```

📝 Note: You can also use the force:navigateToURL event to make an element behave like a URL link. For more information, see force:navigateToURL.

Binding Field Values

You can bind field values to a field in an object using expressions such as `{!v.myAttribute.Name}` or `{!v.myAttribute.namespace__MyField__c}`, and saving an input value via an Apex controller. For an example, see Create a Standalone Lightning App on page 9.

Styling Your Text Fields

You can style the appearance of your text field and output. In the CSS file of your component, add the corresponding class selectors.

For example, to style the `ui:inputPhone` component, use `.THIS .uiInputPhone`, or `.THIS.uiInputPhone` if it's a top-level element.

The following example provides styles to a `ui:inputText` component with the `myStyle` selector.

```
<!-- Component markup-->
<ui:inputText class="myStyle" label="Name"/>

/* CSS */
.THIS .myStyle {
  border: 1px solid #dce4ec;
  border-radius: 4px;
}
```

SEE ALSO:

Rich Text Fields

Input Component Labels

Handling Events with Client-Side Controllers

Localization

CSS in Components

Rich Text Fields

`ui:inputRichText` is an input field for entering rich text. The following code shows a basic implementation of this component, which is rendered as a text area and button. A button click runs the client-side controller action that returns the input value in a `ui:outputRichText` component. In this case, the value returns "Aura" in bold, and "input rich text demo" in red.

```
<!--Rich text demo-->
  <ui:inputRichText isRichText="false" aura:id="inputRT" label="Rich
Text Demo"
    cols="50" rows="5" value="&lt;b&gt;Aura&lt;/b&gt;, &lt;span
style='color:red'&gt;input rich text demo&lt;/span&gt;"/>
  <ui:button aura:id="outputButton"
    buttonTitle="Click to see what you put into the rich text field"

    label="Display" press="{!c.getInput}"/>
  <ui:outputRichText aura:id="outputRT" value=" "/>
```

```
/*Client-side controller*/
  getInput : function(cmp) {
```

```
    var userInput = cmp.find("inputRT").get("v.value");
    var output = cmp.find("outputRT");
    output.set("v.value", userInput);
}
```

In this demo, the `isRichText="false"` attribute replaces the component with the `ui:inputTextArea` component. The WYSIWYG rich text editor is provided when this attribute is not set, as shown below.

The width and height of the rich text editor are independent of those on the `ui:inputTextArea` component. To set the width and height of the component when you set `isRichText="false"`, use the `cols` and `rows` attributes. Otherwise, use the `width` and `height` attributes.

SEE ALSO:

Text Fields

Checkboxes

Checkboxes are clickable and actionable, and they can be presented in a group for multiple selection. You can create a checkbox with `ui:inputCheckbox`, which inherits the behavior and events from `ui:input`. The `value` and `disabled` attributes control the state of a checkbox, and events such as `click` and `change` determine its behavior. Events must be used separately on each checkbox.

Here are several basic ways to set up a checkbox.

Checked

To select the checkbox, set `value="true"`. This example sets the inital value of the checkbox.

```
<aura:attribute name="check" type="Boolean" default="true"/>
<ui:inputcheckbox value="{!v.check}"/>
```

Disabled State

```
<ui:inputCheckbox disabled="true" label="Select" />
```

The previous example results in the following HTML.

```
<div class="uiInput uiInputCheckbox uiInput--default uiInput--checkbox">
<label class="uiLabel-left form-element__label uiLabel"
for="globalId"><span>Select</span></label>
<input disabled="disabled" type="checkbox" id="globalId">
```

Working with Events

Common events for ui:inputCheckbox include the click and change events. For example, click="{!c.done}" calls the client-side controller action with the function name, done.

The following code crosses out the checkbox item.

```
<!--The checkbox-->
    <ui:inputCheckbox label="Cross this out" click="{!c.crossout}"
class="line" />

    /*The controller action*/
    crossout : function(cmp, event){
        var cmpSource = event.getSource();
        $A.util.toggleClass(cmpSource, "done");
    }
```

Styling Your Checkboxes

The ui:inputCheckbox component is customizable with regular CSS styling. This example shows a checkbox with the following image.

```
<ui:inputCheckbox labelClass="check"
                  label="Select?" value="true" />
```

The following CSS style replaces the default checkbox with the given image.

```
.THIS input[type="checkbox"] {
    display: none;
}
```

```
.THIS .check span {
    margin: 20px;
}

.THIS input[type="checkbox"]+label {
    display: inline-block;
    width: 20px;
    height: 20px;
    vertical-align: middle;
    background: url('images/checkbox.png') top left;
        cursor: pointer;
}

.THIS input[type="checkbox"]:checked+label {
    background:url('images/checkbox.png') bottom left;
}
```

SEE ALSO:

Handling Events with Client-Side Controllers

CSS in Components

Radio Buttons

Radio buttons are clickable and actionable, and they can only be individually selected when presented in a group. You can create a radio button with `ui:inputRadio`, which inherits the behavior and events from `ui:input`. The `value` and `disabled` attributes control the state of a radio button, and events such as `click` and `change` determine its behavior. Events must be used separately on each radio button.

If you want to use radio buttons in a menu, use `ui:radioMenuItem` instead.

Here are several basic ways to set up a radio button.

Selected

To select the radio button, set `value="true"`.

```
<ui:inputRadio value="true" label="Select?"/>
```

Disabled State

```
<ui:inputRadio label="Select" disabled="true"/>
```

The previous example results in the following HTML.

```
<div class="uiInput uiInputRadio uiInput--default uiInput--radio">
    <label class="uiLabel-left form-element__label uiLabel"
for="globalId"><span>Select</span></label>
<input type="radio" id="globalId">
```

Providing Labels using An Attribute

You can also initialize the label values using an attribute. This example uses an attribute to populate the radio button labels and wire them up to a client-side controller action when the radio button is selected or deselected.

```
<!--c:labelsAttribute-->
<aura:component>
    <aura:attribute name="stages" type="String[]"
default="Any,Open,Closed,Closed,Closed Won"/>
    <aura:iteration items="{!v.stages}" var="stage">
        <ui:inputRadio label="{!stage}" change="{!c.doSomething}"/>
    </aura:iteration>
</aura:component>
```

Working with Events

Common events for `ui:inputRadio` include the `click` and `change` events. For example, `click="{!c.showItem}"` calls the client-side controller action with the fuction name, `showItem`.

The following code updates the CSS class of a component when the radio button is clicked.

```
<!--The radio button-->
    <ui:inputRadio click="{!c.showItem}" label="Show Item"/>
```

```
/* The controller action */
showItem : function(cmp, event) {
    var myCmp = cmp.find('myCmp');
    $A.util.toggleClass(myCmp, "cssClass");
}
```

SEE ALSO:

Handling Events with Client-Side Controllers

CSS in Components

Buttons

A button is clickable and actionable, providing a textual label, an image, or both. You can create a button in three different ways:

- Text-only Button

```
<ui:button label="Find" />
```

- Image-only Button

```
<!-- Component markup -->
<ui:button label="Find" labelClass="assistiveText" class="img" />

/** CSS **/
THIS.uiButton.img {
    background: url(/path/to/img) no-repeat;
    width:50px;
    height:25px;
}
```

The `assistiveText` class hides the label from view but makes it available to assistive technologies.

- Button with Text and Image

```
<!-- Component markup -->
<ui:button label="Find" />

/** CSS **/
THIS.uiButton {
    background: url(/path/to/img) no-repeat;
}
```

HTML Rendering

The markup for a button with text and image results in the following HTML.

```
<button class="default uiBlock uiButton" accesskey type="button">
  <span class="label bBody truncate" dir="ltr">Find</span>
</button>
```

Working with Click Events

The `press` event on the `ui:button` component is fired when the user clicks the button. In the following example, `press="{!c.getInput}"` calls the client-side controller action with the function name, `getInput`, which outputs the input text value.

```
<aura:component>
  <ui:inputText aura:id="name" label="Enter Name:" placeholder="Your
Name" />
  <ui:button aura:id="button" label="Click me" press="{!c.getInput}"/>

  <ui:outputText aura:id="outName" value="" class="text"/>
</aura:component>
```

```
/* Client-side controller */
({
    getInput : function(cmp, evt) {
        var myName = cmp.find("name").get("v.value");
        var myText = cmp.find("outName");
        var greet = "Hi, " + myName;
        myText.set("v.value", greet);
    }
```

Styling Your Buttons

The `ui:button` component is customizable with regular CSS styling. In the CSS resource of your component, add the following class selector.

```
.THIS.uiButton {
    margin-left: 20px;
}
```

Note that no space is added in the `.THIS.uiButton` selector if your button component is a top-level element.

To override the styling for all `ui:button` components in your app, in the CSS resource of your app, add the following class selector.

```
.THIS .uiButton {
    margin-left: 20px;
}
```

SEE ALSO:

> Handling Events with Client-Side Controllers
>
> CSS in Components
>
> Which Button Was Pressed?

Drop-down Lists

Drop-down lists display a dropdown menu with options you can select.

Both single and multiple selections are supported. You can create a drop-down list using `ui:inputSelect`, which inherits the behavior and events from `ui:input`.

Here are a few basic ways to set up a drop-down list.

For multiple selections, set the `multiple` attribute to `true`.

Single Selection

```
<ui:inputSelect>
        <ui:inputSelectOption text="Red"/>
        <ui:inputSelectOption text="Green" value="true"/>
        <ui:inputSelectOption text="Blue"/>
</ui:inputSelect>
```

Multiple Selection

```
<ui:inputSelect multiple="true">
    <ui:inputSelectOption text="All Primary" label="All Contacts"/>

    <ui:inputSelectOption text="All Primary" label="All Primary"/>
    <ui:inputSelectOption text="All Secondary" label="All
Secondary"/>
</ui:inputSelect>
```

Each option is represented by `ui:inputSelectOption`. The default selected value is specified by `value="true"` on the option.

Note: `v.value` represents the option's HTML `selected` attribute, and `v.text` represents the option's HTML `value` attribute.

Generating Options with `aura:iteration`

You can use `aura:iteration` to iterate over a list of items to generate options. This example iterates over a list of items and conditionally renders the options.

```
<aura:attribute name="contacts" type="String[]" default="All
Contacts,Others"/>
<ui:inputSelect>
    <aura:iteration items="{!v.contacts}" var="contact">
        <aura:if isTrue="{!contact == 'All Contacts'}">
            <ui:inputSelectOption text="{!contact}" label="{!contact}"/>

            <aura:set attribute="else">
                <ui:inputSelectOption text="All Primary" label="All
Primary"/>
                <ui:inputSelectOption text="All Secondary" label="All
 Secondary"/>
            </aura:set>
        </aura:if>
    </aura:iteration>
</ui:inputSelect>
```

Generating Options Dynamically

Generate the options dynamically on component initialization.

```
<aura:component>
  <aura:handler name="init" value="{!this} action="{!c.doInit}"/>
  <ui:inputSelect label="Select me:" class="dynamic"
aura:id="InputSelectDynamic""/>
</aura:component>
```

The following client-side controller generates options using `v.options` on the `ui:inputSelect` component by creating the `opts` object with several parameters. `v.options` takes in the list of objects and converts them into list options. Although the sample code generates the options during initialization, the list of options can be modified anytime when you manipulate the list in `v.options`. The component automatically updates itself and rerenders with the new options.

```
({
    doInit : function(cmp) {
```

```
        var opts = [
            { class: "optionClass", label: "Option1", value: "opt1"},

            { class: "optionClass", label: "Option2", value: "opt2"
},
            { class: "optionClass", label: "Option3", value: "opt3" }


        ];
        cmp.find("InputSelectDynamic").set("v.options", opts);
    }
})
```

> 📝 Note: `class` is a reserved word that might not work with older versions of Internet Explorer. We recommend using `"class"` with double quotes.

The list options support these parameters.

Parameter	Type	Description
class	String	The CSS class for the option.
disabled	Boolean	Indicates whether the option is disabled.
label	String	The label of the option to display on the user interface.
selected	Boolean	Indicates whether the option is selected.
value	String	Required. The value of the option.

Using Options On Multiple Lists

If you're reusing the same set of options on multiple drop-down lists, use different attributes for each set of options. Otherwise, selecting a different option in one list also updates other list options bound to the same attribute.

```
<aura:attribute name="options1" type="String" />
<aura:attribute name="options2" type="String" />
<ui:inputSelect aura:id="Select1" label="Select1"
options="{!v.options1}" />
```

```
<ui:inputSelect aura:id="Select2" label="Select2"
options="{!v.options2}" />
```

Working with Events

Common events for `ui:inputSelect` include the `change` and `click` events. For example, `change="{!c.onSelectChange}"` calls the client-side controller action with the function name, `onSelectChange`, when a user changes a selection.

Styling Your Field-level Errors

The `ui:inputSelect` component is customizable with regular CSS styling. The following CSS sample adds a fixed width to the drop-down menu.

```
.THIS.uiInputSelect {
    width: 200px;
    height: 100px;
}
```

Alternatively, use the `class` attribute to specify your own CSS class.

SEE ALSO:

Handling Events with Client-Side Controllers

CSS in Components

Generating Drop-Down Lists Using Record Field Values

Use an Apex controller if you want to use your record data in list options.

Bind a record field to the `ui:inputSelectOption` component to display its values. Wire up the component to the Apex controller using the `controller` attribute, and invoke it during component initialization.

Let's create a drop-down list that displays your contact names.

```
<aura:component controller="ContactController">
    <!-- Handle component initialization in a client-side controller
-->
    <aura:handler name="init" value="{!this}" action="{!c.doInit}"/>

    <!-- The list of contacts to display -->
    <aura:attribute name="contacts" type="Contact[]"/>
```

```
    <ui:inputSelect aura:id="opt" label="Contacts"
change="{!c.onSelectChange}">
        <aura:iteration items="{!v.contacts}" var="contact">
            <ui:inputSelectOption text="{!contact.Name}"
label="{!contact.Name}" />
        </aura:iteration>
    </ui:inputSelect>
</aura:component>
```

This client-side controller initializes the option values by calling a helper and prints out the selected value when a select change event occurs.

```
({
    doInit : function(component, event, helper) {
        // Retrieve contacts during component initialization
        helper.getMyContacts(component);
    },

    onSelectChange : function(component, event, helper) {
        // Print out the selected value
        var selected = component.find("opt").get("v.value");
        console.log(selected);
    }
})
```

The helper function calls the Apex controller `getContacts()` method to load the contact names.

```
({
    getMyContacts : function(cmp) {
        // Load all contact data
        var action = cmp.get("c.getContacts");
        action.setCallback(this, function(response){
            var state = response.getState();
            if (state === "SUCCESS") {
                cmp.set("v.contacts", response.getReturnValue());
            }
        });
        $A.enqueueAction(action);
    }
})
```

Finally, the Apex controller queries and returns a list of contacts. Your controller name must correspond with your component's `controller` attribute.

```
public with sharing class ContactController {
    @AuraEnabled
    public static List<Contact> getContacts() {
        List<Contact> contacts = [SELECT Id, Name FROM Contact];

        //Add isAccessible() check
        return contacts;
    }
}
```

Field-level Errors

Field-level errors are displayed when a validation error occurs on the field after a user input. The framework creates a default error component, `ui:inputDefaultError`, which provides basic events such as `click` and `mouseover`. See Validating Fields for more information.

Alternatively, you can use `ui:message` for field-level errors by toggling visibility of the message when an error condition is met. See Dynamically Showing or Hiding Markup for more information.

> **Invalid password**
> Your password should be at least 6 alphanumeric characters long.

Working with Events

Common events for `ui:message` include the `click` and `mouseover` events. For example, `click="{!c.revalidate}"` calls the client-side controller action with the fuction name, `revalidate`, when a user clicks on the error message.

SEE ALSO:

Handling Events with Client-Side Controllers

CSS in Components

Menus

A menu is a drop-down list with a trigger that controls its visibility. You must provide the trigger and list of menu items. The dropdown menu and its menu items are hidden by default. You can change this by setting the `visible` attribute on the `ui:menuList` component to `true`. The menu items are shown only when you click the `ui:menuTriggerLink` component.

This example creates a menu with several items.

```
<ui:menu>
    <ui:menuTriggerLink aura:id="trigger" label="Opportunity Status"/>

        <ui:menuList class="actionMenu" aura:id="actionMenu">
            <ui:actionMenuItem aura:id="item2" label="Open"
click="{!c.updateTriggerLabel}"/>
            <ui:actionMenuItem aura:id="item3" label="Closed"
click="{!c.updateTriggerLabel}"/>
            <ui:actionMenuItem aura:id="item4" label="Closed Won"
click="{!c.updateTriggerLabel}"/>
        </ui:menuList>
</ui:menu>
```

You can display a list of items from an object. This example displays a list of contact names in a menu using `aura:iteration`.

```
<aura:component>
    <aura:attribute name="contacts" type="String[]"
default="All,Primary,Secondary"/>
    <ui:menu>
        <ui:menuTriggerLink label="Select Contact"/>
        <ui:menuList>
            <aura:iteration var="contact" items="{!v.contacts}">
                <ui:actionMenuItem label="{!contact}"/>
            </aura:iteration>
        </ui:menuList>
    </ui:menu>
</aura:component>
```

The following components are nested in `ui:menu`.

Component	Description
ui:menu	A drop-down list with a trigger that controls its visibility
ui:menuList	A list of menu items
ui:actionMenuItem	A menu item that triggers an action

Component	Description
`ui:checkboxMenuItem`	A menu item that supports multiple selection and can be used to trigger an action
`ui:radioMenuItem`	A menu item that supports single selection and can be used to trigger an action
`ui:menuItemSeparator`	A visual separator for menu items
`ui:menuItem`	An abstract and extensible component for menu items in a `ui:menuList` component
`ui:menuTrigger`	A trigger that expands and collapses a menu
`ui:menuTriggerLink`	A link that triggers a dropdown menu. This component extends `ui:menuTrigger`

Supporting Accessibility

When customizing components, be careful in preserving code that ensures accessibility, such as the `aria` attributes. See Working with UI Components for components you can use in your apps.

Accessible software and assistive technology enable users with disabilities to use and interact with the products you build. Aura components are created according to W3C specifications so that they work with common assistive technologies. While we always recommend that you follow the WCAG Guidelines for accessibility when developing with the Lightning Component framework, this guide explains the accessibility features that you can leverage when using components in the `ui` namespace.

IN THIS SECTION:

Button Labels

Help and Error Messages

Audio Messages

Forms, Fields, and Labels

Events

Menus

Button Labels

Buttons may be designed to appear with just text, an image and text, or an image without text. To create an accessible button, use `ui:button` and set a textual label using the `label` attribute. The text is available to assistive technologies, but not visible on screen.

```
<ui:button label="Search"
iconImgSrc="/auraFW/resources/aura/images/search.png"/>
```

When using `ui:button`, assign a non-empty string to label attribute. These examples show how a `ui:button` should render:

```
<!-- Good: using alt attribute to provide a invisible label -->
<button>
    <img src="search.png" alt="Search"/>
</button>
```

```
<!-- Good: using span/assistiveText to hide the label visually, but
show it to screen readers -->
<button>
 ::before
    <span class="assistiveText">Search</span>
</button>
```

SEE ALSO:

Buttons

Help and Error Messages

However, If you want to use the input component to create and handle the `ui:inputDefaultError` component, the error messages will automatically get the `ariaDescribedby` attribute. If, however, you want to manually manage the action, you will need to make the connection between the `ui:inputDefaultError` component and the associated output.

If your code failed, check to see if `ariaDescribedby` is missing. Your component should render like this example:

```
<!-- Good: aria-describedby is used to associate error message -->
<label for="fname">Contact name</label>
<input name="" type="text" id="fname" aria-describedby="msgid">
<ul class="uiInputDefaultError" id="msgid">
```

```
  <li>Please enter the contact name</li>
</ul>
```

SEE ALSO:

Validating Fields

Audio Messages

To convey audio notifications, use the `ui:message` component, which has `role="alert"` set on the component by default. The `"alert"` `aria` role will take any text inside the div and read it out loud to screen readers without any additional action by the user.

```
<ui:message title="Error" severity="error" closable="true">
     This is an error message.
</ui:message>
```

Forms, Fields, and Labels

Input components are designed to make it easy to assign labels to form fields. Labels build a programmatic relationship between a form field and its textual label. When using a placeholder in an input component, set the `label` attribute for accessibility.

Use the input components that extend `ui:input`, except when `type="file"`. For example, use `ui:inputTextarea` in preference to the `<textarea>` tag for multi-line text input or the `ui:inputSelect` component in preference to the `<select>` tag.

If your code failed, check the label element during component rendering. A label element should have the `for` attribute and match the value of input control id attribute, OR the label should be wrapped around an input. Input controls include `<input>`, `<textarea>`, and `<select>`.

```
<!-- Good: using label/for= -->
<label for="fullname">Enter your full name:</label>
<input type="text" id="fullname" />

<!-- Good: --using implicit label>
<label>Enter your full name:
```

```
    <input type="text" id="fullname"/>
</label>
```

SEE ALSO:

Using Labels

Events

Although you can attach an `onclick` event to any type of element, for accessibility, consider only applying this event to elements that are actionable in HTML by default, such as `<a>`, `<button>`, or `<input>` tags in component markup. You can use an `onclick` event on a `<div>` tag to prevent event bubbling of a click.

Menus

A menu is a drop-down list with a trigger that controls its visibility. You must provide the trigger and list of menu items. The drop-down menu and its menu items are hidden by default. You can change this by setting the `visible` attribute on the `ui:menuList` component to `true`. The menu items are shown only when you click the `ui:menuTriggerLink` component.

This example code creates a menu with several items:

```
<ui:menu>
    <ui:menuTriggerLink aura:id="trigger" label="Opportunity Status"/>

        <ui:menuList class="actionMenu" aura:id="actionMenu">
            <ui:actionMenuItem aura:id="item2" label="Open"
click="{!c.updateTriggerLabel}"/>
            <ui:actionMenuItem aura:id="item3" label="Closed"
click="{!c.updateTriggerLabel}"/>
            <ui:actionMenuItem aura:id="item4" label="Closed Won"
click="{!c.updateTriggerLabel}"/>
        </ui:menuList>
</ui:menu>
```

Different menus achieve different goals. Make sure you use the right menu for the desired behavior. The three types of menus are:

Actions

Use the `ui:actionMenuItem` for items that create an action, like print, new, or save.

Radio button

If you want users to pick only one from a list several items, use `ui:radioMenuItem`.

Checkbox style

If users can pick multiple items from a list of several items, use `ui:checkboxMenuItem`. Checkboxes can also be used to turn one item on or off.

CHAPTER 4 Using Components

In this chapter ...

- Adding Components to Apps
- Add Lightning Components to Salesforce1
- Add Lightning Components to Lightning Experience
- Use Lightning Components in Visualforce Pages
- Add Lightning Components to Any App with Lightning Out (Beta)
- Configure Components for Communities
- Configure Components for Lightning Pages and the Lightning App Builder

You can use components in many different contexts. This section shows you how.

Adding Components to Apps

When you're ready to add components to your app, you should first look at the out-of-the-box components that come with the framework. You can also leverage these components by extending them or using composition to add them to custom components that you're building.

 Note: For all the out-of-the-box components, see the `Components` folder at
`https://<myDomain>.lightning.force.com/auradocs/reference.app`,
where `<myDomain>` is the name of your custom Salesforce domain. The `ui` namespace includes many components that are common on Web pages.

Components are encapsulated and their internals stay private, while their public shape is visible to consumers of the component. This strong separation gives component authors freedom to change the internal implementation details and insulates component consumers from those changes.

The public shape of a component is defined by the attributes that can be set and the events that interact with the component. The shape is essentially the API for developers to interact with the component. To design a new component, think about the attributes that you want to expose and the events that the component should initiate or respond to.

Once you have defined the shape of any new components, developers can work on the components in parallel. This is a useful approach if you have a team working on an app.

To add a new custom component to your app, see Using the Developer Console on page 4.

SEE ALSO:

Component Composition

Using Object-Oriented Development

Component Attributes

Communicating with Events

Add Lightning Components to Salesforce1

Make your Lightning components available for Salesforce1 users.

In the component you wish to add, include `implements="force:appHostable"` in your `aura:component` tag and save your changes.

EDITIONS

Available in: Salesforce Classic and Lightning Experience

Available for use in: **Contact Manager, Group, Professional, Enterprise, Performance, Unlimited,** and **Developer** Editions

Create Lightning components using the UI in **Enterprise, Performance, Unlimited, Developer** Editions or a sandbox.

USER PERMISSIONS

To create Lightning Component Tabs:
- "Customize Application"

```
<aura:component implements="force:appHostable">
```

The `appHostable` interface makes the component available as a custom tab.

Use the Developer Console to create Lightning components.

Include your components in the Salesforce1 navigation menu by following these steps.

1. Create a custom Lightning component tab for the component. From Setup, enter *Tabs* in the `Quick Find` box, then select **Tabs**.

    Note: You must create a custom Lightning component tab before you can add your component to the Salesforce1 navigation menu. Accessing your Lightning component from the full Salesforce site is not supported.

2. Add your Lightning component to the Salesforce1 navigation menu.

a. From Setup, enter `Navigation` in the `Quick Find` box, then select **Salesforce1 Navigation**.

b. Select the custom tab you just created and click **Add**.

c. Sort items by selecting them and clicking **Up** or **Down**.

In the navigation menu, items appear in the order you specify. The first item in the Selected list becomes your users' Salesforce1 landing page.

3. Check your output by going to the Salesforce1 mobile browser app. Your new menu item should appear in the navigation menu.

 Note: By default, the mobile browser app is turned on for your org. For more information on using the Salesforce1 mobile browser app, see the *Salesforce1 App Developer Guide*.

Add Lightning Components to Lightning Experience

Make your Lightning components available for Lightning Experience users.

EDITIONS

Available in: Salesforce Classic and Lightning Experience

Available for use in: **Contact Manager, Group, Professional, Enterprise, Performance, Unlimited,** and **Developer** Editions

Create Lightning components using the UI in **Enterprise, Performance, Unlimited, Developer** Editions or a sandbox.

USER PERMISSIONS

To create Lightning Component Tabs:
- "Customize Application"

In the components you wish to include in Lightning Experience, add
`implements="force:appHostable"` in the `aura:component` tag and save your changes.

```
<aura:component implements="force:appHostable">
```

Use the Developer Console to create Lightning components.

Follow these steps to include your components in Lightning Experience and make them available to users
in your organization.

1. Create a custom tab for this component.

    a. From Setup, enter *Tabs* in the `Quick Find` box, then select **Tabs**.

    b. Click **New** in the Lightning Component Tabs related list.

    c. Select the Lightning component that you want to make available to users.

    d. Enter a label to display on the tab.

    e. Select the tab style and click **Next**.

    f. When prompted to add the tab to profiles, accept the default and click **Save**.

2. Add your Lightning components to the App Launcher.

    a. From Setup, enter *Apps* in the `Quick Find` box, then select **Apps**.

    b. Click **New**. Select *Custom app* and then click **Next**.

    c. Enter *Lightning* for App Label and click **Next**.

    d. In the `Available Tabs` dropdown menu, select the Lightning Component tab you
    created and click the right arrow button to add it to the custom app.

    e. Click **Next**. Select the `Visible` checkbox to assign the app to profiles and then **Save**.

3. Check your output by navigating to the App Launcher in Lightning Experience. Your custom app
should appear in theApp Launcher. Click the custom app to see the components you added.

Use Lightning Components in Visualforce Pages

Add Lightning components to your Visualforce pages to combine features you've built using both solutions.
Implement new functionality using Lightning components and then use it with existing Visualforce pages.

There are three steps to add Lightning components to a Visualforce page.

1. Add the `<apex:includeLightning />` component to your Visualforce page.

2. Reference a Lightning app that declares your component dependencies with
`$Lightning.use()`.

3. Write a function that creates the component on the page with
`$Lightning.createComponent()`.

Adding `<apex:includeLightning>`

Add `<apex:includeLightning />` at the beginning of your page. This component loads the JavaScript file used by Lightning Components for Visualforce.

Referencing a Lightning App

To use Lightning Components for Visualforce, define component dependencies by referencing a Lightning dependency app. This app is globally accessible and extends `ltng:outApp`. The app declares dependencies on any Lightning definitions (like components) that it uses. Here's an example of a simple app called `lcvfTest.app`. The app uses the `<aura:dependency>` tag to indicate that it uses the standard Lightning component, `ui:button`.

```
<aura:application access="GLOBAL" extends="ltng:outApp">
    <aura:dependency resource="ui:button"/>
</aura:application>
```

To reference this app, use the following markup where *theNamespace* is the namespace prefix for the app. That is, either your org's namespace, or the namespace of the managed package that provides the app.

```
$Lightning.use("theNamespace:lcvfTest", function() {});
```

If the app is defined in your org (that is, not in a managed package), you can use the default "c" namespace instead, as shown in the next example. If your org doesn't have a namespace defined, you *must* use the default namespace.

Creating a Component on a Page

Finally, create your component on a page using `$Lightning.createComponent(String type, Object attributes, String locator, function callback)`. This function is similar to `$A.createComponent()`, but includes an additional parameter, `domLocator`, which specifies the DOM element where you want the component inserted.

Let's look at a sample Visualforce page that creates a `ui:button` using the `lcvfTest.app` from the previous example.

```
<apex:page>
    <apex:includeLightning />

    <div id="lightning" />

    <script>
        $Lightning.use("c:lcvfTest", function() {
          $Lightning.createComponent("ui:button",
          { label : "Press Me!" },
          "lightning",
          function(cmp) {
            // do some stuff
          });
        });
    </script>
</apex:page>
```

This code creates a DOM element with the ID "lightning", which is then referenced in the `$Lightning.createComponent()` method. This method creates a `ui:button` that says "Press Me!", and then executes the callback function.

🚫 **Important:** You can call `$Lightning.use()` multiple times on a page, but all calls must reference the same Lightning dependency app.

SEE ALSO:

Lightning Out Dependencies

Lightning Out Markup

Add Lightning Components to Any App with Lightning Out (Beta)

Lightning Out Considerations and Limitations

Add Lightning Components to Any App with Lightning Out (Beta)

Use Lightning Out to run Lightning components apps outside of Salesforce servers. Whether it's a Node.js app running on Heroku, a department server inside the firewall, or even SharePoint, build your custom app with Force.com and run it wherever your users are.

Note: This release contains a beta version of Lightning Out, which means it's a high quality feature with known limitations. You can provide feedback and suggestions for Lightning Out on the IdeaExchange.

Developing Lightning components that you can deploy anywhere is for the most part the same as developing them to run within Salesforce. Everything you already know about Lightning components development still applies. The only real difference is in how you embed your Lightning components app in the remote web container, or *origin server*.

Lightning Out is added to external apps in the form of a JavaScript library you include in the page on the origin server, and markup you add to configure and activate your Lightning components app. Once initialized, Lightning Out pulls in your Lightning components app over a secure connection, spins it up, and inserts it into the DOM of the page it's running on. Once it reaches this point, your "normal" Lightning components code takes over and runs the show.

 Note: This approach is quite different from embedding an app using an iframe. Lightning components running via Lightning Out are full citizens on the page. If you choose to, you can enable interaction between your Lightning components app and the page or app you've embedded it in. This interaction is handled using Lightning events.

In addition to some straightforward markup, there's a modest amount of setup and preparation within Salesforce to enable the secure connection between Salesforce and the origin server. And, because the origin server is hosting the app, you need to manage authentication with your own code.

This setup process is similar to what you'd do for an application that connects to Salesforce using the Force.com REST API, and you should expect it to require an equivalent amount of work.

IN THIS SECTION:

Lightning Out Requirements

Deploying a Lightning components app using Lightning Out has a few modest requirements to ensure connectivity and security.

Lightning Out Dependencies

Create a special Lightning dependency app to describe the component dependencies of a Lightning components app to be deployed using Lightning Out or Lightning Components for Visualforce.

Lightning Out Markup

Lightning Out requires some simple markup on the page, and is activated using two straightforward JavaScript functions.

Authentication from Lightning Out

Lightning Out doesn't handle authentication. Instead, you manually provide a Salesforce session ID or security token when you initialize a Lightning Out app.

Lightning Out Considerations and Limitations

Creating an app using Lightning Out is, for the most part, much like creating any app with Lightning components. However, because your components are running "outside" of Salesforce, there are a few issues you want to be aware of. And it's possible there are changes you might need to make to your components or your app.

SEE ALSO:

Idea Exchange: Lightning Components Anywhere / Everywhere

Lightning Out Requirements

Deploying a Lightning components app using Lightning Out has a few modest requirements to ensure connectivity and security.

The remote web container, or *origin server*, must support the following.

- Ability to modify the markup served to the client browser, including both HTML and JavaScript. You need to be able to add the Lightning Out markup.
- Ability to acquire a valid Salesforce session ID. This will most likely require you to configure a Connected App for the origin server.
- Ability to access your Salesforce instance. For example, if the origin server is behind a firewall, it needs permission to access the Internet, at least to reach Salesforce.

Your Salesforce org must be configured to allow the following.

- The ability for the origin server to authenticate and connect. This will most likely require you to configure a Connected App for the origin server.
- The origin server must be added to the Cross-Origin Resource Sharing (CORS) whitelist.

Finally, you create a special Lightning components app that contains dependency information for the Lightning components to be hosted on the origin server. This app is only used by Lightning Out or Lightning Components for Visualforce.

Lightning Out Dependencies

Create a special Lightning dependency app to describe the component dependencies of a Lightning components app to be deployed using Lightning Out or Lightning Components for Visualforce.

When a Lightning components app is initialized using Lightning Out, Lightning Out loads the definitions for the components in the app. To do this efficiently, Lightning Out requires you to specify the component dependencies in advance, so that the definitions can be loaded once, at startup time.

145

The mechanism for specifying dependencies is a *Lightning dependency app*. A dependency app is simply an `<aura:application>` with a few attributes, and the dependent components described using the `<aura:dependency>` tag. A Lightning dependency app isn't one you'd ever actually deploy as an app for people to use directly. It's used only to specify the dependencies for Lightning Out, or for Lightning Components for Visualforce, which uses Lightning Out under the covers.

A basic Lightning dependency app looks like the following.

```
<aura:application access="GLOBAL" extends="ltng:outApp">
    <aura:dependency resource="c:myAppComponent"/>
</aura:application>
```

In this example, `<c:myAppComponent>` is the top-level component for the Lightning components app you are planning to create on the origin server using `$Lightning.createComponent()`. Create a dependency for each different component you add to the page with `$Lightning.createComponent()`.

 Note: Don't worry about what additional components are included within the top-level component. The Lightning Component framework handles dependency resolution for child components.

SEE ALSO:

Creating a Connected App

Use CORS to Access Supported Salesforce APIs, Apex REST, and Lightning Out

aura:dependency

Lightning Out Markup

Lightning Out requires some simple markup on the page, and is activated using two straightforward JavaScript functions.

The markup and JavaScript functions in the Lightning Out library are the only things specific to Lightning Out. Everything else is the Lightning components code you already know and love.

Adding the Lightning Out Library to the Page

Enable an origin server for use with Lightning Out by including the Lightning Out JavaScript library in the app or page hosting your Lightning components app. Including the library requires a single line of markup.

```
<script
src="https://myDomain.my.salesforce.com/lightning/lightning.out.js"></script>
```

🛈 Important: Use **your** custom domain for the host. Don't copy-and-paste someone else's instance from example source code. If you do this, your app will break whenever there's a version mismatch between your Salesforce instance and the instance from which you're loading the Lightning Out library. This happens at least three times a year, during regular upgrades of Salesforce. Don't do it!

Loading and Initializing Your Lightning Components App

Load and initialize the Lightning Component framework and your Lightning components app with the `$Lightning.use()` function.

The `$Lightning.use()` function takes four arguments.

Name	Type	Description
`appName`	string	Required. The name of your Lightning dependency app, including the namespace. For example, `"c:expenseAppDependencies"`.
`callback`	function	A function to call once the Lightning Component framework and your app have fully loaded. The callback receives no arguments.
		This callback is usually where you call `$Lightning.createComponent()` to add your app to the page (see the next section). You might also update your display in other ways, or otherwise respond to your Lightning components app being ready.
`lightningEndPointURI`	string	The URL for the Lightning domain on your Salesforce instance. For example, "https://*myDomain*.lightning.force.com".
`authToken`	string	The session ID or OAuth access token for a valid, active Salesforce session.
		📝 Note: You must obtain this token in your own code. Lightning Out doesn't handle authentication for you. See Authentication from Lightning Out.

`appName` is required. The other three parameters are optional. In normal use you provide all four parameters.

Note: You can't use more than one Lightning dependency app on a page. You can call `$Lightning.use()` more than once, but you must reference the same dependency app in every call.

Adding Your Lightning Components to the Page

Add to and activate your Lightning components on the page with the `$Lightning.createComponent()` function.

The `$Lightning.createComponent()` function takes four arguments.

Name	Type	Description
componentName	string	Required. The name of the Lightning component to add to the page, including the namespace. For example, `"c:newExpenseForm"`.
attributes	Object	Required. The attributes to set on the component when it's created. For example, `{ name: theName, amount: theAmount }`. If the component doesn't require any attributes, pass in an empty object, `{ }`.
domLocator	Element or string	Required. The DOM element or element ID that indicates where on the page to insert the created component.
callback	function	A function to call once the component is added to and active on the page. The callback receives the component created as its only argument.

Note: You can add more than one Lightning component to a page. That is, you can call `$Lightning.createComponent()` multiple times, with multiple DOM locators, to add components to different parts of the page. Each component created this way must be specified in the page's Lightning dependency app.

Behind the scenes `$Lightning.createComponent()` calls the standard `$A.createComponent()` function. Except for the DOM locator, the arguments are the same. And except for wrapping the call in some Lightning Out semantics, the behavior is the same, too.

SEE ALSO:

Dynamically Creating Components

Authentication from Lightning Out

Lightning Out doesn't handle authentication. Instead, you manually provide a Salesforce session ID or security token when you initialize a Lightning Out app.

An authenticated session is normally obtained using OAuth, following the same process you'd use to obtain an authenticated session to use with the Force.com REST API. If you're using something besides OAuth, that's fine too. Whatever works to acquire an authenticated session ID. This process lets you manage authentication with your own code, according to your organization's security infrastructure, practices, and policies.

The key thing to understand is that Lightning Out isn't in the business of authentication. The `$Lightning.use()` function simply passes along to the security subsystem whatever authentication token you provide it. For most organizations, this will be a session ID or an OAuth token.

Lightning Out Considerations and Limitations

Creating an app using Lightning Out is, for the most part, much like creating any app with Lightning components. However, because your components are running "outside" of Salesforce, there are a few issues you want to be aware of. And it's possible there are changes you might need to make to your components or your app.

The issues you should be aware of can be divided into two categories.

Considerations for Using Lightning Out

Because Lightning Out apps run outside of any Salesforce container, there are things you need to keep in mind, and possibly address.

The most obvious issue is authentication. There's no Salesforce container to handle authentication for you, so you have to handle it yourself. This essential topic is discussed in detail in "Authentication from Lightning Out."

Another important consideration is more subtle. Many important actions your apps support are accomplished by firing various Lightning events. But events are sort of like that tree that falls in the forest. If no one's listening, does it have an effect? In the case of many core Lightning events, the "listener" is the `one.app` container. And if `one.app` isn't there to handle the events, they indeed have no effect. Firing those events silently fails.

Standard events are listed in "Event Reference." Events not supported for use in Lightning Out include the following note:

 Note: This event is handled by the `one.app` container. It's supported in Lightning Experience and Salesforce1 only. If used outside of Lightning Experience or Salesforce1, this event won't be handled automatically. To use this event outside of `one.app`, create and wire up an event handler of your own.

Limitations During the Lightning Out Beta

While the core Lightning Out functionality is stable and complete, there are a few interactions with other Salesforce features that we're still working on.

Chief among these is the standard components built into the Lightning Component framework. At this time, a number of the standard components don't behave correctly when used in a stand-alone context, such as Lightning Out, and Lightning Components for Visualforce, which is based on Lightning Out. This is because the components implicitly depend on resources available in the `one.app` container, instead of explicitly defining their dependencies.

Avoid this issue with your components by making their dependencies explicit. Use `ltng:require` to reference all required JavaScript and CSS resources that aren't embedded in the component itself.

If you're using standard components in your apps, they might not be fully styled, or behave as documented, when they're used in Lightning Out or Lightning Components for Visualforce.

SEE ALSO:
   Authentication from Lightning Out
   Use Lightning Components in Visualforce Pages

Configure Components for Communities

Make your custom Lightning components available for drag and drop in the Community Builder.

Add a New Interface to Your Component

To appear in the Community Builder, a component must implement the `forceCommunity:availableForAllPageTypes` interface.

Here's the sample code for a simple "Hello World" component.

```
<aura:component implements="forceCommunity:availableForAllPageTypes"
access="global">
    <aura:attribute name="greeting" type="String" default="Hello"
access="global" />
    <aura:attribute name="subject" type="String" default="World"
```

```
access="global" />

    <div style="box">
      <span class="greeting">{!v.greeting}</span>, {!v.subject}!
    </div>
</aura:component>
```

> Note: Mark your resources, such as a component, with `access="global"` to make the resource usable outside of your own org; for example, if you want a component to be usable in an installed package or by a Lightning App Builder user or a Community Builder user in another org.

Next, add a design resource to your component bundle. A design resource describes the design-time behavior of a Lightning component—information that visual tools need to allow adding the component to a page or app. It contains attributes that are available for administrators to edit in the Community Builder.

Adding this resource is similar to adding it for the Lightning App Builder. For more information, see Configure Components for Lightning Pages and the Lightning App Builder.

IN THIS SECTION:

Create Custom Page Layout Components for Communities
Community Builder includes several ready-to-use layouts that let you quickly change the look of your community's pages. However, if you need a layout that's customized for your community, create a custom layout component to use when building new pages in Community Builder. You can also update the layout of the default pages that come with your community template.

SEE ALSO:

Component Bundles
Standard Design Tokens for Communities

Create Custom Page Layout Components for Communities

Community Builder includes several ready-to-use layouts that let you quickly change the look of your community's pages. However, if you need a layout that's customized for your community, create a custom layout component to use when building new pages in Community Builder. You can also update the layout of the default pages that come with your community template.

When you create a custom layout component in the Developer Console, it appears in Community Builder in:

* The Create New Page dialog box. To view the custom layout, select the Custom view in the Layouts tab.

- The Change Layout dialog box. To view the custom layout, select the Custom tab.

1. Add a New Interface to Your Layout Component

To appear in the Create New Page and Change Layout dialog boxes in Community Builder, a custom layout component must implement the `forceCommunity:layout` interface.

Here's the sample code for a simple two-column layout.

```
<aura:component implements="forceCommunity:layout" access="global">
    <aura:attribute name="column1" type="Aura.Component[]"
required="false"></aura:attribute>
    <aura:attribute name="column2" type="Aura.Component[]"
required="false"></aura:attribute>

    <div class="container">
        <div class='contentPanel'>
            <div class='left'>
                {!v.column1}
            </div>
            <div class='right'>
                {!v.column2}
            </div>
        </div>
    </div>
</aura:component>
```

Note: Mark your resources, such as a component, with `access="global"` to make the resource usable outside of your own org; for example, if you want a component to be usable in an installed package or by a Lightning App Builder user or a Community Builder user in another org.

2. Add a CSS Resource to Your Component Bundle

Next, add a CSS resource to style the layout as needed.

Here's the sample CSS for our simple two-column layout.

```
.THIS .ui-widget {
    margin: 36px 0;
}
.THIS .contentPanel:before,
.THIS .contentPanel:after {
    content: " ";
    display: table;
```

```
}
.THIS .contentPanel:after {
    clear: both;
}
.THIS .left {
    float: left;
    width: 50%;
}
.THIS .right {
    float: right;
    width: 50%;
}
```

CSS resources must be named `componentName.css`. For example, the CSS resource for the component `communityLayout.cmp` is `communityLayout.css`.

3 Optional: Add an SVG Resource to Your Component Bundle

You can include an SVG resource in your component bundle to define a custom icon for the layout component when it appears in the Community Builder.

The recommended image size for a layout component in Community Builder is 155px by 120px. However, if the image has different dimensions, Community Builder scales the image to fit.

SVG resources must be named `componentName.svg`.

SEE ALSO:

Component Bundles

Standard Design Tokens for Communities

Configure Components for Lightning Pages and the Lightning App Builder

There are three steps you must take before you can use your custom Lightning components in either Lightning Pages or the Lightning App Builder.

1. Enable My Domain in Your Org

You must enable My Domain in your org if you want to use Lightning components in Lightning tabs, Lightning Pages, or as standalone apps.

For more information about My Domain, see the Salesforce Help.

2. Add a New Interface to Your Component

To appear in the Lightning App Builder or a Lightning Page, a component must implement the `flexipage:availableForAllPageTypes` interface.

Here's the sample code for a simple "Hello World" component.

```
<aura:component implements="flexipage:availableForAllPageTypes"
access="global">
    <aura:attribute name="greeting" type="String" default="Hello"
access="global" />
    <aura:attribute name="subject" type="String" default="World"
access="global" />

    <div style="box">
      <span class="greeting">{!v.greeting}</span>, {!v.subject}!
    </div>
</aura:component>
```

 Note: Mark your resources, such as a component, with `access="global"` to make the resource usable outside of your own org; for example, if you want a component to be usable in an installed package or by a Lightning App Builder user or a Community Builder user in another org.

3. Add a Design Resource to Your Component Bundle

You must include a design resource in the component bundle to make your Lightning component usable in Lightning Pages and the Lightning App Builder. A design resource describes the design-time behavior of a Lightning component—information that visual tools need to allow adding the component to a page or app.

To make a Lightning component attribute available for administrators to edit in the Lightning App Builder, add a `design:attribute` node for the attribute into the design resource. An attribute marked as required in the component definition automatically appears for users in the Lightning App Builder, unless it has a default value assigned to it. Required attributes with default values and attributes not marked as required in the component definition must be specified in the design resource or they won't appear for users.

Here's the design resource that goes in the bundle with the "Hello World" component.

```
<design:component label="Hello World">
    <design:attribute name="subject" label="Subject" description="Name
 of the person you want to greet" />
    <design:attribute name="greeting" label="Greeting" />
</design:component>
```

To render a field as a picklist, add a `datasource` onto the attribute in the design resource, like this:

```
<design:attribute name="Name" datasource="value1,value2,value3" />
```

Any string attribute with a `datasource` in a design resource is treated as a picklist.

You can set a default value on an attribute in a design resource, like this:

```
<design:attribute name="Name" datasource="value1,value2,value3"
default="value1" />
```

A design resource supports only attributes of type `int`, `string`, or `boolean`.

Design resources must be named `componentName.design`.

Optional: Add an SVG Resource to Your Component Bundle

You can use an SVG resource to define a custom icon for your component when it appears in the Lightning App Builder's component pane. Just include it in the component bundle.

Here's a simple red circle SVG resource to go with the "Hello World" component.

```
<?xml version="1.0"?>
<!DOCTYPE svg PUBLIC "-//W3C//DTD SVG 1.1//EN"
  "http://www.w3.org/Graphics/SVG/1.1/DTD/svg11.dtd">

<svg xmlns="http://www.w3.org/2000/svg"
     width="400" height="400">
  <circle cx="100" cy="100" r="50" stroke="black"
    stroke-width="5" fill="red" />
</svg>
```

SVG resources must be named `componentName.svg`.

IN THIS SECTION:

Configure Components for Lightning Experience Record Home Pages
With a few tweaks to your component, you can make it work on a record page in Lightning Experience.

Tips and Considerations for Configuring Components for Lightning App Builder

Keep these guidelines in mind when creating components and component bundles for the Lightning App Builder.

SEE ALSO:

Component Bundles

Tips and Considerations for Configuring Components for Lightning App Builder

Configure Components for Lightning Experience Record Home Pages

With a few tweaks to your component, you can make it work on a record page in Lightning Experience.

Before your component can work on a record page in Lightning Experience, configure the component so it works in Lightning App Builder. See Configure Components for Lightning Pages and the Lightning App Builder on page 153 for more information.

Once your component is compatible with Lightning App Builder, use these guidelines to adjust it so it works on record pages in Lightning Experience.

Record pages are different from app pages in a key way: they have the context of a record. To make your components display content that is based on the current record, use a combination of an interface and an attribute.

- If your component is available for both record pages and any other type of page, implement `flexipage:availableForAllPageTypes`.
- If your component is designed just for record pages, implement the `flexipage:availableForRecordHome` interface instead of `flexipage:availableForAllPageTypes`.
- If your component needs the record ID, also implement the `force:hasRecordId` interface.
- If your component needs the object's API name, also implement the `force:hasSObjectName` interface.

 Note: If your managed component implements the `flexipage` or `forceCommunity` interfaces, its upload is blocked if the component and its attributes aren't set to `access="global"`. For more information on access checks, see Controlling Access.

force:hasRecordId

Useful for record page components. Implement this interface if you want your component to receive the ID of the currently displaying record.

This interface adds an attribute named `recordId` to your component. This attribute is of type String, and its value is an 18-character Salesforce record ID, like this: 001xx000003DGSWAA4. Don't expose the `recordId` attribute to the Lightning App Builder—don't put it in the component's design file. You don't want admins supplying a record ID.

```
<aura:attribute name="recordId" type="String" />
```

The record ID is populated only when you place the component on a record page. In all other cases, the record ID isn't populated, such as when you create this component programmatically inside another component.

force:hasSObjectName

Useful for record page components. Implement this interface if your component needs to know the API name of the object of the currently displaying record.

This interface adds an attribute named `sObjectName` to your component. This attribute is of type String, and its value is the API name of an object, such as `Account` or `myNamespace__myObject__c`.

```
<aura:attribute name="sObjectName" type="String" />
```

The `sObjectName` attribute is populated only when you place the component on a record page. In all other cases, `sObjectName` isn't populated, such as when you create this component programmatically inside another component.

 Tip: Some components only work with a specific object. The mechanism for restricting components to specific objects isn't yet available. In the meantime, we recommend using the Entity Context to check the object. Then, display a message in the component to gracefully handle the case where the component has been added to an incompatible object page.

SEE ALSO:

Configure Components for Lightning Pages and the Lightning App Builder

Tips and Considerations for Configuring Components for Lightning App Builder

Working with Salesforce Records

Tips and Considerations for Configuring Components for Lightning App Builder

Keep these guidelines in mind when creating components and component bundles for the Lightning App Builder.

 Note: Mark your resources, such as a component, with `access="global"` to make the resource usable outside of your own org; for example, if you want a component to be usable in an installed package or by a Lightning App Builder user or a Community Builder user in another org.

Components

- Set a friendly name for the component using the `label` attribute in the element in the design file, such as `<design:component label="foo">`.
- Design your components to fill 100% of the width (including margins) of the region that they display in.
- Components should provide an appropriate placeholder behavior in declarative tools if they require interaction.
- A component should never display a blank box. Think of how other sites work. For example, Facebook displays an outline of the feed before the actual feed items come back from the server. This improves the user's perception of UI responsiveness.
- If the component depends on a fired event, then give it a default state that displays before the event fires.
- Style components in a manner consistent with the styling of Lightning Experience and consistent with the Salesforce Design System.

Attributes

- Use the design file to control which attributes are exposed to the App Builder.
- Make your attributes easy to use and understandable to an administrator. Don't expose SOQL queries, JSON objects, or APEX class names.
- Give your required attributes default values. When a component that has required attributes with no default values is added to the App Builder, it appears invalid, which is a poor user experience.
- Use basic supported types (string, integer, boolean) for any exposed attributes.
- Specify a min and max attribute for integer attributes in the `<design:attribute>` element to control the range of accepted values.

- String attributes can provide a datasource with a set of predefined values allowing the attribute to expose its configuration as a picklist.

- Give all attributes a label with a friendly display name.

- Provide descriptions to explain the expected data and any guidelines, such as data format or expected range of values. Description text appears as a tooltip in the Property Editor.

- To delete a design attribute for a component that implements the `flexipage:availableForAllPageTypes` or `forceCommunity:availableForAllPageTypes` interface, first remove the interface from the component before deleting the design attribute. Then reimplement the interface. If the component is referenced in a Lightning Page, you must remove the component from the page before you can change it.

SEE ALSO:

Configure Components for Lightning Pages and the Lightning App Builder

Configure Components for Lightning Experience Record Home Pages

CHAPTER 5   Communicating with Events

In this chapter ...

- Handling Events with Client-Side Controllers
- Actions and Events
- Component Events
- Application Events
- Event Handling Lifecycle
- Advanced Events Example
- Firing Lightning Events from Non-Lightning Code
- Events Best Practices
- Events Fired During the Rendering Lifecycle
- Salesforce1 Events
- System Events

The framework uses event-driven programming. You write handlers that respond to interface events as they occur. The events may or may not have been triggered by user interaction.

In the Lightning Component framework, events are fired from JavaScript controller actions. Events can contain attributes that can be set before the event is fired and read when the event is handled.

Events are declared by the `aura:event` tag in a `.evt` resource, and they can have one of two types: component or application.

Component Events

A component event is fired from an instance of a component. A component event can be handled by the component that fired the event or by a component in the containment hierarchy that receives the bubbled event.

Application Events

Application events follow a traditional publish-subscribe model. An application event is fired from an instance of a component. All components that provide a handler for the event are notified.

> Note: Always try to use a component event instead of an application event, if possible. Component events can only be handled by components above them in the containment hierarchy so their usage is more localized to the components that need to know about them. Application events are best used for something that should be handled at the application level, such as navigating to a specific record.

Handling Events with Client-Side Controllers

A client-side controller handles events within a component. It's a JavaScript resource that defines the functions for all of the component's actions.

Client-side controllers are surrounded by brackets and curly braces to denote a JSON object containing a map of name-value pairs.

```
({
    myAction : function(cmp, event, helper) {
        // add code for the action
    }
})
```

Each action function takes in three parameters:

1. `cmp`—The component to which the controller belongs.

2. `event`—The event that the action is handling.

3. `helper`—The component's helper, which is optional. A helper contains functions that can be reused by any JavaScript code in the component bundle.

Creating a Client-Side Controller

A client-side controller is part of the component bundle. It is auto-wired via the naming convention, *componentName*`Controller.js`.

To create a client-side controller using the Developer Console, click **CONTROLLER** in the sidebar of the component.

Calling Client-Side Controller Actions

The following example component creates two buttons to contrast an HTML button with a `<ui:button>`, which is a standard Lightning component. Clicking on these buttons updates the `text` component attribute with the specified values. `target.get("v.label")` refers to the `label` attribute value on the button.

Component source

```
<aura:component>
    <aura:attribute name="text" type="String" default="Just a string.
 Waiting for change."/>
    <input type="button" value="Flawed HTML Button"
```

```
        onclick="alert('this will not work')"/>
    <br/>
    <ui:button label="Framework Button" press="{!c.handleClick}"/>
    <br/>
    {!v.text}
</aura:component>
```

If you know some JavaScript, you might be tempted to write something like the first "Flawed" button because you know that HTML tags are first-class citizens in the framework. However, the "Flawed" button won't work because arbitrary JavaScript, such as the `alert()` call, in the component is ignored.

The framework has its own event system. DOM events are mapped to Lightning events, since HTML tags are mapped to Lightning components.

Any browser DOM element event starting with `on`, such as `onclick` or `onkeypress`, can be wired to a controller action. You can only wire browser events to controller actions.

The "Framework" button wires the `press` attribute in the `<ui:button>` component to the `handleClick` action in the controller.

Client-side controller source

```
({
    handleClick : function(cmp, event) {
        var attributeValue = cmp.get("v.text");
        console.log("current text: " + attributeValue);

        var target = event.getSource();
        cmp.set("v.text", target.get("v.label"));
    }
})
```

The `handleClick` action uses `event.getSource()` to get the source component that fired this component event. In this case, the source component is the `<ui:button>` in the markup.

The code then sets the value of the `text` component attribute to the value of the button's `label` attribute. The `text` component attribute is defined in the `<aura:attribute>` tag in the markup.

Handling Framework Events

Handle framework events using actions in client-side component controllers. Framework events for common mouse and keyboard interactions are available with out-of-the-box components.

Tip: Use unique names for client-side and server-side actions in a component. A JavaScript function (client-side action) with the same name as a server-side action (Apex method) can lead to hard-to-debug issues.

Accessing Component Attributes

In the `handleClick` function, notice that the first argument to every action is the component to which the controller belongs. One of the most common things you'll want to do with this component is look at and change its attribute values.

`cmp.get("v.`***attributeName***`")` returns the value of the ***attributeName*** attribute.

`cmp.set("v.`***attributeName***`",  "attribute value")` sets the value of the ***attributeName*** attribute.

Invoking Another Action in the Controller

To call an action method from another method, put the common code in a helper function and invoke it using `helper.someFunction(cmp)`.

SEE ALSO:

Sharing JavaScript Code in a Component Bundle

Event Handling Lifecycle

Creating Server-Side Logic with Controllers

Actions and Events

The framework uses events to relay data between components, which are usually triggered by a user action. Here are some considerations for working with actions and events.

Actions

User interaction with an element on a component or app. User actions trigger events, but events are not always explicitly triggered by user actions. Note that this type of action is *not* the same as a client-side JavaScript controller, which is sometimes known as a *controller action*. The following button is wired up to a browser `onclick` event in response to a button click.

```
<ui:button label = "Click Me" press = "{!c.handleClick}" />
```

Clicking the button invokes the `handeClick` method in the component's client-side controller.

Events

A notification by the browser regarding an action. Browser events are handled by client-side JavaScript controllers, as shown in the previous example. Note that a browser event is not the same as a *component event* or *application event*, which you can create and fire on your own in a JavaScript controller to communicate data between components. For example, you can wire up the click event of a checkbox to a client-side controller, which then fires a component event to communicate relevant data to a parent component.

Another type of event, known as a *system event*, is fired automatically by the framework during its lifecycle, such as during component initialization, change of an attribute value, and rendering. Components can handle a system event by registering the event in the component markup.

The following diagram describes what happens when a user clicks a button that requires the component to retrieve data from the server.

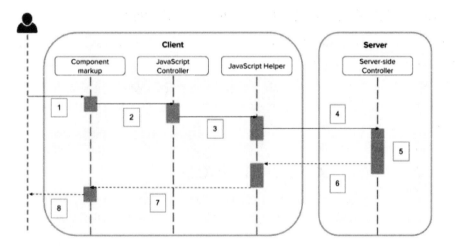

1. User clicks a button or interacts with a component, triggering a browser event. For example, you want to save data from the server when the button is clicked.

2. The button click invokes a client-side JavaScript controller, which provides some custom logic before invoking a helper function.

3. The JavaScript controller invokes a helper function. Note that a helper function improves code reuse but it's optional for this example.

4. The helper function calls an Apex controller method and queues the action.

5. The Apex method is invoked and data is returned.

6. A JavaScript callback function is invoked when the Apex method completes.

7. The JavaScript callback function evaluates logic and updates the component's UI.

8. User sees the updated component.

Alternatively, consider an attribute value on a component that changes without a user action directly causing it, which then automatically fires a `change` event. When the attribute value changes, the component that registers a `change` event handles this event by invoking a JavaScript controller that contains custom logic, which could then proceed from step (3) onwards to retrieve data from the server.

SEE ALSO:

Handling Events with Client-Side Controllers

Detecting Data Changes

Calling a Server-Side Action

Events Fired During the Rendering Lifecycle

Component Events

A component event is fired from an instance of a component. A component event can be handled by the component that fired the event or by a component in the containment hierarchy that receives the bubbled event.

Create Custom Component Event

You can create custom component events using the `<aura:event>` tag in a `.evt` resource. Events can contain attributes that can be set before the event is fired and read when the event is handled.

Use `type="COMPONENT"` in the `<aura:event>` tag for a component event. For example, this is a `c:compEvent` component event with one `message` attribute.

```
<!--c:compEvent-->
<aura:event type="COMPONENT">
    <!-- add aura:attribute tags to define event shape.
      One sample attribute here -->
    <aura:attribute name="message" type="String"/>
</aura:event>
```

The component that handles an event can retrieve the event data. To retrieve the attribute in this event, call `event.getParam("message")` in the handler's client-side controller.

Register Component Event

A component registers that it may fire an event by using `<aura:registerEvent>` in its markup.
For example:

```
<aura:registerEvent name="sampleComponentEvent" type="c:compEvent"/>
```

We'll see how the value of the `name` attribute is used for firing and handling events.

Fire Component Event

To get a reference to a component event in JavaScript, use `getEvent("evtName")` where `evtName`
matches the `name` attribute in `<aura:registerEvent>`. Use `fire()` to fire the event from an
instance of a component. For example, in an action function in a client-side controller:

```
var compEvent = cmp.getEvent("sampleComponentEvent");
// Optional: set some data for the event (also known as event shape)
// compEvent.setParams({"myParam" : myValue });
compEvent.fire();
```

Get the Source of a Component Event

In a handler component, use `evt.getSource()` in JavaScript to find out which component fired the
component event, where `evt` is a reference to the event. To retrieve the source element, use
`evt.getSource().getElement()`.

IN THIS SECTION:

Handling Component Events
A component event can be handled by the component that fired the event or by a component in the
containment hierarchy that receives the bubbled event.

SEE ALSO:

aura:method
Application Events
Handling Events with Client-Side Controllers
Advanced Events Example
What is Inherited?

Handling Component Events

A component event can be handled by the component that fired the event or by a component in the containment hierarchy that receives the bubbled event.

IN THIS SECTION:

Component Handling Its Own Event

A component can handle its own event by using the `<aura:handler>` tag in its markup.

Component Event Bubbling

Component event bubbling is similar to standard event bubbling in browsers. When a component event is fired, the component that fired the event can handle it. The event then bubbles up and can be handled by a component in the containment hierarchy that receives the bubbled event.

Handling Component Events Dynamically

A component can have its handler bound dynamically via JavaScript. This is useful if a component is created in JavaScript on the client-side.

Component Handling Its Own Event

A component can handle its own event by using the `<aura:handler>` tag in its markup.

The `action` attribute of `<aura:handler>` sets the client-side controller action to handle the event. For example:

```
<aura:registerEvent name="sampleComponentEvent" type="c:compEvent"/>
<aura:handler name="sampleComponentEvent"
action="{!c.handleSampleEvent}"/>
```

 Note: The `name` attributes in `<aura:registerEvent>` and `<aura:handler>` must match, since each event is defined by its name.

Component Event Bubbling

Component event bubbling is similar to standard event bubbling in browsers. When a component event is fired, the component that fired the event can handle it. The event then bubbles up and can be handled by a component in the containment hierarchy that receives the bubbled event.

Event Bubbling Rules

A component event can't be handled by every parent in the containment hierarchy. Instead, it bubbles to every facet value provider in the containment hierarchy. A facet value provider is the outermost component containing the markup that references the component firing the event. Confused? It makes more sense when you look at an example.

`c:eventBubblingParent` contains `c:eventBubblingChild`, which in turn contains `c:eventBubblingGrandchild`.

```
<!--c:eventBubblingParent-->
<aura:component>
    <c:eventBubblingChild>
        <c:eventBubblingGrandchild />
    </c:eventBubblingChild>
</aura:component>
```

If `c:eventBubblingGrandchild` fires a component event, it can handle the event itself. The event then bubbles up the containment hierarchy. `c:eventBubblingChild` contains `c:eventBubblingGrandchild` but it's not the facet value provider as it's not the outermost component in the markup so it can't handle the bubbled event. `c:eventBubblingParent` is the facet value provider as `c:eventBubblingChild` is in its markup. `c:eventBubblingParent` can handle the event.

Handle Bubbled Event

A component that fires a component event registers that it fires the event by using the `<aura:registerEvent>` tag.

```
<aura:component>
    <aura:registerEvent name="bubblingEvent" type="c:compEvent" />
</aura:component>
```

A component handling the bubbled component event uses the `<aura:handler>` tag to assign a handling action in its client-side controller.

```
<aura:component>
    <aura:handler name="bubblingEvent" event="c:compEvent"
action="{!c.handleBubbling}"/>
</aura:component>
```

Note: The `name` attribute in `<aura:handler>` must match the `name` attribute in the `<aura:registerEvent>` tag in the component that fires the event.

Event Bubbling Example

Let's go through all the code for this example so you can play around with it yourself.

 Note: This sample code uses the default c namespace. If your org has a namespace, use that namespace instead.

First, we define a simple component event.

```
<!--c:compEvent-->
<aura:event type="COMPONENT">
    <!--simple event with no attributes-->
</aura:event>
```

c:eventBubblingEmitter is the component that fires c:compEvent.

```
<!--c:eventBubblingEmitter-->
<aura:component>
    <aura:registerEvent name="bubblingEvent" type="c:compEvent" />
    <ui:button press="{!c.fireEvent}" label="Start Bubbling"/>
</aura:component>
```

Here is the controller for c:eventBubblingEmitter. When you press the button, it fires the bubblingEvent event registered in the markup.

```
/*eventBubblingEmitterController.js*/
{
    fireEvent : function(cmp) {
        var cmpEvent = cmp.getEvent("bubblingEvent");
        cmpEvent.fire();
    }
}
```

c:eventBubblingGrandchild contains c:eventBubblingEmitter and uses <aura:handler> to assign a handler for the event.

```
<!--c:eventBubblingGrandchild-->
<aura:component>
    <aura:handler name="bubblingEvent" event="c:compEvent"
action="{!c.handleBubbling}"/>

    <div class="grandchild">
        <c:eventBubblingEmitter />
    </div>
</aura:component>
```

Here is the controller for c:eventBubblingGrandchild.

```
/*eventBubblingGrandchildController.js*/
{
    handleBubbling : function(component, event) {
        console.log("Grandchild handler for " + event.getName());
    }
}
```

The controller logs the event name when the handler is called.

Here is the markup for c:eventBubblingChild. We will pass c:eventBubblingGrandchild in as the body of c:eventBubblingChild when we create c:eventBubblingParent later in this example.

```
<!--c:eventBubblingChild-->
<aura:component>
    <aura:handler name="bubblingEvent" event="c:compEvent"
action="{!c.handleBubbling}"/>

    <div class="child">
        {!v.body}
    </div>
</aura:component>
```

Here is the controller for c:eventBubblingChild.

```
/*eventBubblingChildController.js*/
{
    handleBubbling : function(component, event) {
        console.log("Child handler for " + event.getName());
    }
}
```

c:eventBubblingParent contains c:eventBubblingChild, which in turn contains c:eventBubblingGrandchild.

```
<!--c:eventBubblingParent-->
<aura:component>
    <aura:handler name="bubblingEvent" event="c:compEvent"
action="{!c.handleBubbling}"/>

    <div class="parent">
        <c:eventBubblingChild>
            <c:eventBubblingGrandchild />
        </c:eventBubblingChild>
```

```
        </div>
</aura:component>
```

Here is the controller for `c:eventBubblingParent`.

```
/*eventBubblingParentController.js*/
{
    handleBubbling : function(component, event) {
        console.log("Parent handler for " + event.getName());
    }
}
```

Now, let's see what happens when you run the code.

1. In your browser, navigate to `c:eventBubblingParent`. Create a `.app` resource that contains `<c:eventBubblingParent />`.

2. Click the **Start Bubbling** button that is part of the markup in `c:eventBubblingEmitter`.

3. Note the output in your browser's console:

```
Grandchild handler for bubblingEvent
Parent handler for bubblingEvent
```

The `c:compEvent` event is bubbled to `c:eventBubblingGrandchild` and `c:eventBubblingParent` as they are facet value providers in the containment hierarchy. The event is not handled by `c:eventBubblingChild` as `c:eventBubblingChild` is in the markup for `c:eventBubblingParent` but it's not a facet value provider as it's not the outermost component in that markup.

Stop Event Propagation

Use the `stopPropagation()` method in the `Event` object to stop the event bubbling to other components.

For example, edit the controller for `c:eventBubblingGrandchild` to stop propagation.

```
/*eventBubblingGrandchildController.js*/
{
    handleBubbling : function(component, event) {
        console.log("Grandchild handler for " + event.getName());
        event.stopPropagation();
    }
}
```

Now, navigate to `c:eventBubblingParent` and click the **Start Bubbling** button.

Note the output in your browser's console:

```
Grandchild handler for bubblingEvent
```

The event no longer bubbles up to the `c:eventBubblingParent` component.

Handling Component Events Dynamically

A component can have its handler bound dynamically via JavaScript. This is useful if a component is created in JavaScript on the client-side.

For more information, see Dynamically Adding Event Handlers on page 276.

Component Event Example

Here's a simple use case of using a component event to update an attribute in another component.

1. A user clicks a button in the notifier component, `ceNotifier.cmp`.
2. The client-side controller for `ceNotifier.cmp` sets a message in a component event and fires the event.
3. The handler component, `ceHandler.cmp`, contains the notifier component, and handles the fired event.
4. The client-side controller for `ceHandler.cmp` sets an attribute in `ceHandler.cmp` based on the data sent in the event.

 Note: The event and components in this example use the default `c` namespace. If your org has a namespace, use that namespace instead.

Component Event

The `ceEvent.evt` component event has one attribute. We'll use this attribute to pass some data in the event when it's fired.

```
<!--c:ceEvent-->
<aura:event type="COMPONENT">
    <aura:attribute name="message" type="String"/>
</aura:event>
```

Notifier Component

The `c:ceNotifier` component uses `aura:registerEvent` to declare that it may fire the component event.

The button in the component contains a `press` browser event that is wired to the `fireComponentEvent` action in the client-side controller. The action is invoked when you click the button.

```
<!--c:ceNotifier-->
<aura:component>
    <aura:registerEvent name="cmpEvent" type="c:ceEvent"/>

    <h1>Simple Component Event Sample</h1>
    <p><ui:button
        label="Click here to fire a component event"
        press="{!c.fireComponentEvent}" />
    </p>
</aura:component>
```

The client-side controller gets an instance of the event by calling `cmp.getEvent("cmpEvent")`, where `cmpEvent` matches the value of the name attribute in the `<aura:registerEvent>` tag in the component markup. The controller sets the `message` attribute of the event and fires the event.

```
/* ceNotifierController.js */
{
    fireComponentEvent : function(cmp, event) {
        // Get the component event by using the
        // name value from aura:registerEvent
        var cmpEvent = cmp.getEvent("cmpEvent");
        cmpEvent.setParams({
            "message" : "A component event fired me. " +
            "It all happened so fast. Now, I'm here!" });
        cmpEvent.fire();
    }
}
```

Handler Component

The `c:ceHandler` handler component contains the `c:ceNotifier` component. The `<aura:handler>` tag uses the same value of the `name` attribute, `cmpEvent`, from the `<aura:registerEvent>` tag in `c:ceNotifier`. This wires up `c:ceHandler` to handle the event bubbled up from `c:ceNotifier`.

When the event is fired, the `handleComponentEvent` action in the client-side controller of the handler component is invoked.

```
<!--c:ceHandler-->
<aura:component>
    <aura:attribute name="messageFromEvent" type="String"/>
    <aura:attribute name="numEvents" type="Integer" default="0"/>

    <!-- Note that name="cmpEvent" in aura:registerEvent
     in ceNotifier.cmp -->
    <aura:handler name="cmpEvent" event="c:ceEvent"
action="{!c.handleComponentEvent}"/>

    <!-- handler contains the notifier component -->
    <c:ceNotifier />

    <p>{!v.messageFromEvent}</p>
    <p>Number of events: {!v.numEvents}</p>

</aura:component>
```

The controller retrieves the data sent in the event and uses it to update the `messageFromEvent` attribute in the handler component.

```
/* ceHandlerController.js */
{
    handleComponentEvent : function(cmp, event) {
        var message = event.getParam("message");

        // set the handler attributes based on event data
        cmp.set("v.messageFromEvent", message);
        var numEventsHandled = parseInt(cmp.get("v.numEvents")) + 1;
        cmp.set("v.numEvents", numEventsHandled);
    }
}
```

Put It All Together

Add the `c:ceHandler` component to a `c:ceHandlerApp` application. Navigate to the application and click the button to fire the component event.

`https://<myDomain>.lightning.force.com/c/ceHandlerApp.app`, where `<myDomain>` is the name of your custom Salesforce domain.

If you want to access data on the server, you could extend this example to call a server-side controller from the handler's client-side controller.

SEE ALSO:

Component Events

Creating Server-Side Logic with Controllers

Application Event Example

Application Events

Application events follow a traditional publish-subscribe model. An application event is fired from an instance of a component. All components that provide a handler for the event are notified.

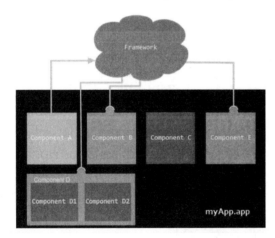

Create Custom Application Event

You can create custom application events using the `<aura:event>` tag in a `.evt` resource. Events can contain attributes that can be set before the event is fired and read when the event is handled.

Use `type="APPLICATION"` in the `<aura:event>` tag for an application event. For example, this is a `c:appEvent` application event with one `message` attribute.

```
<!--c:appEvent-->
<aura:event type="APPLICATION">
    <!-- add aura:attribute tags to define event shape.
        One sample attribute here -->
```

```
    <aura:attribute name="message" type="String"/>
</aura:event>
```

The component that handles an event can retrieve the event data. To retrieve the attribute in this event, call `event.getParam("message")` in the handler's client-side controller.

Register Application Event

A component registers that it may fire an application event by using `<aura:registerEvent>` in its markup. Note that the `name` attribute is required but not used for application events. The `name` attribute is only relevant for component events. This example uses `name="appEvent"` but the value is not used anywhere.

```
<aura:registerEvent name="appEvent" type="c:appEvent"/>
```

Fire Application Event

Use `$A.get("e.myNamespace:myAppEvent")` in JavaScript to get an instance of the `myAppEvent` event in the `myNamespace` namespace. Use `fire()` to fire the event.

```
var appEvent = $A.get("e.c:appEvent");
// Optional: set some data for the event (also known as event shape)
//appEvent.setParams({ "myParam" : myValue });
appEvent.fire();
```

Get the Source of an Application Event

Note that `evt.getSource()` doesn't work for application events It only works for component events.

A component event is usually fired by code like `cmp.getEvent('cmpEvent').fire()` so it's obvious who fired the event. However, it's relatively opaque which component fired an application event. It's fired by code like `$A.get('e.c.appEvent').fire();`

If you need to find the source of an application event, you could use `evt.setParams()` to set the source component in the event data before firing it. For example, `evt.setParams("source" :` `sourceCmp)`, where `sourceCmp` is a reference to the source component.

Events Fired on App Rendering

Several events are fired when an app is rendering. All `init` events are fired to indicate the component or app has been initialized. If a component is contained in another component or app, the inner component is initialized first. If any server calls are made during rendering, `aura:waiting` is fired. Finally, `aura:doneWaiting` and `aura:doneRendering` are fired in that order to indicate that all rendering has been completed. For more information, see Events Fired During the Rendering Lifecycle on page 192.

IN THIS SECTION:

Handling Application Events
Use `<aura:handler>` in the markup of the handler component.

SEE ALSO:

Component Events
Handling Events with Client-Side Controllers
Advanced Events Example
What is Inherited?

Handling Application Events

Use `<aura:handler>` in the markup of the handler component.

The `action` attribute of `<aura:handler>` sets the client-side controller action to handle the event. For example:

```
<aura:handler event="c:appEvent" action="{!c.handleApplicationEvent}"/>
```

When the event is fired, the `handleApplicationEvent` client-side controller action is called.

Application Event Example

Here's a simple use case of using an application event to update an attribute in another component.

1. A user clicks a button in the notifier component, `aeNotifier.cmp`.

2. The client-side controller for `aeNotifier.cmp` sets a message in a component event and fires the event.

3. The handler component, `aeHandler.cmp`, handles the fired event.

4. The client-side controller for `aeHandler.cmp` sets an attribute in `aeHandler.cmp` based on the data sent in the event.

Note: The event and components in this example use the default `c` namespace. If your org has a namespace, use that namespace instead.

Application Event

The `aeEvent.evt` application event has one attribute. We'll use this attribute to pass some data in the event when it's fired.

```
<!--c:aeEvent-->
<aura:event type="APPLICATION">
    <aura:attribute name="message" type="String"/>
</aura:event>
```

Notifier Component

The `aeNotifier.cmp` notifier component uses `aura:registerEvent` to declare that it may fire the application event. Note that the `name` attribute is required but not used for application events. The `name` attribute is only relevant for component events.

The button in the component contains a `press` browser event that is wired to the `fireApplicationEvent` action in the client-side controller. Clicking this button invokes the action.

```
<!--c:aeNotifier-->
<aura:component>
    <aura:registerEvent name="appEvent" type="c:aeEvent"/>

    <h1>Simple Application Event Sample</h1>
    <p><ui:button
        label="Click here to fire an application event"
        press="{!c.fireApplicationEvent}" />
    </p>
</aura:component>
```

The client-side controller gets an instance of the event by calling `$A.get("e.c:aeEvent")`. The controller sets the `message` attribute of the event and fires the event.

```
/* aeNotifierController.js */
{
    fireApplicationEvent : function(cmp, event) {
        // Get the application event by using the
        // e.<namespace>.<event> syntax
        var appEvent = $A.get("e.c:aeEvent");
        appEvent.setParams({
```

179

```
            "message" : "An application event fired me. " +
            "It all happened so fast. Now, I'm everywhere!" });
        appEvent.fire();
    }
}
```

Handler Component

The `aeHandler.cmp` handler component uses the `<aura:handler>` tag to register that it handles the application event.

When the event is fired, the `handleApplicationEvent` action in the client-side controller of the handler component is invoked.

```
<!--c:aeHandler-->
<aura:component>
    <aura:attribute name="messageFromEvent" type="String"/>
    <aura:attribute name="numEvents" type="Integer" default="0"/>

    <aura:handler event="c:aeEvent"
action="{!c.handleApplicationEvent}"/>

    <p>{!v.messageFromEvent}</p>
    <p>Number of events: {!v.numEvents}</p>
</aura:component>
```

The controller retrieves the data sent in the event and uses it to update the `messageFromEvent` attribute in the handler component.

```
/* aeHandlerController.js */
{
    handleApplicationEvent : function(cmp, event) {
        var message = event.getParam("message");

        // set the handler attributes based on event data
        cmp.set("v.messageFromEvent", message);
        var numEventsHandled = parseInt(cmp.get("v.numEvents")) + 1;
        cmp.set("v.numEvents", numEventsHandled);
    }
}
```

Container Component

The `aeContainer.cmp` container component contains the notifier and handler components. This is different from the component event example where the handler contains the notifier component.

```
<!--c:aeContainer-->
<aura:component>
    <c:aeNotifier/>
    <c:aeHandler/>
</aura:component>
```

Put It All Together

You can test this code by adding `<c:aeContainer>` to a sample `aeWrapper.app` application and navigating to the application.

`https://<myDomain>.lightning.force.com/c/aeWrapper.app`, where `<myDomain>` is the name of your custom Salesforce domain.

If you want to access data on the server, you could extend this example to call a server-side controller from the handler's client-side controller.

SEE ALSO:

  Application Events

  Creating Server-Side Logic with Controllers

  Component Event Example

Event Handling Lifecycle

The following chart summarizes how the framework handles events.

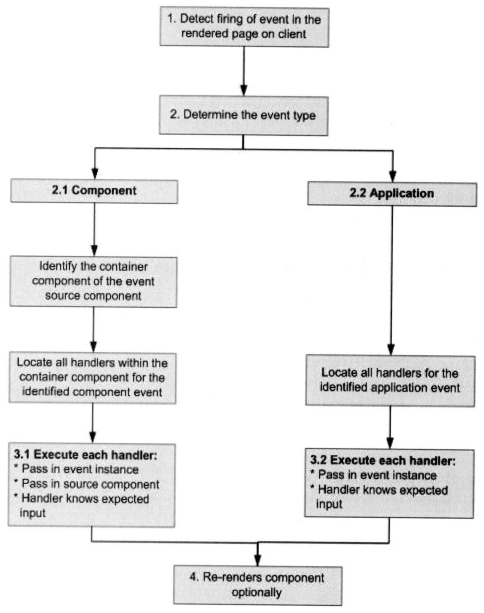

1 Detect Firing of Event

The framework detects the firing of an event. For example, the event could be triggered by a button click in a notifier component.

2 Determine the Event Type

2.1 Component Event

The parent or container component instance that fired the event is identified. This container component locates all relevant event handlers for further processing.

2.2 Application Event

Any component can have an event handler for this event. All relevant event handlers are located.

3 Execute each Handler

3.1 Executing a Component Event Handler

Each of the event handlers defined in the container component for the event are executed by the handler controller, which can also:

- Set attributes or modify data on the component (causing a re-rendering of the component).
- Fire another event or invoke a client-side or server-side action.

3.2 Executing an Application Event Handler

All event handlers are executed. When the event handler is executed, the event instance is passed into the event handler.

4 Re-render Component (optional)

After the event handlers and any callback actions are executed, a component might be automatically re-rendered if it was modified during the event handling process.

SEE ALSO:

Client-Side Rendering to the DOM

Advanced Events Example

This example builds on the simpler component and application event examples. It uses one notifier component and one handler component that work with both component and application events. Before we see a component wired up to events, let's look at the individual resources involved.

This table summarizes the roles of the various resources used in the example. The source code for these resources is included after the table.

Resource	Resource Name	Usage
Event files	Component event (`compEvent.evt`) and application event (`appEvent.evt`)	Defines the component and application events in separate resources. `eventsContainer.cmp` shows how to use both component and application events.
Notifier	Component (`eventsNotifier.cmp`) and its controller (`eventsNotifierController.js`)	The notifier contains an `onclick` browser event to initiate the event. The controller fires the event.
Handler	Component (`eventsHandler.cmp`) and its controller (`eventsHandlerController.js`)	The handler component contains the notifier component (or a `<aura:handler>` tag for application events), and calls the controller action that is executed after the event is fired.
Container Component	`eventsContainer.cmp`	Displays the event handlers on the UI for the complete demo.

The definitions of component and application events are stored in separate `.evt` resources, but individual notifier and handler component bundles can contain code to work with both types of events.

The component and application events both contain a `context` attribute that defines the shape of the event. This is the data that is passed to handlers of the event.

Component Event

Here is the markup for `compEvent.evt`.

```
<!--c:compEvent-->
<aura:event type="COMPONENT">
    <!-- pass context of where the event was fired to the handler. -->

    <aura:attribute name="context" type="String"/>
</aura:event>
```

Application Event

Here is the markup for `appEvent.evt`.

```
<!--c:appEvent-->
<aura:event type="APPLICATION">
    <!-- pass context of where the event was fired to the handler. -->

    <aura:attribute name="context" type="String"/>
</aura:event>
```

Notifier Component

The `eventsNotifier.cmp` notifier component contains buttons to initiate a component or application event.

The notifier uses `aura:registerEvent` tags to declare that it may fire the component and application events. Note that the `name` attribute is required but the value is only relevant for the component event; the value is not used anywhere else for the application event.

The `parentName` attribute is not set yet. We will see how this attribute is set and surfaced in `eventsContainer.cmp`.

```
<!--c:eventsNotifier-->
<aura:component>
  <aura:attribute name="parentName" type="String"/>
  <aura:registerEvent name="componentEventFired" type="c:compEvent"/>

  <aura:registerEvent name="appEvent" type="c:appEvent"/>

  <div>
    <h3>This is {!v.parentName}'s eventsNotifier.cmp instance</h3>
    <p><ui:button
        label="Click here to fire a component event"
        press="{!c.fireComponentEvent}" />
    </p>
    <p><ui:button
        label="Click here to fire an application event"
        press="{!c.fireApplicationEvent}" />
    </p>
  </div>
</aura:component>
```

CSS source

The CSS is in `eventsNotifier.css`.

```
/* eventsNotifier.css */
.cEventsNotifier {
    display: block;
    margin: 10px;
    padding: 10px;
    border: 1px solid black;
}
```

Client-side controller source

The `eventsNotifierController.js` controller fires the event.

```
/* eventsNotifierController.js */
{
    fireComponentEvent : function(cmp, event) {
        var parentName = cmp.get("v.parentName");

        // Look up event by name, not by type
        var compEvents = cmp.getEvent("componentEventFired");

        compEvents.setParams({ "context" : parentName });
        compEvents.fire();
    },

    fireApplicationEvent : function(cmp, event) {
        var parentName = cmp.get("v.parentName");

        // note different syntax for getting application event
        var appEvent = $A.get("e.c:appEvent");

        appEvent.setParams({ "context" : parentName });
        appEvent.fire();
    }
}
```

You can click the buttons to fire component and application events but there is no change to the output because we haven't wired up the handler component to react to the events yet.

The controller sets the `context` attribute of the component or application event to the `parentName` of the notifier component before firing the event. We will see how this affects the output when we look at the handler component.

Handler Component

The `eventsHandler.cmp` handler component contains the `c:eventsNotifier` notifier component and `<aura:handler>` tags for the application and component events.

```
<!--c:eventsHandler-->
<aura:component>
  <aura:attribute name="name" type="String"/>
  <aura:attribute name="mostRecentEvent" type="String" default="Most
recent event handled:"/>
  <aura:attribute name="numComponentEventsHandled" type="Integer"
default="0"/>
  <aura:attribute name="numApplicationEventsHandled" type="Integer"
default="0"/>

  <aura:handler event="c:appEvent"
action="{!c.handleApplicationEventFired}"/>
  <aura:handler name="componentEventFired" event="c:compEvent"
action="{!c.handleComponentEventFired}"/>

  <div>
    <h3>This is {!v.name}</h3>
    <p>{!v.mostRecentEvent}</p>
    <p># component events handled: {!v.numComponentEventsHandled}</p>

    <p># application events handled:
{!v.numApplicationEventsHandled}</p>
    <c:eventsNotifier parentName="{!v.name}" />
  </div>
</aura:component>
```

CSS source

The CSS is in `eventsHandler.css`.

```
/* eventsHandler.css */
.cEventsHandler {
  display: block;
  margin: 10px;
  padding: 10px;
  border: 1px solid black;
}
```

Client-side controller source

The client-side controller is in `eventsHandlerController.js`.

```
/* eventsHandlerController.js */
{
    handleComponentEventFired : function(cmp, event) {
        var context = event.getParam("context");
        cmp.set("v.mostRecentEvent",
            "Most recent event handled: COMPONENT event, from " +
context);

        var numComponentEventsHandled =
            parseInt(cmp.get("v.numComponentEventsHandled")) + 1;
        cmp.set("v.numComponentEventsHandled",
numComponentEventsHandled);
    },

    handleApplicationEventFired : function(cmp, event) {
        var context = event.getParam("context");
        cmp.set("v.mostRecentEvent",
            "Most recent event handled: APPLICATION event, from " +
context);

        var numApplicationEventsHandled =
            parseInt(cmp.get("v.numApplicationEventsHandled")) + 1;
        cmp.set("v.numApplicationEventsHandled",
numApplicationEventsHandled);
    }
}
```

The `name` attribute is not set yet. We will see how this attribute is set and surfaced in `eventsContainer.cmp`.

You can click buttons and the UI now changes to indicate the type of event. The click count increments to indicate whether it's a component or application event. We aren't finished yet though. Notice that the source of the event is undefined as the event `context` attribute hasn't been set .

Container Component

Here is the markup for `eventsContainer.cmp`.

```
<!--c:eventsContainer-->
<aura:component>
    <c:eventsHandler name="eventsHandler1"/>
```

```
    <c:eventsHandler name="eventsHandler2"/>
</aura:component>
```

The container component contains two handler components. It sets the `name` attribute of both handler components, which is passed through to set the `parentName` attribute of the notifier components. This fills in the gaps in the UI text that we saw when we looked at the notifier or handler components directly.

Add the `c:eventsContainer` component to a `c:eventsContainerApp` application. Navigate to the application.

`https://<myDomain>.lightning.force.com/c/eventsContainerApp.app`, where `<myDomain>` is the name of your custom Salesforce domain.

Click the **Click here to fire a component event** button for either of the event handlers. Notice that the **# component events handled** counter only increments for that component because only the firing component's handler is notified.

Click the **Click here to fire an application event** button for either of the event handlers. Notice that the **# application events handled** counter increments for both the components this time because all the handling components are notified.

SEE ALSO:

Component Event Example

Application Event Example

Event Handling Lifecycle

Firing Lightning Events from Non-Lightning Code

You can fire Lightning events from JavaScript code outside a Lightning app. For example, your Lightning app might need to call out to some non-Lightning code, and then have that code communicate back to your Lightning app once it's done.

For example, you could call external code that needs to log into another system and return some data to your Lightning app. Let's call this event `mynamespace:externalEvent`. You'll fire this event when your non-Lightning code is done by including this JavaScript in your non-Lightning code.

```
var myExternalEvent;
    if(window.opener.$A &&
      (myExternalEvent =
window.opener.$A.get("e.mynamespace:externalEvent"))) {
        myExternalEvent.setParams({isOauthed:true});
```

```
            myExternalEvent.fire();
        }
```

`window.opener.$A.get()` references the master window where your Lightning app is loaded.

SEE ALSO:

Application Events

Modifying Components Outside the Framework Lifecycle

Events Best Practices

Here are some best practices for working with events.

Use Component Events Whenever Possible

Always try to use a component event instead of an application event, if possible. Component events can only be handled by components above them in the containment hierarchy so their usage is more localized to the components that need to know about them. Application events are best used for something that should be handled at the application level, such as navigating to a specific record.

Separate Low-Level Events from Business Logic Events

It's a good practice to handle low-level events, such as a click, in your event handler and refire them as higher-level events, such as an `approvalChange` event or whatever is appropriate for your business logic.

Dynamic Actions based on Component State

If you need to invoke a different action on a click event depending on the state of the component, try this approach:

1. Store the component state as a discrete value, such as New or Pending, in a component attribute.

2. Put logic in your client-side controller to determine the next action to take.

3. If you need to reuse the logic in your component bundle, put the logic in the helper.

For example:

1. Your component markup contains `<ui:button label="do something"`
   `press="{!c.click}" />`.

2. In your controller, define the `click` function, which delegates to the appropriate helper function or potentially fires the correct event.

Using a Dispatcher Component to Listen and Relay Events

If you have a large number of handler component instances listening for an event, it may be better to identify a dispatcher component to listen for the event. The dispatcher component can perform some logic to decide which component instances should receive further information and fire another component or application event targeted at those component instances.

SEE ALSO:

Handling Events with Client-Side Controllers

Events Anti-Patterns

Events Anti-Patterns

These are some anti-patterns that you should avoid when using events.

Don't Fire an Event in a Renderer

Firing an event in a renderer can cause an infinite rendering loop.

Don't do this!

```
afterRender: function(cmp, helper) {
    this.superAfterRender();
    $A.get("e.myns:mycmp").fire();
}
```

Instead, use the `init` hook to run a controller action after component construction but before rendering. Add this code to your component:

```
<aura:handler name="init" value="{!this}" action="{!c.doInit}"/>
```

For more details, see .Invoking Actions on Component Initialization on page 262.

Don't Use `onclick` and `ontouchend` Events

You can't use different actions for `onclick` and `ontouchend` events in a component. The framework translates touch-tap events into clicks and activates any `onclick` handlers that are present.

SEE ALSO:

Client-Side Rendering to the DOM

Events Best Practices

Events Fired During the Rendering Lifecycle

A component is instantiated, rendered, and rerendered during its lifecycle. A component is rerendered only when there's a programmatic or value change that would require a rerender, such as when a browser event triggers an action that updates its data.

Component Creation

The component lifecycle starts when the client sends an HTTP request to the server and the component configuration data is returned to the client. No server trip is made if the component definition is already on the client from a previous request and the component has no server dependencies.

Let's look at an app with several nested components. The framework instantiates the app and goes through the children of the `v.body` facet to create each component, First, it creates the component definition, its entire parent hierarchy, and then creates the facets within those components. The framework also creates any component dependencies on the server, including definitions for attributes, interfaces, controllers, and actions..

The following image lists the order of component creation.

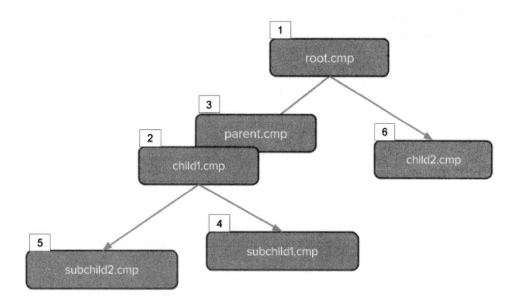

After creating a component instance, the serialized component definitions and instances are sent down to the client. Definitions are cached but not the instance data. The client deserializes the response to create the JavaScript objects or maps, resulting in an instance tree that's used to render the component instance. When the component tree is ready, the `init` event is fired for all the components, starting from the children component and finishing in the parent component.

Component Rendering

The following image depicts a typical rendering lifecycle of a component on the client, after the component definitions and instances are deserialized.

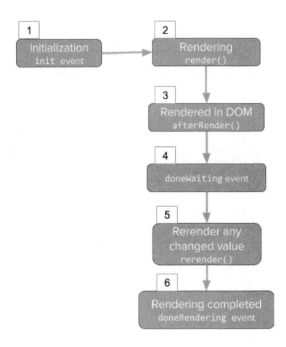

1. The `init` event is fired by the component service that constructs the components to signal that initialization has completed.

    ```
    <aura:handler name="init" value="{!this}" action="{!.c.doInit}"/>
    ```

    You can customize the `init` handler and add your own controller logic before the component starts rendering. For more information, see Invoking Actions on Component Initialization on page 262.

2. For each component in the tree, the base implementation of `render()` or your custom renderer is called to start component rendering. For more information, see Client-Side Rendering to the DOM on page 258. Similar to the component creation process, rendering starts at the root component, its children components and their super components, if any, and finally the subchildren components.

3. Once your components are rendered to the DOM, `afterRender()` is called to signal that rendering is completed for each of these component definitions. It enables you to interact with the DOM tree after the framework rendering service has created the DOM elements.

4. To indicate that the client is done waiting for a response to the server request XHR, the `doneWaiting` event is fired. You can handle this event by adding a handler wired to a client-side controller action.

5. The framework checks whether any components need to be rerendered and rerenders any "dirtied" components to reflect any updates to attribute values. This rerender check is done even if there's no dirtied components or values.

6. Finally, the `doneRendering` event is fired at the end of the rendering lifecycle.

Let's see what happens when a `ui:button` component is returned from the server and any rerendering that occurs when the button is clicked to update its label.

```
<!-- The uiExamples:buttonExample container component -->
<aura:component>
    <aura:attribute name="num" type="Integer" default="0"/>
    <ui:button aura:id="button" label="{!v.num}" press="{!c.update}"/>
</aura:component>
```

```
/** Client-side Controller **/
({
    update : function(cmp, evt) {
        cmp.set("v.num", cmp.get("v.num")+1);
    }
})
```

> Note: It's helpful to refer to the `ui:button` source to understand the component definitions to be rendered. For more information, see
> https://github.com/forcedotcom/aura/blob/master/aura-components/src/main/components/ui/button/button.cmp.

After initialization, `render()` is called to render `ui:button`. `ui:button` doesn't have a custom renderer, and uses the base implementation of `render()`. In this example, `render()` is called eight times in the following order.

Component	Description
`uiExamples:buttonExample`	The top-level component that contains the `ui:button` component
`ui:button`	The `ui:button` component that's in the top-level component
`aura:html`	Renders the `<button>` tag.
`aura:if`	The first `aura:if` tag in `ui:button`, which doesn't render anything since the button contains no image
`aura:if`	The second `aura:if` tag in `ui:button`

Component	Description
`aura:html`	The `<span>` tag for the button label, nested in the `<button>` tag
`aura:expression`	The `v.num` expression
`aura:expression`	Empty `v.body` expression

HTML tags in the markup are converted to `aura:html`, which has a `tag` attribute that defines the HTML tag to be generated. When rendering is done, this example calls `afterRender()` eight times for these component definitions. The `doneWaiting` event is fired, followed by the `doneRendering` event.

Clicking the button updates its label, which checks for any "dirtied" components and fires `rerender()` to rerender these components, followed by the `doneRendering` event. In this example, `rerender()` is called eight times. All changed values are stored in a list on the rendering service, resulting in the rerendering of any "dirtied" components.

 Note: Firing an event in a custom renderer is not recommended. For more information, see Events Anti-Patterns.

Rendering Nested Components

Let's say that you have an app `myApp.app` that contains a component `myCmp.cmp` with a `ui:button` component.

During initialization, the `init()` event is fired in this order: `ui:button`, `ui:myCmp`, and `myApp.app`. The `doneWaiting` event is fired in the same order. Finally, the `doneRendering` event is also called in the same order.

SEE ALSO:

Client-Side Rendering to the DOM

Salesforce1 Events

Lightning components interact with Salesforce1 via events.

You can fire the following events, which are automatically handled by Salesforce1. If you fire these events in your Lightning apps or components outside of Salesforce1, you must handle them as necessary.

Event Name	Description
`force:createRecord`	Opens the page to create a record for the specified `entityApiName`, for example, "Account" or "myNamespace__MyObject__c".
`force:editRecord`	Opens the page to edit the record specified by `recordId`.
`force:navigateToList`	Navigates to the list view specified by `listViewId`.
`force:navigateToObjectHome`	Navigates to the object home specified by the `scope` attribute.
`force:navigateToRelatedList`	Navigates to the related list specified by `parentRecordId`.
`force:navigateToSObject`	Navigates to an sObject record specified by `recordId`.
`force:navigateToURL`	Navigates to the specified URL.
`force:recordSave`	Saves a record.
`force:recordSaveSuccess`	Indicates that the record has been successfully saved.
`force:refreshView`	Reloads the view.
`force:showToast`	Displays a toast notification with a message.

Customizing Client-Side Logic for Salesforce1 and a Standalone App

Since Salesforce1 automatically handles many events, you have to do extra work if your component runs in a standalone app. Instantiating a Salesforce1 event using `$A.get()` can help you determine if your component is running within Salesforce1 or a standalone app. For example, you want to display a toast when a component loads in Salesforce1 and in a standalone app. You can fire the `force:showToast` event and set its parameters for Salesforce1 and create your own implementation for a standalone app.

```
displayToast : function (component, event, helper) {
    var toast = $A.get("e.force:showToast");
    if (toast){
        //fire the toast event in Salesforce1
        toast.setParams({
            "title": "Success!",
            "message": "The component loaded successfully."
        });
        toast.fire();
    } else {
        //your toast implementation for a standalone app here
    }
}
```

System Events

The framework fires several system events during its lifecycle.

You can handle these events in your Lightning apps or components, and within Salesforce1.

Event Name	Description
aura:doneRendering	Indicates that the initial rendering of the root application or root component has completed.
aura:doneWaiting	Indicates that the app or component is done waiting for a response to a server request. This event is preceded by an aura:waiting event.
aura:locationChange	Indicates that the hash part of the URL has changed.
aura:noAccess	Indicates that a requested resource is not accessible due to security constraints on that resource.

Event Name	Description
aura:systemError	Indicates that an error has occurred.
aura:valueChange	Indicates that a value has changed.
aura:valueDestroy	Indicates that a value is being destroyed.
aura:valueInit	Indicates that a value has been initialized.
aura:waiting	Indicates that the app or component is waiting for a response to a server request.

CHAPTER 6   Creating Apps

In this chapter ...

- App Overview
- Designing App UI
- Creating App Templates
- Developing Secure Code
- Styling Apps
- Using JavaScript
- JavaScript Cookbook
- Using Apex
- Controlling Access
- Using Object-Oriented Development
- Caching with Storage Service
- Using the AppCache
- Distributing Applications and Components

Components are the building blocks of an app. This section shows you a typical workflow to put the pieces together to create a new app.

First, you should decide whether you're creating a component for a standalone app or for Salesforce apps, such as Lightning Experience or Salesforce1. Both components can access your Salesforce data, but only a component created for Lightning Experience or Salesforce1 can automatically handle Salesforce events that take advantage of record create and edit pages, among other benefits.

The Quick Start on page 7 walks you through creating components for a standalone app and components for Salesforce1 to help you determine which one you need.

App Overview

An app is a special top-level component whose markup is in a `.app` resource.

On a production server, the `.app` resource is the only addressable unit in a browser URL. Access an app using the URL:

`https://<myDomain>.lightning.force.com/<namespace>/<appName>.app,`
where `<myDomain>` is the name of your custom Salesforce domain

SEE ALSO:

aura:application

Designing App UI

Design your app's UI by including markup in the `.app` resource, which starts with the `<aura:application>` tag.

Let's take a look at the `accounts.app` resource created in Create a Standalone Lightning App.

```
<aura:application>
    <h1>Accounts</h1>
    <div class="container">
        <!-- Other components or markup here -->
    </div>
</aura:application>
```

`accounts.app` contains HTML tags and component markup. You can use HTML tags like `<div class="container">` to design the layout of your app.

SEE ALSO:

aura:application

Creating App Templates

An app template bootstraps the loading of the framework and the app. Customize an app's template by creating a component that extends the default `aura:template` template.

A template must have the `isTemplate` system attribute in the `<aura:component>` tag set to `true`. This informs the framework to allow restricted items, such as `<script>` tags, which aren't allowed in regular components.

For example, a sample app has a `np:template` template that extends `aura:template`. `np:template` looks like:

```
<aura:component isTemplate="true" extends="aura:template">
    <aura:set attribute="title" value="My App"/>

    ...
</aura:component>
```

Note how the component extends `aura:template` and sets the `title` attribute using `aura:set`.

The app points at the custom template by setting the `template` system attribute in `<aura:application>`.

```
<aura:application template="np:template">
    ...
</aura:application>
```

A template can only extend a component or another template. A component or an application can't extend a template.

Developing Secure Code

The framework uses Content Security Policy (CSP) to control the source of content that can be loaded on a page.

The LockerService architectural layer enhances security by isolating individual Lightning components in their own containers and enforcing coding best practices.

IN THIS SECTION:

Content Security Policy Overview
The framework uses Content Security Policy (CSP) to control the source of content that can be loaded on a page.

LockerService Rules for Writing Secure Code
LockerService is a powerful security architecture for Lightning components. LockerService enhances security by isolating individual Lightning components in their own containers. LockerService also promotes best practices that improve the supportability of your code by only allowing access to supported APIs and eliminating access to non-published framework internals.

Salesforce Lightning CLI

Use Lightning CLI, a code linting tool, to validate your code for use within the LockerService security architecture. Lightning CLI is a Heroku Toolbelt plugin that lets you scan your code for Lightning-specific issues. This tool is extremely useful for preparing your Lightning code for LockerService enablement.

Content Security Policy Overview

The framework uses Content Security Policy (CSP) to control the source of content that can be loaded on a page.

CSP is a Candidate Recommendation of the W3C working group on Web Application Security. The framework uses the `Content-Security-Policy` HTTP header recommended by the W3C.

The framework's CSP covers these resources:

JavaScript Libraries

All JavaScript libraries must be uploaded to Salesforce static resources. For more information, see Using External JavaScript Libraries on page 251.

HTTPS Connections for Resources

All external fonts, images, frames, and CSS must use an HTTPS URL.

Inline Scripts

LockerService tightens CSP to eliminate the possibility of cross-site scripting attacks by removing the `unsafe-inline` and `unsafe-eval` keywords for inline scripts (`script-src`).

Browser Support

CSP is not enforced for all browsers. For a list of browsers that enforce CSP, see `caniuse.com`.

 Note: IE11 doesn't support CSP, so we recommend using other supported browsers for enhanced security.

Finding CSP Violations

Any policy violations are logged in the browser's developer console. The violations look like this:

```
Refused to load the script
'https://externaljs.docsample.com/externalLib.js'
because it violates the following Content Security Policy directive:
...
```

If your app's functionality isn't affected, you can ignore the CSP violation.

LockerService Rules for Writing Secure Code

LockerService is a powerful security architecture for Lightning components. LockerService enhances security by isolating individual Lightning components in their own containers. LockerService also promotes best practices that improve the supportability of your code by only allowing access to supported APIs and eliminating access to non-published framework internals.

LockerService enforces a number of security features in your code.

JavaScript ES5 Strict Mode Enforcement

JavaScript ES5 strict mode is implicitly enabled. You don't need to specify `"use strict"` in your code. Enforcement includes declaration of variables with the `var` keyword and other JavaScript coding best practices. The libraries that your components use must also work in strict mode.

DOM Access Containment

A component can only traverse the DOM and access elements created by that component. This behavior prevents the anti-pattern of reaching into DOM elements owned by other components.

Stricter Content Security Policy (CSP)

LockerService tightens CSP to eliminate the possibility of cross-site scripting attacks by removing the `unsafe-inline` and `unsafe-eval` keywords for inline scripts (`script-src`).

 Note: IE11 doesn't support CSP, so we recommend using other supported browsers for enhanced security.

Restrictions to Global References

LockerService applies restrictions to global references. You can access intrinsic objects, such as `Array`. LockerService provides secure versions of non-intrinsic objects, such as `window`. The secure object versions automatically and seamlessly control access to the object and its properties.

Use the Salesforce Lightning CLI tool to scan your code for Lightning-specific issues.

Access to Supported JavaScript API Framework Methods Only

You can access published, supported JavaScript API framework methods only. These methods are published in the reference doc app at `https://`*yourDomain*`.lightning.force.com/auradocs/reference.app`. Previously, unsupported methods were accessible, which exposed your code to the risk of breaking when unsupported methods were changed or removed.

Don't Use `instanceof`

When LockerService is enabled, the `instanceof` operator is unreliable due to the potential presence of multiple windows or frames. To determine a variable type, use `typeof` or a standard JavaScript method, such as `Array.isArray()`, instead.

Activate the Critical Update

LockerService is a critical update for this release.

We recommend that you test this update in a sandbox or Developer Edition org to verify correct behavior of your components before enabling it in your production org.

To activate this critical update:

1. From Setup, enter `Critical Updates` in the `Quick Find` box, and then select **Critical Updates**.

2. For "Enable Lightning LockerService Security", click **Activate**.

3. Refresh your browser page to proceed with LockerService enabled.

> **Note:** LockerService is automatically enabled for:
>
> - New orgs created after the Summer '16 release
> - All Developer Edition orgs
> - All existing orgs with no custom Lightning components
>
> If you don't see this critical update in your org, LockerService has been automatically enabled. Automatic enablement occurs within 24 hours after the release.

SEE ALSO:

Content Security Policy Overview

Reference Doc App

Salesforce Lightning CLI

Use Lightning CLI, a code linting tool, to validate your code for use within the LockerService security architecture. Lightning CLI is a Heroku Toolbelt plugin that lets you scan your code for Lightning-specific issues. This tool is extremely useful for preparing your Lightning code for LockerService enablement.

Lightning CLI is a linting tool based on the open source ESLint project. Like ESLint, it flags issues it finds in your code. Lightning CLI alerts you to specific issues related to LockerService. Issues that are flagged include incorrect Lightning components code, use of unsupported or private Lightning APIs, and a number of general JavaScript coding issues. Lightning CLI installs into the Heroku Toolbelt, and is used on the command line.

IN THIS SECTION:

Install Salesforce Lightning CLI

Install Lightning CLI as a Heroku Toolbelt plugin. Then, update the Heroku Toolbelt to get the latest Lightning CLI rules.

Use Salesforce Lightning CLI

Run Lightning CLI just like any other lint command line tool. The only trick is invoking it through the `heroku` command. Your shell window shows the results.

Review and Resolve Problems

When you run Lightning CLI on your Lightning components code, the tool outputs results for each issue found in the files scanned. Review the results and resolve problems in your code.

Salesforce Lightning CLI Rules

Rules built into Lightning CLI cover restrictions under LockerService, correct use of Lightning APIs, and a number of best practices for writing Lightning components code. Each rule, when triggered by your code, points to an area where your code might have an issue.

Salesforce Lightning CLI Options

There are several options that modify the behavior of Lightning CLI.

Install Salesforce Lightning CLI

Install Lightning CLI as a Heroku Toolbelt plugin. Then, update the Heroku Toolbelt to get the latest Lightning CLI rules.

Lightning CLI relies on Heroku Toolbelt. Make sure that you have the `heroku` command installed correctly before attempting to use Lightning CLI. More information about Heroku Toolbelt is available here:

`https://devcenter.heroku.com/articles/getting-started-with-nodejs#set-up`

After getting Heroku Toolbelt up and running, install the Lightning CLI plugin using the following command:

```
heroku plugins:install salesforce-lightning-cli
```

Once installed, the plugin is updated whenever you update the Heroku Toolbelt using the `heroku update` command. Run the update command every week or so to make sure you've got the latest Lightning CLI rules.

Use Salesforce Lightning CLI

Run Lightning CLI just like any other lint command line tool. The only trick is invoking it through the `heroku` command. Your shell window shows the results.

Normal Use

You can run the Lightning CLI linter on any folder that contains Lightning components:

```
heroku lightning:lint ./path/to/lightning/components/
```

 Note: Lightning CLI runs only on local files. Download your component code to your machine using the Metadata API, or a tool such as the Force.com IDE, the Force.com Migration Tool, or any of a number of third-party options.

See "Review and Resolve Problems" for what to do with the output of running Lightning CLI.

Common Options

Filtering Files

Sometimes you just want to scan a particular kind of file. The `--files` argument allows you to set a pattern to match files against.

For example, the following command allows you to scan controllers only:

```
heroku lightning:lint ./path/to/lightning/components/ --files
**/*Controller.js
```

Ignoring Warnings

Sometimes you just want to focus on the errors. The `--quiet` argument allows you to ignore warning messages during the linting process.

SEE ALSO:

Salesforce Lightning CLI Options

Review and Resolve Problems

When you run Lightning CLI on your Lightning components code, the tool outputs results for each issue found in the files scanned. Review the results and resolve problems in your code.

For example, here is some example output.

```
error      secure-document      Invalid SecureDocument API
  Line:109:29
  scrapping = document.innerHTML;
  ^


  warning    no-plusplus    Unary operator '++' used
```

```
Line:120:50
for (var i = (index+1); i < sibs.length; i++) {
^


error    secure-window   Invalid SecureWindow API
Line:33:21
var req = new XMLHttpRequest();
^


error   default-case   Expected a default case
Line:108:13
switch (e.keyCode) {
^
```

Issues are displayed, one for each warning or error. Each issue includes the line number, severity, and a brief description of the issue. It also includes the rule name, which you can use to look up a more detailed description of the issue. See "Salesforce Lightning CLI Rules" for the rules applied by Lightning CLI, as well as possible resolutions and options for further reading.

Your mission is to review each issue, examine the code in question, and to revise it to eliminate all of the genuine problems.

While no automated tool is perfect, we expect that most errors and warnings generated by Lightning CLI will point to genuine issues in your code, which you should plan to fix before using the code with LockerService enabled.

SEE ALSO:

Salesforce Lightning CLI Rules

Salesforce Lightning CLI Rules

Rules built into Lightning CLI cover restrictions under LockerService, correct use of Lightning APIs, and a number of best practices for writing Lightning components code. Each rule, when triggered by your code, points to an area where your code might have an issue.

In addition to the Lightning-specific rules we've created, other rules are active in Lightning CLI, included from ESLint. Documentation for these rules is available on the ESLint project site. When you encounter an error or warning from a rule not described here, search for it on the ESLint Rules page.

IN THIS SECTION:

Validate JavaScript Intrinsic APIs (ecma-intrinsics)

This rule deals with the intrinsic APIs in JavaScript, more formally known as ECMAScript.

Disallow instanceof (no-instanceof)

This rule aims to eliminate the use of `instanceof`, and direct comparison with `Array` or `Object` primitives.

Validate Aura API (aura-api)

This rule verifies that use of the framework APIs is according to the published documentation. The use of undocumented or private features is disallowed.

Validate Lightning Component Public API (secure-component)

This rule validates that only public, supported framework API functions and properties are used.

Validate Secure Document Public API (secure-document)

This rule validates that only supported functions and properties of the `document` global are accessed.

Validate Secure Window Public API (secure-window)

This rule validates that only supported functions and properties of the `window` global are accessed.

Custom "House Style" Rules

Customize the JavaScript style rules that Salesforce Lightning CLI applies to your code.

Validate JavaScript Intrinsic APIs (`ecma-intrinsics`)

This rule deals with the intrinsic APIs in JavaScript, more formally known as ECMAScript.

When LockerService is enabled, the framework prevents the use of unsupported API objects or calls. That means your Lightning components code is allowed to use:

* Features built into JavaScript ("intrinsic" features)
* Published, supported features built into the Lightning Component framework
* Published, supported features built into LockerService *SecureObject* objects

What exactly are these "intrinsic APIs"? They're the APIs defined in the ECMAScript Language Specification. That is, things built into JavaScript. This includes Annex B of the specification, which deals with legacy browser features that aren't part of the "core" of JavaScript, but are nevertheless still supported for JavaScript running inside a web browser.

Note that some features of JavaScript that you might consider intrinsic—for example, the `window` and `document` global variables—are superceded by *SecureObject* objects, which offer a more constrained API.

Rule Details

This rule verifies that use of the intrinsic JavaScript APIs is according to the published specification. The use of non-standard, deprecated, and removed language features is disallowed.

Further Reading

- ECMAScript specification
- Annex B: Additional ECMAScript Features for Web Browsers
- Intrinsic Objects (JavaScript)

SEE ALSO:

Validate Aura API (aura-api)

Validate Lightning Component Public API (secure-component)

Validate Secure Document Public API (secure-document)

Validate Secure Window Public API (secure-window)

Disallow `instanceof` (`no-instanceof`)

This rule aims to eliminate the use of `instanceof`, and direct comparison with `Array` or `Object` primitives.

The framework sometimes, for security reasons, evaluates a component's code in a different iframe or worker. As a result your code might fail under certain conditions. For these reasons, it's a best practice to avoid using `instanceof`.

Why is this? Different scopes have different execution environments. This means that they have different built-ins—different global objects, different constructors, etc. This can produce results you might, at first, find unintuitive. For example, `[] instanceof window.parent.Array` returns `false`, because `Array.prototype !== window.parent.Array`, and arrays inherit from the former.

You'll encounter this issue when you're dealing with multiple frames or windows in your script and pass objects from one context to another via functions. Because the security infrastructure of the framework does this automatically, you want to write code that behaves consistently no matter what context it executes in.

Rule Details

The following patterns are considered problematic:

```
if (foo instanceof bar) {
    // do something!
```

```
}
if (foo.prototype === Array) {
    // do something
}
if (foo.prototype === Object) {
    // do something else
}
```

The following patterns make use of built in JavaScript or Lightning components utility functions, and are a suggested alternative:

```
if (Array.isArray(foo)) {
    // do something
}
if ($A.util.isPlainObject(foo)) {
    // do something else
}
```

Further Reading

- instanceof
- Array.isArray
- typeof

Validate Aura API (`aura-api`)

This rule verifies that use of the framework APIs is according to the published documentation. The use of undocumented or private features is disallowed.

When LockerService is enabled, the framework prevents the use of unsupported API objects or calls. That means your Lightning components code is allowed to use:

- Features built into JavaScript ("intrinsic" features)
- Published, supported features built into the Lightning Component framework
- Published, supported features built into LockerService *SecureObject* objects

This rule deals with the supported, public framework APIs, for example, those available through the framework global `$A`.

Why is this rule called "Aura API"? Because the core of the the Lightning Component framework is the open source Aura Framework. And this rule verifies permitted uses of that framework, rather than anything specific to Lightning Components.

Rule Details

The following patterns are considered problematic:

```
Aura.something(); // Use $A instead
$A.util.fake(); // fake is not available in $A.util
```

Further Reading

For details of all of the methods available in the framework, including $A, see the JavaScript API at `https://myDomain.lightning.force.com/auradocs/reference.app`, where *myDomain* is the name of your custom Salesforce domain.

SEE ALSO:

Validate Lightning Component Public API (secure-component)

Validate Secure Document Public API (secure-document)

Validate Secure Window Public API (secure-window)

Validate Lightning Component Public API (`secure-component`)

This rule validates that only public, supported framework API functions and properties are used.

When LockerService is enabled, the framework prevents the use of unsupported API objects or calls. That means your Lightning components code is allowed to use:

- Features built into JavaScript ("intrinsic" features)
- Published, supported features built into the Lightning Component framework
- Published, supported features built into LockerService *SecureObject* objects

Prior to LockerService, when you created or obtained a reference to a component, you could call any function and access any property available on that component, even if it wasn't public. When LockerService is enabled, components are "wrapped" by a new SecureComponent object, which controls access to the component and its functions and properties. SecureComponent restricts you to using only published, supported component API.

Rule Details

Supported component functions and properties include the following:

- addHandler
- addValueProvider

213

- autoDestroy
- clearReference
- destroy
- find
- get
- getConcreteComponent
- getElement
- getElements
- getEvent
- getGlobalId
- getLocalId
- getReference
- getSuper
- getVersion
- isConcrete
- isInstanceOf
- isRendered
- isValid
- set

The following patterns are considered problematic as `find().find()` is an anti-pattern that breaks encapsulation by reaching into another component:

```
{
    onclick: function (cmp, evt, help) {
        cmp.find('foo').find('bar');
    }
}
```

The following patterns make correct use of component functions, and are a suggested alternative:

```
{
    onclick: function (cmp, evt, help) {
        cmp.find('foo');
    }
}
```

Further Reading

- SecureComponent.js Implementation

SEE ALSO:

Validate Aura API (aura-api)

Validate Secure Document Public API (secure-document)

Validate Secure Window Public API (secure-window)

Validate Secure Document Public API (`secure-document`)

This rule validates that only supported functions and properties of the `document` global are accessed.

When LockerService is enabled, the framework prevents the use of unsupported API objects or calls. That means your Lightning components code is allowed to use:

- Features built into JavaScript ("intrinsic" features)
- Published, supported features built into the Lightning Component framework
- Published, supported features built into LockerService *SecureObject* objects

Prior to LockerService, when you accessed the `document` global, you could call any function and access any property available. When LockerService is enabled, the `document` global is "wrapped" by a new SecureDocument object, which controls access to `document` and its functions and properties. SecureDocument restricts you to using only "safe" features of the `document` global.

Rule Details

Supported `document` functions and properties include the following:

- addEventListener
- createComment
- createDocumentFragment
- createElement
- createTextNode
- documentElement
- getElementById
- getElementsByClassName
- getElementsByName
- getElementsByTagName

- querySelector
- querySelectorAll
- head
- title
- body
- childNodes
- nodeType
- cookie

The following patterns are considered problematic:

```
{
    onclick: function (cmp, evt, help) {
        var content = document.innerHTML;
    }
}
```

The following patterns are supported:

```
{
    onclick: function (cmp, evt, help) {
        var el = document.getElementById('foo');
    }
}
```

Further Reading

- SecureDocument.js Implementation

SEE ALSO:

Validate Aura API (aura-api)

Validate Lightning Component Public API (secure-component)

Validate Secure Window Public API (secure-window)

Validate Secure Window Public API (`secure-window`)

This rule validates that only supported functions and properties of the `window` global are accessed.

When LockerService is enabled, the framework prevents the use of unsupported API objects or calls. That means your Lightning components code is allowed to use:

- Features built into JavaScript ("intrinsic" features)
- Published, supported features built into the Lightning Component framework
- Published, supported features built into LockerService *SecureObject* objects

Prior to LockerService, when you accessed the `window` global, you could call any function and access any property available. When LockerService is enabled, the `window` global is "wrapped" by a new SecureWindow object, which controls access to `window` and its functions and properties. SecureWindow restricts you to using only "safe" features of the `window` global.

Rule Details

Supported `window` functions and properties include the following:

- addEventListener
- setInterval
- setTimeout
- $A
- document
- location
- navigator
- window

The following patterns are considered problematic:

```
{
    onclick: function (cmp, evt, help) {
        window.open ('bar');
    }
}
```

The following patterns use features of the Lightning Components framework and are suggested as an alternative:

```
{
    onclick: function (cmp, evt, help) {
        setTimeout(function () {}, 100);
    }
}
```

Further Reading

- SecureWindow.js Implementation

SEE ALSO:

Validate Aura API (aura-api)

Validate Lightning Component Public API (secure-component)

Validate Secure Document Public API (secure-document)

Custom "House Style" Rules

Customize the JavaScript style rules that Salesforce Lightning CLI applies to your code.

It's common that different organizations or projects will adopt different JavaScript rules. The Lightning CLI tool is here to help you get ready for LockerService, not enforce Salesforce coding conventions. To that end, the Lightning CLI rules are divided into two sets, *security* rules and *style* rules. The security rules can't be modified, but you can modify or add to the style rules.

Use the `--config` argument to provide a custom rules configuration file. A custom rules configuration file allows you to define your own code style rules, which affect the **style** rules used by the Lightning CLI tool.

The Lightning CLI default style rules are provided below. Copy the rules to a new file, and modify them to match your preferred style rules. Alternatively, you can use your existing ESLint rule configuration file directly. For example:

```
heroku lightning:lint ./path/to/lightning/components/ --config
~/.eslintrc
```

📝 Note: Not all ESLint rules can be added or modified using `--config`. Only rules that we consider benign or neutral in the context of Lightning Platform are activated by Lightning CLI. And again, you can't override the security rules.

Default Style Rules

Here are the default style rules used by Lightning CLI.

```
/*
 * Copyright (C) 2016 salesforce.com, inc.
 *
 * Licensed under the Apache License, Version 2.0 (the "License");
 * you may not use this file except in compliance with the License.
 * You may obtain a copy of the License at
```

```
 *
 *          http://www.apache.org/licenses/LICENSE-2.0
 *
 * Unless required by applicable law or agreed to in writing, software
 * distributed under the License is distributed on an "AS IS" BASIS,
 * WITHOUT WARRANTIES OR CONDITIONS OF ANY KIND, either express or
implied.
 * See the License for the specific language governing permissions and
 * limitations under the License.
 */

module.exports = {
    rules: {
        // code style rules, these are the default value, but the user
can
        // customize them via --config in the linter by providing
custom values
        // for each of these rules.
        "no-trailing-spaces": 1,
        "no-spaced-func": 1,
        "no-mixed-spaces-and-tabs": 0,
        "no-multi-spaces": 0,
        "no-multiple-empty-lines": 0,
        "no-lone-blocks": 1,
        "no-lonely-if": 1,
        "no-inline-comments": 0,
        "no-extra-parens": 0,
        "no-extra-semi": 1,
        "no-warning-comments": [0, { "terms": ["todo", "fixme", "xxx"],
 "location": "start" }],
        "block-scoped-var": 1,
        "brace-style": [1, "1tbs"],
        "camelcase": 1,
        "comma-dangle": [1, "never"],
        "comma-spacing": 1,
        "comma-style": 1,
        "complexity": [0, 11],
        "consistent-this": [0, "that"],
        "curly": [1, "all"],
        "eol-last": 0,
        "func-names": 0,
        "func-style": [0, "declaration"],
```

```
        "generator-star-spacing": 0,
        "indent": 0,
        "key-spacing": 0,
        "keyword-spacing": [0, "always"],
        "max-depth": [0, 4],
        "max-len": [0, 80, 4],
        "max-nested-callbacks": [0, 2],
        "max-params": [0, 3],
        "max-statements": [0, 10],
        "new-cap": 0,
        "newline-after-var": 0,
        "one-var": [0, "never"],
        "operator-assignment": [0, "always"],
        "padded-blocks": 0,
        "quote-props": 0,
        "quotes": 0,
        "semi": 1,
        "semi-spacing": [0, {"before": false, "after": true}],
        "sort-vars": 0,
        "space-after-function-name": [0, "never"],
        "space-before-blocks": [0, "always"],
        "space-before-function-paren": [0, "always"],
        "space-before-function-parentheses": [0, "always"],
        "space-in-brackets": [0, "never"],
        "space-in-parens": [0, "never"],
        "space-infix-ops": 0,
        "space-unary-ops": [1, { "words": true, "nonwords": false }],

        "spaced-comment": [0, "always"],
        "vars-on-top": 0,
        "valid-jsdoc": 0,
        "wrap-regex": 0,
        "yoda": [1, "never"]
    }
};
```

Salesforce Lightning CLI Options

There are several options that modify the behavior of Lightning CLI.

The following options are available.

Option	Description
`-i, --ignore IGNORE`	Pattern to ignore some folders. For example: ```--ignore **/foo/**```
`--files FILES`	Pattern to include only specific files. Defaults to all `.js` files. For example: ```--files **/*Controller.js```
`-j, --json`	Output JSON to facilitate integration with other tools. Without this option, defaults to standard text output format.
`--config CONFIG`	Path to a custom ESLint configuration. Only code styles rules are picked up, the rest are ignored. For example: ```--config path/to/.eslintrc```
`--quiet`	Report errors only. By default, Lightning CLI reports both errors and warnings.

Lightning CLI also provides some built-in help, which you can access at any time with the following commands:

```
heroku lightning --help
heroku lightning:lint --help
```

SEE ALSO:

Use Salesforce Lightning CLI

Styling Apps

An app is a special top-level component whose markup is in a `.app` resource. Just like any other component, you can put CSS in its bundle in a resource called `<appName>.css`.

For example, if the app markup is in `notes.app`, its CSS is in `notes.css`.

When viewed in Salesforce1 and Lightning Experience, the UI components include styling that matches those visual themes. For example, the `ui:button` includes the `button--neutral` class to display a neutral style. The input components that extend `ui:input` include the `uiInput--input` class to display the input fields using a custom font in addition to other styling.

 Note: Styles added to UI components in Salesforce1 and Lightning Experience don't apply to components in standalone apps.

IN THIS SECTION:

More Readable Styling Markup with the join Expression

Markup can get messy when you specify the class names to apply based on the component attribute values. Try using a `join` expression for easier-to-read markup.

Using External CSS

To reference an external CSS resource that you've uploaded as a static resource, use a `<ltng:require>` tag in your `.cmp` or `.app` markup.

Tips for CSS in Components

Here are some tips for configuring the CSS for components that you plan to use in Lightning Pages, the Lightning App Builder, or the Community Builder.

Styling with Design Tokens

Capture the essential values of your visual design into named tokens. Define the token values once and reuse them throughout your Lightning components CSS resources. Tokens make it easy to ensure that your design is consistent, and even easier to update it as your design evolves.

SEE ALSO:

CSS in Components

Add Lightning Components to Salesforce1

More Readable Styling Markup with the `join` Expression

Markup can get messy when you specify the class names to apply based on the component attribute values. Try using a `join` expression for easier-to-read markup.

This example sets the class names based on the component attribute values. It's readable, but the spaces between class names are easy to forget.

```
<li class="{! 'calendarEvent ' +
    v.zoomDirection + ' ' +
    (v.past ? 'pastEvent ' : '') +
    (v.zoomed ? 'zoom ' : '') +
    (v.multiDayFragment ? 'multiDayFragment ' : '')}">
```

```
        <!-- content here -->
</li>
```

Sometimes, if the markup is not broken into multiple lines, it can hurt your eyes or make you mutter profanities under your breath.

```
<li class="{! 'calendarEvent ' + v.zoomDirection + ' ' + (v.past ?
'pastEvent ' : '') + (v.zoomed ? 'zoom ' : '') + (v.multiDayFragment
? 'multiDayFragment ' : '')}">
    <!-- content here -->
</li>
```

Try using a `join` expression instead for easier-to-read markup. This example `join` expression sets ' ' as the first argument so that you don't have to specify it for each subsequent argument in the expression.

```
<li
    class="{! join(' ',
        'calendarEvent',
        v.zoomDirection,
        v.past ? 'pastEvent' : '',
        v.zoomed ? 'zoom' : '',
        v.multiDayFragment ? 'multiDayFragment' : ''
    )}">
    <!-- content here -->
</li>
```

You can also use a `join` expression for dynamic styling.

```
<div style="{! join(';',
    'top:' + v.timeOffsetTop + '%',
    'left:' + v.timeOffsetLeft + '%',
    'width:' + v.timeOffsetWidth + '%'
)}">
    <!-- content here -->
</div>
```

SEE ALSO:

Expression Functions Reference

Using External CSS

To reference an external CSS resource that you've uploaded as a static resource, use a `<ltng:require>` tag in your `.cmp` or `.app` markup.

Here's an example of using `<ltng:require>`:

```
<ltng:require styles="{!$Resource.resourceName}" />
```

`resourceName` is the `Name` of the static resource. In a managed packaged, the resource name must include the package namespace prefix, such as `$Resource.yourNamespace__resourceName`. For a stand-alone static resource, such as an individual graphic or script, that's all you need. To reference an item within an archive static resource, add the rest of the path to the item using string concatenation.

Here are some considerations for loading styles:

Loading Sets of CSS

Specify a comma-separated list of resources in the `styles` attribute to load a set of CSS.

 Note: Due to a quirk in the way `$Resource` is parsed in expressions, use the `join` operator to include multiple `$Resource` references in a single attribute. For example, if you have more than one style sheet to include into a component the `styles` attribute should be something like the following.

```
styles="{!join(',',
    $Resource.myStyles + '/stylesheetOne.css',
    $Resource.myStyles + '/moreStyles.css')}"
```

Loading Order

The styles are loaded in the order that they are listed.

One-Time Loading

The styles load only once, even if they're specified in multiple `<ltng:require>` tags in the same component or across different components.

Encapsulation

To ensure encapsulation and reusability, add the `<ltng:require>` tag to every `.cmp` or `.app` resource that uses the CSS resource.

`<ltng:require>` also has a `scripts` attribute to load a list of JavaScript libraries. The `afterScriptsLoaded` event enables you to call a controller action after the `scripts` are loaded. It's only triggered by loading of the `scripts` and is never triggered when the CSS in `styles` is loaded.

For more information on static resources, see "Static Resources" in the Salesforce online help.

Styling Components for Lightning Experience or Salesforce1

To prevent styling conflicts in Lightning Experience or Salesforce1, prefix your external CSS with a unique namespace. For example, if you prefix your external CSS declarations with `.myBootstrap`, wrap your component markup with a `<div>` tag that specifies the `myBootstrap` class.

```
<ltng:require styles="{!$Resource.bootstrap}"/>
<div class="myBootstrap">
    <c:myComponent />
    <!-- Other component markup -->
</div>
```

> Note: Prefixing your CSS with a unique namespace only applies to external CSS. If you're using CSS within a component bundle, the `.THIS` keyword becomes `.namespaceComponentName` during runtime.

SEE ALSO:

Using External JavaScript Libraries

CSS in Components

$Resource

Tips for CSS in Components

Here are some tips for configuring the CSS for components that you plan to use in Lightning Pages, the Lightning App Builder, or the Community Builder.

Components must be set to 100% width

Because they can be moved to different locations on a Lightning Page, components must not have a specific width nor a left or right margin. Components should take up 100% of whatever container they display in. Adding a left or right margin changes the width of a component and can break the layout of the page.

Don't remove HTML elements from the flow of the document

Some CSS rules remove the HTML element from the flow of the document. For example:

```
float: left;
float: right;
position: absolute;
position: fixed;
```

Because they can be moved to different locations on the page as well as used on different pages entirely, components must rely on the normal document flow. Using floats and absolute or fixed positions breaks the layout of the page the component is on. Even if they don't break the layout of the page *you're* looking at, they will break the layout of *some* page the component can be put on.

Child elements shouldn't be styled to be larger than the root element

The Lightning Page maintains consistent spacing between components, and can't do that if child elements are larger than the root element.

For example, avoid these patterns:

```
<div style="height: 100px">
  <div style="height: 200px">
    <!--Other markup here-->
  </div>
</div>
```

```
<!--Margin increases the element's effective size-->
<div style="height: 100px">
  <div style="height: 100px margin: 10px">
    <!--Other markup here-->
  </div>
</div>
```

Vendor Prefixes

Vendor prefixes, such as —moz— and —webkit— among many others, are automatically added in Lightning.

You only need to write the unprefixed version, and the framework automatically adds any prefixes that are necessary when generating the CSS output. If you choose to add them, they are used as-is. This enables you to specify alternative values for certain prefixes.

 Example: For example, this is an unprefixed version of border-radius.

```
.class {
  border-radius: 2px;
}
```

The previous declaration results in the following declarations.

```
.class {
  -webkit-border-radius: 2px;
  -moz-border-radius: 2px;
  border-radius: 2px;
}
```

Styling with Design Tokens

Capture the essential values of your visual design into named tokens. Define the token values once and reuse them throughout your Lightning components CSS resources. Tokens make it easy to ensure that your design is consistent, and even easier to update it as your design evolves.

Design tokens are visual design "atoms" for building a design for your components or apps. Specifically, they're named entities that store visual design attributes, such as pixel values for margins and spacing, font sizes and families, or hex values for colors. Tokens are a terrific way to centralize the low-level values, which you then use to compose the styles that make up the design of your component or app.

IN THIS SECTION:

Tokens Bundles

Tokens are a type of bundle, just like components, events, and interfaces.

Create a Tokens Bundle

Create a tokens bundle in your org using the Developer Console.

Defining and Using Tokens

A token is a name-value pair that you specify using the `<aura:token>` component. Define tokens in a tokens bundle, and then use tokens in your components' CSS styles resources.

Using Expressions in Tokens

Tokens support a restricted set of expressions. Use expressions to reuse one token value in another token, or to combine tokens to form a more complex style property.

Extending Tokens Bundles

Use the `extends` attribute to extend one tokens bundle from another.

Using Standard Design Tokens

Salesforce exposes a set of "base" tokens that you can access in your component style resources. Use these standard tokens to mimic the look-and-feel of the Salesforce Lightning Design System (SLDS) in your own custom components. As the SLDS evolves, components that are styled using the standard design tokens will evolve along with it.

Tokens Bundles

Tokens are a type of bundle, just like components, events, and interfaces.

A tokens bundle contains only one resource, a tokens collection definition.

Resource	Resource Name	Usage
Tokens Collection	`defaultTokens.tokens`	The only required resource in a tokens bundle. Contains markup for one or more tokens. Each tokens bundle contains only one tokens resource.

> 📝 Note: You can't edit the tokens bundle name or description in the Developer Console after you create it. The bundle's `AuraBundleDefinition` can be modified using the Metadata API.

A tokens collection starts with the `<aura:tokens>` tag. It can only contain `<aura:token>` tags to define tokens.

Tokens collections have restricted support for expressions; see Using Expressions in Tokens. You can't use other markup, renderers, controllers, or anything else in a tokens collection.

SEE ALSO:

Using Expressions in Tokens

Create a Tokens Bundle

Create a tokens bundle in your org using the Developer Console.

To create a tokens bundle:

1. In the Developer Console, select **File** > **New** > **Lightning Tokens**.

2. Enter a name for the tokens bundle.

    Your first tokens bundle should be named *defaultTokens*. The tokens defined within `defaultTokens` are automatically accessible in your Lightning components. Tokens defined in any other bundle won't be accessible in your components unless you import them into the `defaultTokens` bundle.

You have an empty tokens bundle, ready to edit.

```
<aura:tokens>

</aura:tokens>
```

> 📝 Note: You can't edit the tokens bundle name or description in the Developer Console after you create it. The bundle's `AuraBundleDefinition` can be modified using the Metadata API. Although you can set a version on a tokens bundle, doing so has no effect.

Defining and Using Tokens

A token is a name-value pair that you specify using the `<aura:token>` component. Define tokens in a tokens bundle, and then use tokens in your components' CSS styles resources.

Defining Tokens

Add new tokens as child components of the bundle's `<aura:tokens>` component. For example:

```
<aura:tokens>
    <aura:token name="myBodyTextFontFace"
            value="'Salesforce Sans', Helvetica, Arial, sans-serif"/>

    <aura:token name="myBodyTextFontWeight" value="normal"/>
    <aura:token name="myBackgroundColor" value="#f4f6f9"/>
    <aura:token name="myDefaultMargin" value="6px"/>
</aura:tokens>
```

The only allowed attributes for the `<aura:token>` tag are `name` and `value`.

Using Tokens

Tokens created in the `defaultTokens` bundle are automatically available in components in your namespace. To use a design token, reference it using the `token()` function and the token name in the CSS resource of a component bundle. For example:

```
.THIS p {
    font-family: token(myBodyTextFontFace);
    font-weight: token(myBodyTextFontWeight);
}
```

If you prefer a more concise function name for referencing tokens, you can use the `t()` function instead of `token()`. The two are equivalent. If your token names follow a naming convention or are sufficiently descriptive, the use of the more terse function name won't affect the clarity of your CSS styles.

Using Expressions in Tokens

Tokens support a restricted set of expressions. Use expressions to reuse one token value in another token, or to combine tokens to form a more complex style property.

Cross-Referencing Tokens

To reference one token's value in another token's definition, wrap the token to be referenced in standard expression syntax.

In the following example, we'll reference tokens provided by Salesforce in our custom tokens. Although you can't see the standard tokens directly, we'll imagine they look something like the following.

```
<!-- force:base tokens (SLDS standard tokens) -->
<aura:tokens>
  ...
  <aura:token name="colorBackground" value="rgb(244, 246, 249)" />
  <aura:token name="fontFamily" value="'Salesforce Sans', Arial,
sans-serif" />
  ...
</aura:tokens>
```

With the preceding in mind, you can reference the standard tokens in your custom tokens, as in the following.

```
<!-- defaultTokens.tokens (your tokens) -->
<aura:tokens extends="force:base">
  <aura:token name="mainColor" value="{! colorBackground }" />
  <aura:token name="btnColor" value="{! mainColor }" />
  <aura:token name="myFont" value="{! fontFamily }" />
</aura:tokens>
```

You can only cross-reference tokens defined in the same file or a parent.

Expression syntax in tokens resources is restricted to references to other tokens.

Combining Tokens

To support combining individual token values into more complex CSS style properties, the `token()` function supports string concatenation. For example, if you have the following tokens defined:

```
<!-- defaultTokens.tokens (your tokens) -->
<aura:tokens>
  <aura:token name="defaultHorizonalSpacing" value="12px" />
  <aura:token name="defaultVerticalSpacing" value="6px" />
</aura:tokens>
```

You can combine these two tokens in a CSS style definition. For example:

```
/* myComponent.css */
.THIS div.notification {
```

```
    margin: token(defaultVerticalSpacing + ' ' + defaultHorizonalSpacing);

    /* more styles here */
}
```

You can mix tokens with strings as much as necessary to create the right style definition. For example, use `margin: token(defaultVerticalSpacing + ' ' + defaultHorizonalSpacing + ' 3px');` to hard code the bottom spacing in the preceding definition.

The only operator supported within the `token()` function is "+" for string concatenation.

SEE ALSO:

  Defining and Using Tokens

Extending Tokens Bundles

Use the `extends` attribute to extend one tokens bundle from another.

To add tokens from one bundle to another, extend the "child" tokens bundle from the "parent" tokens, like this.

```
<aura:tokens extends="yourNamespace:parentTokens">
    <!-- additional tokens here -->
</aura:tokens>
```

Overriding tokens values works mostly as you'd expect: tokens in a child tokens bundle override tokens with the same name from a parent bundle. The exception is if you're using standard tokens. You can't override standard tokens in Lightning Experience or Salesforce1.

 Important: Overriding standard token values is undefined behavior and unsupported. If you create a token with the same name as a standard token, it overrides the standard token's value in some contexts, and has no effect in others. This behavior will change in a future release. Don't use it.

SEE ALSO:

  Using Standard Design Tokens

Using Standard Design Tokens

Salesforce exposes a set of "base" tokens that you can access in your component style resources. Use these standard tokens to mimic the look-and-feel of the Salesforce Lightning Design System (SLDS) in your own custom components. As the SLDS evolves, components that are styled using the standard design tokens will evolve along with it.

To add the standard tokens to your org, extend a tokens bundle from the base tokens, like so.

```
<aura:tokens extends="force:base">
    <!-- your own tokens here -->
</aura:tokens>
```

Once added to `defaultTokens` (or another tokens bundle that `defaultTokens` extends) you can reference tokens from `force:base` just like your own tokens, using the `token()` function and token name. For example:

```
.THIS p {
    font-family: token(fontFamily);
    font-weight: token(fontWeightRegular);
}
```

You can mix-and-match your tokens with the standard tokens. It's a best practice to develop a naming system for your own tokens to make them easily distinguishable from standard tokens. Consider prefixing your token names with "my", or something else easily identifiable.

 Important: Overriding standard token values is undefined behavior and unsupported. If you create a token with the same name as a standard token, it overrides the standard token's value in some contexts, and has no effect in others. This behavior will change in a future release. Don't use it.

IN THIS SECTION:

Standard Design Tokens—force:base

The standard tokens available are a subset of the design tokens offered in the Salesforce Lightning Design System (SLDS). The following tokens are available when extending from `force:base`.

Standard Design Tokens for Communities

Use a subset of the standard design tokens to make your components compatible with the Branding Editor in Community Builder. The Branding Editor enables administrators to quickly style an entire community using branding properties. Each property in the Branding Editor maps to one or more standard design tokens. When an administrator updates a property in the Branding Editor, the system automatically updates any Lightning components that use the tokens associated with that branding property.

SEE ALSO:

Extending Tokens Bundles

Standard Design Tokens—`force:base`

The standard tokens available are a subset of the design tokens offered in the Salesforce Lightning Design System (SLDS). The following tokens are available when extending from `force:base`.

Available Tokens

🛈 **Important:** The standard token values evolve along with SLDS. Available tokens and their values can change without notice. Token values presented here are for example only.

Token Name	Example Value
`elevation3Below`	-3
`elevation0`	0
`elevation2`	2
`elevation4`	4
`elevation8`	8
`elevation16`	16
`elevation32`	32
`elevationShadow3Below`	inset 0px 3px 3px 0px rgba(0,0,0,.16)
`elevationShadow0`	none
`elevationShadow2`	0px 2px 2px 0px rgba(0,0,0,.16)

Token Name	Example Value
elevationShadow4	0px 4px 4px 0px rgba(0,0,0,.16)
elevationShadow8	0px 8px 8px 0px rgba(0,0,0,.16)
elevationShadow16	0px 16px 16px 0px rgba(0,0,0,.16)
elevationShadow32	0px 32px 32px 0px rgba(0,0,0,.16)
elevationInverseShadow3Below	inset 0px -3px 3px 0px rgba(0,0,0,.16)
elevationInverseShadow0	none
elevationInverseShadow2	0px -2px 2px 0px rgba(0,0,0,.16)
elevationInverseShadow4	0px -4px 4px 0px rgba(0,0,0,.16)
elevationInverseShadow8	0px -8px 8px 0px rgba(0,0,0,.16)
elevationInverseShadow16	0px -16px 16px 0px rgba(0,0,0,.16)
elevationInverseShadow32	0px -32px 32px 0px rgba(0,0,0,.16)
colorBackground	rgb(244, 246, 249)
colorBackgroundAlt	rgb(255, 255, 255)
colorBackgroundAlt2	rgb(238, 241, 246)
colorBackgroundAltInverse	rgb(22, 50, 92)
colorBackgroundRowHover	rgb(244, 246, 249)
colorBackgroundRowActive	rgb(238, 241, 246)
colorBackgroundRowSelected	rgb(240, 248, 252)
colorBackgroundRowNew	rgb(217, 255, 223)
colorBackgroundInverse	rgb(6, 28, 63)
colorBackgroundAnchor	rgb(244, 246, 249)
colorBackgroundBrowser	rgb(84, 105, 141)
colorBackgroundChromeMobile	rgb(0, 112, 210)
colorBackgroundChromeDesktop	rgb(255, 255, 255)

Token Name	Example Value
colorBackgroundCustomer	rgb(255, 154, 60)
colorBackgroundHighlight	rgb(250, 255, 189)
colorBackgroundActionbarIconUtility	rgb(84, 105, 141)
colorBackgroundIndicatorDot	rgb(159, 170, 181)
colorBackgroundModal	rgb(255, 255, 255)
colorBackgroundModalBrand	rgb(0, 112, 210)
colorBackgroundNotificationBadge	rgb(194, 57, 52)
colorBackgroundNotificationBadgeHover	rgb(0, 95, 178)
colorBackgroundNotificationBadgeFocus	rgb(0, 95, 178)
colorBackgroundNotificationBadgeActive	rgb(0, 57, 107)
colorBackgroundNotificationNew	rgb(240, 248, 252)
colorBackgroundOrgSwitcherArrow	rgb(6, 28, 63)
colorBackgroundPayload	rgb(244, 246, 249)
colorBackgroundShade	rgb(224, 229, 238)
colorBackgroundShadeDark	rgb(216, 221, 230)
colorBackgroundStencil	rgb(238, 241, 246)
colorBackgroundStencilAlt	rgb(224, 229, 238)
colorBackgroundTempModal	rgba(126, 140, 153, 0.8)
colorBackgroundTempModalTint	rgba(126, 140, 153, 0.8)
colorBackgroundTempModalTintAlt	rgba(255, 255, 255, 0.75)
colorBackgroundScrollbar	rgb(224, 229, 238)
colorBackgroundScrollbarTrack	rgb(168, 183, 199)
colorBrand	rgb(21, 137, 238)
colorBrandDark	rgb(0, 112, 210)

Token Name	Example Value
colorBrandDarker	rgb(0, 95, 178)
colorBrandToggle	rgb(159, 170, 181)
colorBrandToggleDisabled	rgb(159, 170, 181)
colorBrandToggleHover	rgb(126, 140, 153)
colorBrandToggleActive	rgb(0, 112, 210)
colorBrandToggleActiveHover	rgb(0, 0, 0)
colorBackgroundContextBar	rgb(22, 50, 92)
colorBackgroundContextBarShadow	rgba(0, 0, 0, 0.25)
colorBackgroundContextBarHighlight	rgba(255, 255, 255, 0.2)
colorBackgroundPageHeader	rgb(247, 249, 251)
borderWidthThin	1px
borderWidthThick	2px
borderRadiusSmall	.125rem
borderRadiusMedium	.25rem
borderRadiusLarge	.5rem
borderRadiusPill	15rem
borderRadiusCircle	50%
colorBorder	rgb(216, 221, 230)
colorBorderBrand	rgb(21, 137, 238)
colorBorderBrandDark	rgb(0, 112, 210)
colorBorderCustomer	rgb(255, 154, 60)
colorBorderDestructive	rgb(194, 57, 52)
colorBorderDestructiveHover	rgb(166, 26, 20)
colorBorderDestructiveActive	rgb(135, 5, 0)

Token Name	Example Value
colorBorderInfo	rgb(84, 105, 141)
colorBorderError	rgb(194, 57, 52)
colorBorderErrorAlt	rgb(234, 130, 136)
colorBorderErrorDark	rgb(234, 130, 136)
colorBorderOffline	rgb(68, 68, 68)
colorBorderSuccess	rgb(75, 202, 129)
colorBorderSuccessDark	rgb(4, 132, 75)
colorBorderWarning	rgb(255, 183, 93)
colorBorderInverse	rgb(6, 28, 63)
colorBorderTabSelected	rgb(0, 112, 210)
colorBorderSeparator	rgb(244, 246, 249)
colorBorderSeparatorAlt	rgb(216, 221, 230)
colorBorderSeparatorAlt2	rgb(168, 183, 199)
colorBorderSeparatorInverse	rgb(42, 66, 108)
colorBorderRowSelected	rgb(0, 112, 210)
colorBorderRowSelectedHover	rgb(21, 137, 238)
colorBorderHint	rgb(42, 66, 108)
colorBorderSelection	rgb(0, 112, 210)
colorBorderSelectionHover	rgb(21, 137, 238)
colorBorderSelectionActive	rgb(244, 246, 249)
colorBorderCanvasElementSelection	rgb(94, 180, 255)
colorBorderCanvasElementSelectionHover	rgb(0, 95, 178)
colorBorderContextBarDivider	rgba(255, 255, 255, 0.2)
colorTextButtonBrand	rgb(255, 255, 255)

Token Name	Example Value
colorTextButtonBrandHover	rgb(255, 255, 255)
colorTextButtonBrandActive	rgb(255, 255, 255)
colorTextButtonBrandDisabled	rgb(255, 255, 255)
colorTextButtonDefault	rgb(0, 112, 210)
colorTextButtonDefaultHover	rgb(0, 112, 210)
colorTextButtonDefaultActive	rgb(0, 112, 210)
colorTextButtonDefaultDisabled	rgb(216, 221, 230)
colorTextButtonDefaultHint	rgb(159, 170, 181)
colorTextButtonInverse	rgb(224, 229, 238)
colorTextButtonInverseDisabled	rgba(255, 255, 255, 0.15)
colorTextIconDefault	rgb(84, 105, 141)
colorTextIconDefaultHint	rgb(159, 170, 181)
colorTextIconDefaultHintBorderless	rgb(224, 229, 238)
colorTextIconDefaultHover	rgb(0, 112, 210)
colorTextIconDefaultActive	rgb(0, 57, 107)
colorTextIconDefaultDisabled	rgb(216, 221, 230)
colorTextIconInverse	rgb(255, 255, 255)
colorTextIconInverseHover	rgb(255, 255, 255)
colorTextIconInverseActive	rgb(255, 255, 255)
colorTextIconInverseDisabled	rgba(255, 255, 255, 0.15)
colorBackgroundButtonBrand	rgb(0, 112, 210)
colorBackgroundButtonBrandActive	rgb(0, 57, 107)
colorBackgroundButtonBrandHover	rgb(0, 95, 178)
colorBackgroundButtonBrandDisabled	rgb(224, 229, 238)

Token Name	Example Value
colorBackgroundButtonDefault	rgb(255, 255, 255)
colorBackgroundButtonDefaultHover	rgb(244, 246, 249)
colorBackgroundButtonDefaultFocus	rgb(244, 246, 249)
colorBackgroundButtonDefaultActive	rgb(238, 241, 246)
colorBackgroundButtonDefaultDisabled	rgb(255, 255, 255)
colorBackgroundButtonIcon	rgba(0, 0, 0, 0)
colorBackgroundButtonIconHover	rgb(244, 246, 249)
colorBackgroundButtonIconFocus	rgb(244, 246, 249)
colorBackgroundButtonIconActive	rgb(238, 241, 246)
colorBackgroundButtonIconDisabled	rgb(255, 255, 255)
colorBackgroundButtonInverse	rgba(0, 0, 0, 0)
colorBackgroundButtonInverseActive	rgba(0, 0, 0, 0.24)
colorBackgroundButtonInverseDisabled	rgba(0, 0, 0, 0)
colorBackgroundModalButton	rgba(0, 0, 0, 0.07)
colorBackgroundModalButtonActive	rgba(0, 0, 0, 0.16)
colorBorderButtonBrand	rgb(0, 112, 210)
colorBorderButtonBrandDisabled	rgba(0, 0, 0, 0)
colorBorderButtonDefault	rgb(216, 221, 230)
colorBorderButtonInverseDisabled	rgba(255, 255, 255, 0.15)
fontFamily	'Salesforce Sans', Arial, sans-serif
fontWeightLight	300
fontWeightRegular	400
fontWeightBold	700
fontSizeXSmall	0.625rem

Token Name	Example Value
fontSizeSmall	0.875rem
fontSizeMedium	1rem
fontSizeMediumA	0.875rem
fontSizeLarge	1.25rem
fontSizeXLarge	1.5rem
fontSizeXxLarge	2rem
lineHeightHeading	1.25
lineHeightText	1.375
lineHeightReset	1
lineHeightTab	2.5rem
lineHeightButton	1.875rem
lineHeightButtonSmall	1.75rem
lineHeightToggle	1.3rem
colorBackgroundInput	rgb(255, 255, 255)
colorBackgroundInputActive	rgb(255, 255, 255)
colorBackgroundInputCheckbox	rgb(255, 255, 255)
colorBackgroundInputCheckboxDisabled	rgb(216, 221, 230)
colorBackgroundInputCheckboxSelected	rgb(21, 137, 238)
colorBackgroundInputDisabled	rgb(224, 229, 238)
colorBackgroundInputError	rgb(255, 221, 225)
colorBackgroundInputSearch	rgba(0, 0, 0, 0.16)
colorBackgroundPill	rgb(255, 255, 255)
colorTextLabel	rgb(84, 105, 141)
colorTextPlaceholder	rgb(84, 105, 141)

Token Name	Example Value
`colorTextPlaceholderInverse`	rgb(224, 229, 238)
`colorTextRequired`	rgb(194, 57, 52)
`colorTextPill`	rgb(0, 112, 210)
`colorBorderInput`	rgb(216, 221, 230)
`colorBorderInputActive`	rgb(21, 137, 238)
`colorBorderInputDisabled`	rgb(168, 183, 199)
`colorBorderInputCheckboxSelectedCheckmark`	rgb(255, 255, 255)
`colorBackgroundDestructive`	rgb(194, 57, 52)
`colorBackgroundDestructiveHover`	rgb(166, 26, 20)
`colorBackgroundDestructiveActive`	rgb(135, 5, 0)
`colorBackgroundInfo`	rgb(84, 105, 141)
`colorBackgroundError`	rgb(212, 80, 76)
`colorBackgroundErrorDark`	rgb(194, 57, 52)
`colorBackgroundErrorAlt`	rgb(234, 130, 136)
`colorBackgroundOffline`	rgb(68, 68, 68)
`colorBackgroundSuccess`	rgb(75, 202, 129)
`colorBackgroundSuccessDark`	rgb(4, 132, 75)
`colorBackgroundToast`	rgb(84, 105, 141)
`colorBackgroundToastSuccess`	rgb(4, 132, 75)
`colorBackgroundToastError`	rgb(194, 57, 52)
`colorBackgroundWarning`	rgb(255, 183, 93)
`opacity5`	0.5
`shadowActionOverflowFooter`	0 -2px 4px #F4F6F9
`shadowOverlay`	0 -2px 4px rgba(0,0,0,.07)

Token Name	Example Value
shadowDrag	0px 2px 4px 0px rgba(0,0,0,.4)
shadowButton	0px 1px 1px 0px rgba(0,0,0,.05)
shadowDropDown	0px 2px 3px 0px rgba(0,0,0,.16)
shadowHeader	0 2px 4px rgba(0,0,0,.07)
shadowButtonFocus	0 0 3px #0070D2
shadowButtonFocusInverse	0 0 3px #E0E5EE
sizeXxSmall	6rem
sizeXSmall	12rem
sizeSmall	15rem
sizeMedium	20rem
sizeLarge	25rem
sizeXLarge	40rem
sizeXxLarge	60rem
squareIconUtilitySmall	1rem
squareIconUtilityMedium	1.25rem
squareIconUtilityLarge	1.5rem
squareIconLargeBoundary	3rem
squareIconLargeBoundaryAlt	5rem
squareIconLargeContent	2rem
squareIconMedium	2.375rem
squareIconMediumBoundary	2rem
squareIconMediumBoundaryAlt	2.25rem
squareIconMediumContent	1rem
squareIconSmall	1rem

Token Name	Example Value
squareIconSmallBoundary	1.5rem
squareIconSmallContent	.75rem
squareIconXSmallBoundary	1.25rem
squareIconXSmallContent	.5rem
squareIconLarge	3.125rem
squareToggleSlider	1.25rem
widthToggle	3.375rem
heightToggle	1.5rem
heightContextBar	2.25rem
spacingNone	0
spacingXxxSmall	0.125rem
spacingXxSmall	0.25rem
spacingXSmall	0.5rem
spacingSmall	0.75rem
spacingMedium	1rem
spacingLarge	1.5rem
spacingXLarge	2rem
spacingXxLarge	3rem
colorTextActionLabel	rgb(84, 105, 141)
colorTextActionLabelActive	rgb(22, 50, 92)
colorTextBrand	rgb(21, 137, 238)
colorTextBrowser	rgb(255, 255, 255)
colorTextBrowserActive	rgba(0, 0, 0, 0.4)
colorTextCustomer	rgb(255, 154, 60)

Token Name	Example Value
colorTextDefault	rgb(22, 50, 92)
colorTextError	rgb(194, 57, 52)
colorTextInputDisabled	rgb(84, 105, 141)
colorTextInputFocusInverse	rgb(22, 50, 92)
colorTextInputIcon	rgb(159, 170, 181)
colorTextInverse	rgb(255, 255, 255)
colorTextInverseWeak	rgb(159, 170, 181)
colorTextInverseActive	rgb(94, 180, 255)
colorTextInverseHover	rgb(159, 170, 181)
colorTextLink	rgb(0, 112, 210)
colorTextLinkActive	rgb(0, 57, 107)
colorTextLinkDisabled	rgb(22, 50, 92)
colorTextLinkFocus	rgb(0, 95, 178)
colorTextLinkHover	rgb(0, 95, 178)
colorTextLinkInverse	rgb(255, 255, 255)
colorTextLinkInverseHover	rgba(255, 255, 255, 0.75)
colorTextLinkInverseActive	rgba(255, 255, 255, 0.5)
colorTextLinkInverseDisabled	rgba(255, 255, 255, 0.15)
colorTextModal	rgb(255, 255, 255)
colorTextModalButton	rgb(84, 105, 141)
colorTextStageLeft	rgb(224, 229, 238)
colorTextTabLabel	rgb(22, 50, 92)
colorTextTabLabelSelected	rgb(0, 112, 210)
colorTextTabLabelHover	rgb(0, 95, 178)

Token Name	Example Value
colorTextTabLabelFocus	rgb(0, 95, 178)
colorTextTabLabelActive	rgb(0, 57, 107)
colorTextTabLabelDisabled	rgb(224, 229, 238)
colorTextToast	rgb(224, 229, 238)
colorTextWarning	rgb(255, 183, 93)
colorTextWeak	rgb(84, 105, 141)
colorTextIconBrand	rgb(0, 112, 210)
colorTextToggleDisabled	rgb(216, 221, 230)
colorTextContextBar	rgb(255, 255, 255)
colorTextContextBarTrigger	rgba(255, 255, 255, 0.4)
durationInstantly	0s
durationImmediately	0.05s
durationQuickly	0.1s
durationPromptly	0.2s
durationSlowly	0.4s
durationPaused	3.2s
zIndexToast	10000
zIndexModal	9000
zIndexOverlay	8000
zIndexDropdown	7000
zIndexDialog	6000
zIndexPopup	5000
zIndexDefault	1
zIndexDeepdive	-99999

For a complete list of the design tokens available in the SLDS, see Design Tokens on the Lightning Design System site.

SEE ALSO:

Extending Tokens Bundles

Standard Design Tokens for Communities

Use a subset of the standard design tokens to make your components compatible with the Branding Editor in Community Builder. The Branding Editor enables administrators to quickly style an entire community using branding properties. Each property in the Branding Editor maps to one or more standard design tokens. When an administrator updates a property in the Branding Editor, the system automatically updates any Lightning components that use the tokens associated with that branding property.

Available Tokens for Communities

For Communities using the Napili template, the following standard tokens are available when extending from `force:base`.

🛈 **Important:** The standard token values evolve along with SLDS. Available tokens and their values can change without notice.

These Branding Editor properties...	...map to these standard design tokens
Text Color	`colorTextDefault`
Detail Text Color	• `colorTextLabel` • `colorTextPlaceholder` • `colorTextWeak`
Action Color	• `colorBackgroundButtonBrand` • `colorBackgroundHighlight` • `colorBorderBrand` • `colorBorderButtonBrand` • `colorBrand` • `colorTextBrand`
Link Color	`colorTextLink`
Overlay Text Color	• `colorTextButtonBrand` • `colorTextButtonBrandHover` • `colorTextInverse`
Border Color	• `colorBorder` • `colorBorderButtonDefault` • `colorBorderInput` • `colorBorderSeparatorAlt`
Primary Font	`fontFamily`

In addition, the following standard tokens are available for derived branding properties in the Napili template. You can indirectly access derived branding properties when you update the properties in the Branding Editor. For example, if you change the Action Color property in the Branding Editor, the system automatically recalculates the token values associated with Action Color Darker based on the new value of Action Color.

These derived branding properties...	...map to these standard design tokens
Action Color Darker (Derived from Action Color)	• colorBackgroundButtonBrandActive • colorBackgroundButtonBrandHover
Hover Color (Derived from Action Color)	• colorBackgroundButtonDefaultHover • colorBackgroundRowHover • colorBackgroundRowSelected • colorBackgroundShade
Link Color Darker (Derived from Link Color)	• colorTextLinkActive • colorTextLinkHover

For a complete list of the design tokens available in the SLDS, see Design Tokens on the Lightning Design System site.

SEE ALSO:

Configure Components for Communities

Using JavaScript

Use JavaScript for client-side code. The $A namespace is the entry point for using the framework in JavaScript code.

For all the methods available in $A, see the JavaScript API at
https://<myDomain>.lightning.force.com/auradocs/reference.app, where
<myDomain> is the name of your custom Salesforce domain.

A component bundle can contain JavaScript code in a client-side controller, helper, or renderer. Client-side controllers are the most commonly used of these JavaScript resources.

Expressions in JavaScript Code

In JavaScript, use string syntax to evaluate an expression. For example, this expression retrieves the `label` attribute in a component.

```
var theLabel = cmp.get("v.label");
```

⚡ Note: Only use the `{! }` expression syntax in markup in `.app` or `.cmp` resources.

IN THIS SECTION:

Accessing the DOM

The Document Object Model (DOM) is the language-independent model for representing and interacting with objects in HTML and XML documents. The framework's rendering service takes in-memory component state and updates the component in the DOM.

Using External JavaScript Libraries

To reference a JavaScript library that you've uploaded as a static resource, use a `<ltng:require>` tag in your `.cmp` or `.app` markup.

Working with Attribute Values in JavaScript

These are useful and common patterns for working with attribute values in JavaScript.

Working with a Component Body in JavaScript

These are useful and common patterns for working with a component's body in JavaScript.

Sharing JavaScript Code in a Component Bundle

Put functions that you want to reuse in the component's helper. Helper functions also enable specialization of tasks, such as processing data and firing server-side actions.

Client-Side Rendering to the DOM

The framework's rendering service takes in-memory component state and updates the component in the Document Object Model (DOM).

Invoking Actions on Component Initialization

Use the `init` event to initialize a component or fire an event after component construction but before rendering.

Modifying Components Outside the Framework Lifecycle

Use `$A.getCallback()` to wrap any code that modifies a component outside the normal rerendering lifecycle, such as in a `setTimeout()` call. The `$A.getCallback()` call ensures that the framework rerenders the modified component and processes any enqueued actions.

Validating Fields

You can validate fields using JavaScript. Typically, you validate the user input, identify any errors, and display the error messages.

Throwing and Handling Errors

The framework gives you flexibility in handling unrecoverable and recoverable app errors in JavaScript code. For example, you can throw these errors in a callback when handling an error in a server-side response.

Calling Component Methods

Use `<aura:method>` to define a method as part of a component's API. This enables you to directly call a method in a component's client-side controller instead of firing and handling a component event. Using `<aura:method>` simplifies the code needed for a parent component to call a method on a child component that it contains.

Making API Calls

You can't make API calls from client-side code. Make API calls, including Salesforce API calls, from server-side controllers instead.

SEE ALSO:

Handling Events with Client-Side Controllers

Accessing the DOM

The Document Object Model (DOM) is the language-independent model for representing and interacting with objects in HTML and XML documents. The framework's rendering service takes in-memory component state and updates the component in the DOM.

The framework automatically renders your components so you don't have to know anything more about rendering unless you need to customize the default rendering behavior for a component.

There are two very important guidelines for accessing the DOM from a component or app.

* You should never modify the DOM outside a renderer. However, you can read from the DOM outside a renderer.
* Use expressions, whenever possible, instead of trying to set a DOM element directly.

Using Renderers

The rendering service is the bridge from the framework to update the DOM. If you modify the DOM from a client-side controller, the changes may be overwritten when the components are rendered, depending on how the component renderers behave. Modify the DOM only in `afterRender()` and `rerender()`. If you need to modify the DOM outside of the renderers, use utilities like `$A.util.addClass()`, `$A.util.removeClass()`, and `$A.util.toggleClass()`. Modify the DOM that belongs to the context component only.

Using Expressions

You can often avoid writing a custom renderer by using expressions in the markup instead. See Dynamically Showing or Hiding Markup on page 277 for more information.

Using External JavaScript Libraries

To reference a JavaScript library that you've uploaded as a static resource, use a `<ltng:require>` tag in your `.cmp` or `.app` markup.

The framework's content security policy mandates that external JavaScript libraries must be uploaded to Salesforce static resources. For more information on static resources, see "Static Resources" in the Salesforce online help.

Here's an example of using `<ltng:require>`.

```
<ltng:require scripts="{!$Resource.resourceName}"
    afterScriptsLoaded="{!c.afterScriptsLoaded}" />
```

resourceName is the `Name` of the static resource. In a managed packaged, the resource name must include the package namespace prefix, such as `$Resource.yourNamespace__resourceName`. For a stand-alone static resource, such as an individual graphic or script, that's all you need. To reference an item within an archive static resource, add the rest of the path to the item using string concatenation.

The `afterScriptsLoaded` action in the client-side controller is called after the scripts are loaded.

Here are some considerations for loading scripts:

Loading Sets of Scripts

Specify a comma-separated list of resources in the `scripts` attribute to load a set of resources.

 Note: Due to a quirk in the way `$Resource` is parsed in expressions, use the `join` operator to include multiple `$Resource` references in a single attribute. For example, if you have more than one JavaScript library to include into a component the `scripts` attribute should be something like the following.

```
scripts="{!join(',',
    $Resource.jsLibraries + '/jsLibOne.js',
    $Resource.jsLibraries + '/jsLibTwo.js')}"
```

Loading Order

The scripts are loaded in the order that they are listed.

One-Time Loading

Scripts load only once, even if they're specified in multiple `<ltng:require>` tags in the same component or across different components.

Parallel Loading

Use separate `<ltng:require>` tags for parallel loading if you have multiple sets of scripts that are not dependent on each other.

Encapsulation

To ensure encapsulation and reusability, add the `<ltng:require>` tag to every `.cmp` or `.app` resource that uses the JavaScript library.

`<ltng:require>` also has a `styles` attribute to load a list of CSS resources. You can set the `scripts` and `styles` attributes in one `<ltng:require>` tag.

If you're using an external library to work with your HTML elements after rendering, use `afterScriptsLoaded` to wire up a client-side controller. The following example sets up a chart using the `Chart.js` library, which is uploaded as a static resource.

```
<ltng:require scripts="{!$Resource.chart}"
             afterScriptsLoaded="{!c.setup}"/>
<canvas aura:id="chart" id="myChart" width="400" height="400"/>
```

The component's client-side controller sets up the chart after component initialization and rendering.

```
setup : function(component, event, helper) {
    var data = {
        labels: ["January", "February", "March"],
        datasets: [{
            data: [65, 59, 80, 81, 56, 55, 40]
        }]
    };
    var el = component.find("chart").getElement();
    var ctx = el.getContext("2d");
```

```
        var myNewChart = new Chart(ctx).Line(data);
}
```

SEE ALSO:

Reference Doc App

Content Security Policy Overview

Using External CSS

$Resource

Working with Attribute Values in JavaScript

These are useful and common patterns for working with attribute values in JavaScript.

`component.get(String key)` and `component.set(String key, Object value)` retrieves and assigns values associated with the specified key on the component. Keys are passed in as an expression, which represents attribute values. To retrieve an attribute value of a component reference, use `component.find("cmpId").get("v.value")`. Similarly, use `component.find("cmpId").set("v.value", myValue)` to set the attribute value of a component reference. This example shows how you can retrieve and set attribute values on a component reference, represented by the button with an ID of `button1`.

```
<aura:component>
    <aura:attribute name="buttonLabel" type="String"/>
    <ui:button aura:id="button1" label="Button 1"/>
    {!v.buttonLabel}
    <ui:button label="Get Label" press="{!c.getLabel}"/>
</aura:component>
```

This controller action retrieves the `label` attribute value of a button in a component and sets its value on the `buttonLabel` attribute.

```
({
    getLabel : function(component, event, helper) {
        var myLabel = component.find("button1").get("v.label");
        component.set("v.buttonLabel", myLabel);
    }
})
```

In the following examples, `cmp` is a reference to a component in your JavaScript code.

Get an Attribute Value

To get the value of a component's `label` attribute:

```
var label = cmp.get("v.label");
```

Set an Attribute Value

To set the value of a component's `label` attribute:

```
cmp.set("v.label","This is a label");
```

Validate that an Attribute Value is Defined

To determine if a component's `label` attribute is defined:

```
var isDefined = !$A.util.isUndefined(cmp.get("v.label"));
```

Validate that an Attribute Value is Empty

To determine if a component's `label` attribute is empty:

```
var isEmpty = $A.util.isEmpty(cmp.get("v.label"));
```

SEE ALSO:

Working with a Component Body in JavaScript

Working with a Component Body in JavaScript

These are useful and common patterns for working with a component's body in JavaScript.

In these examples, `cmp` is a reference to a component in your JavaScript code. It's usually easy to get a reference to a component in JavaScript code. Remember that the `body` attribute is an array of components, so you can use the JavaScript `Array` methods on it.

 Note: When you use `cmp.set("v.body", ...)` to set the component body, you must explicitly include `{!v.body}` in your component markup.

Replace a Component's Body

To replace the current value of a component's body with another component:

```
// newCmp is a reference to another component
cmp.set("v.body", newCmp);
```

Clear a Component's Body

To clear or empty the current value of a component's body:

```
cmp.set("v.body", []);
```

Append a Component to a Component's Body

To append a newCmp component to a component's body:

```
var body = cmp.get("v.body");
// newCmp is a reference to another component
body.push(newCmp);
cmp.set("v.body", body);
```

Prepend a Component to a Component's Body

To prepend a newCmp component to a component's body:

```
var body = cmp.get("v.body");
body.unshift(newCmp);
cmp.set("v.body", body);
```

Remove a Component from a Component's Body

To remove an indexed entry from a component's body:

```
var body = cmp.get("v.body");
// Index (3) is zero-based so remove the fourth component in the body
```

```
body.splice(3, 1);
cmp.set("v.body", body);
```

SEE ALSO:

Component Body

Working with Attribute Values in JavaScript

Sharing JavaScript Code in a Component Bundle

Put functions that you want to reuse in the component's helper. Helper functions also enable specialization of tasks, such as processing data and firing server-side actions.

They can be called from any JavaScript code in a component's bundle, such as from a client-side controller or renderer. Helper functions are similar to client-side controller functions in shape, surrounded by brackets and curly braces to denote a JSON object containing a map of name-value pairs. A helper function can pass in any arguments required by the function, such as the component it belongs to, a callback, or any other objects.

Creating a Helper

A helper resource is part of the component bundle and is auto-wired via the naming convention, `<componentName>Helper.js`.

To create a helper using the Developer Console, click **HELPER** in the sidebar of the component. This helper file is valid for the scope of the component to which it's auto-wired.

Using a Helper in a Renderer

Add a helper argument to a renderer function to enable the function to use the helper. In the renderer, specify `(component, helper)` as parameters in a function signature to enable the function to access the component's helper. These are standard parameters and you don't have to access them in the function. The following code shows an example on how you can override the `afterRender()` function in the renderer and call `open` in the helper method.

detailsRenderer.js

```
({
    afterRender : function(component, helper){
        helper.open(component, null, "new");
```

```
    }
})
```

detailsHelper.js

```
({
    open : function(component, note, mode, sort){
        if(mode === "new") {
            //do something
        }
        // do something else, such as firing an event
    }
})
```

For an example on using helper methods to customize renderers, see Client-Side Rendering to the DOM.

Using a Helper in a Controller

Add a `helper` argument to a controller function to enable the function to use the helper. Specify `(component, event, helper)` in the controller. These are standard parameters and you don't have to access them in the function. You can also pass in an instance variable as a parameter, for example, `createExpense: function(component, expense){...}`, where `expense` is a variable defined in the component.

The following code shows you how to call the `updateItem` helper function in a controller, which can be used with a custom event handler.

```
({
    newItemEvent: function(component, event, helper) {
        helper.updateItem(component, event.getParam("item"));
    }
})
```

Helper functions are local to a component, improve code reuse, and move the heavy lifting of JavaScript logic away from the client-side controller where possible. The following code shows the helper function, which takes in the `value` parameter set in the controller via the `item` argument. The code walks through calling a server-side action and returning a callback but you can do something else in the helper function.

```
({
    updateItem : function(component, item, callback) {
        //Update the items via a server-side action
        var action = component.get("c.saveItem");
        action.setParams({"item" : item});
```

257

```
        //Set any optional callback and enqueue the action
        if (callback) {
            action.setCallback(this, callback);
        }
        $A.enqueueAction(action);
    }
})
```

SEE ALSO:

Client-Side Rendering to the DOM

Component Bundles

Handling Events with Client-Side Controllers

Client-Side Rendering to the DOM

The framework's rendering service takes in-memory component state and updates the component in the Document Object Model (DOM).

The DOM is the language-independent model for representing and interacting with objects in HTML and XML documents. The framework automatically renders your components so you don't have to know anything more about rendering unless you need to customize the default rendering behavior for a component.

You should never modify the DOM outside a renderer. However, you can read from the DOM outside a renderer.

Rendering Lifecycle

The rendering lifecycle automatically handles rendering and rerendering of components whenever the underlying data changes. Here is an outline of the rendering lifecycle.

1. A browser event triggers one or more Lightning events.

2. Each Lightning event triggers one or more actions that can update data. The updated data can fire more events.

3. The rendering service tracks the stack of events that are fired.

4. When all the data updates from the events are processed, the framework rerenders all the components that own modified data.

For more information, see Events Fired During the Rendering Lifecycle .

Base Component Rendering

The base component in the framework is `aura:component`. Every component extends this base component.

The renderer for `aura:component` is in `componentRenderer.js`. This renderer has base implementations for the `render()`, `rerender()`, `afterRender()`, and `unrender()` functions. The framework calls these functions as part of the rendering lifecycle. You can override the base rendering functions in a custom renderer.

 Note: When you create a new component, the framework fires an `init` event, enabling you to update a component or fire an event after component construction but before rendering. The default renderer, `render()`, gets the component body and uses the rendering service to render it.

Creating a Renderer

You don't normally have to write a custom renderer, but if you want to customize rendering behavior, you can create a client-side renderer in a component bundle. A renderer file is part of the component bundle and is auto-wired if you follow the naming convention, `<componentName>Renderer.js`. For example, the renderer for `sample.cmp` would be in `sampleRenderer.js`.

Customizing Component Rendering

Customize rendering by creating a `render()` function in your component's renderer to override the base `render()` function, which updates the DOM.

The `render()` function returns a DOM node, an array of DOM nodes, or nothing. The base HTML component expects DOM nodes when it renders a component.

You generally want to extend default rendering by calling `superRender()` from your `render()` function before you add your custom rendering code. Calling `superRender()` creates the DOM nodes specified in the markup.

 Note: These guidelines are very important when you customize rendering.

- A renderer should only modify DOM elements that are part of the component. You should never break component encapsulation by reaching in to another component and changing its DOM elements, even if you are reaching in from the parent component.
- A renderer should never fire an event. An alternative is to use an `init` event instead.

259

Rerendering Components

When an event is fired, it may trigger actions to change data and call `rerender()` on affected components. The `rerender()` function enables components to update themselves based on updates to other components since they were last rendered. This function doesn't return a value.

The framework automatically calls `rerender()` if you update data in a component.

You generally want to extend default rerendering by calling `superRerender()` from your `renderer()` function before you add your custom rerendering code. Calling `superRerender()` chains the rerendering to the components in the `body` attribute.

Accessing the DOM After Rendering

The `afterRender()` function enables you to interact with the DOM tree after the framework's rendering service has inserted DOM elements. It's not necessarily the final call in the rendering lifecycle; it's simply called after `render()` and it doesn't return a value.

You generally want to extend default after rendering by calling `superAfterRender()` function before you add your custom code.

Unrendering Components

The base `unrender()` function deletes all the DOM nodes rendered by a component's `render()` function. It is called by the framework when a component is being destroyed. Customize this behavior by overriding `unrender()` in your component's renderer. This can be useful when you are working with third-party libraries that are not native to the framework.

You generally want to extend default unrendering by calling `superUnrender()` from your `unrender()` function before you add your custom code.

Rendering Example

Let's look at the button component to see how it customizes the base rendering behavior. It is important to know that every tag in markup, including standard HTML tags, has an underlying component representation. Therefore, the framework's rendering service uses the same process to render standard HTML tags or custom components that you create.

View the source for `ui:button`. Note that the button component includes a `disabled` attribute to track the disabled status for the component in a `Boolean`.

```
<aura:attribute name="disabled" type="Boolean" default="false"/>
```

In `button.cmp`, `onclick` is set to `{!c.press}`.

The renderer for the button component is `buttonRenderer.js`. The button component overrides the default `render()` function.

```
render : function(cmp, helper) {
    var ret = this.superRender();
    helper.updateDisabled(cmp);
    return ret;
},
```

The first line calls the `superRender()` function to invoke the default rendering behavior. The `helper.updateDisabled(cmp)` call invokes a helper function to customize the rendering.

Let's look at the `updateDisabled(cmp)` function in `buttonHelper.js`.

```
updateDisabled: function(cmp) {
    if (cmp.get("v.disabled")) {
        var disabled = $A.util.getBooleanValue(cmp.get("v.disabled"));

        var button = cmp.find("button");
        if (button) {
            var element = button.getElement();
            if (element) {
                if (disabled) {
                    element.setAttribute('disabled', 'disabled');
                } else {
                    element.removeAttribute('disabled');
                }
            }
        }
    }
}
```

The `updateDisabled(cmp)` function translates the `Boolean disabled` value to the value expected in HTML, where the attribute doesn't exist or is set to `disabled`.

It uses `cmp.find("button")` to retrieve a unique component. Note that `button.cmp` uses `aura:id="button"` to uniquely identify the component. `button.getElement()` returns the DOM element.

The `rerender()` function in `buttonRenderer.js` is very similar to the `render()` function. Note that it also calls `updateDisabled(cmp)`.

```
rerender : function(cmp, helper){
    this.superRerender();
```

```
        helper.updateDisabled(cmp);
}
```

Rendering components is part of the lifecycle of the framework and it's a bit trickier to demonstrate than some other concepts. The takeaway is that you don't need to think about it unless you need to customize the default rendering behavior for a component.

SEE ALSO:

Accessing the DOM

Invoking Actions on Component Initialization

Component Bundles

Modifying Components Outside the Framework Lifecycle

Sharing JavaScript Code in a Component Bundle

Invoking Actions on Component Initialization

Use the `init` event to initialize a component or fire an event after component construction but before rendering.

Component source

```
<aura:component>
    <aura:attribute name="setMeOnInit" type="String" default="default
value" />
    <aura:handler name="init" value="{!this}" action="{!c.doInit}"/>

    <p>This value is set in the controller after the component
initializes and before rendering.</p>
    <p><b>{!v.setMeOnInit}</b></p>

</aura:component>
```

Client-side controller source

```
({
    doInit: function(cmp) {
        // Set the attribute value.
        // You could also fire an event here instead.
        cmp.set("v.setMeOnInit", "controller init magic!");
    }
})
```

Let's look at the **Component source** to see how this works. The magic happens in this line.

```
<aura:handler name="init" value="{!this}" action="{!c.doInit}"/>
```

This registers an `init` event handler for the component. `init` is a predefined event sent to every component. After the component is initialized, the `doInit` action is called in the component's controller. In this sample, the controller action sets an attribute value, but it could do something more interesting, such as firing an event.

Setting `value="{!this}"` marks this as a value event. You should always use this setting for an `init` event.

SEE ALSO:

Handling Events with Client-Side Controllers

Client-Side Rendering to the DOM

Component Attributes

Detecting Data Changes

Modifying Components Outside the Framework Lifecycle

Use `$A.getCallback()` to wrap any code that modifies a component outside the normal rerendering lifecycle, such as in a `setTimeout()` call. The `$A.getCallback()` call ensures that the framework rerenders the modified component and processes any enqueued actions.

 Note: `$A.run()` is deprecated. Use `$A.getCallback()` instead.

You don't need to use `$A.getCallback()` if your code is executed as part of the framework's call stack; for example, your code is handling an event or in the callback for a server-side controller action.

An example of where you need to use `$A.getCallback()` is calling `window.setTimeout()` in an event handler to execute some logic after a time delay. This puts your code outside the framework's call stack.

This sample sets the `visible` attribute on a component to `true` after a five-second delay.

```
window.setTimeout(
    $A.getCallback(function() {
        if (cmp.isValid()) {
            cmp.set("v.visible", true);
        }
    }), 5000
);
```

Note how the code updating a component attribute is wrapped in `$A.getCallback()`, which ensures that the framework rerenders the modified component.

 Note: Always add an `isValid()` check if you reference a component in asynchronous code, such as a callback or a timeout. If you navigate elsewhere in the UI while asynchronous code is executing, the framework unrenders and destroys the component that made the asynchronous request. You can still have a reference to that component, but it is no longer valid. Add an `isValid()` call to check that the component is still valid before processing the results of the asynchronous request.

 Warning: Don't save a reference to a function wrapped in `$A.getCallback()`. If you use the reference later to send actions, the saved transaction state will cause the actions to be aborted.

SEE ALSO:

Handling Events with Client-Side Controllers

Firing Lightning Events from Non-Lightning Code

Communicating with Events

Validating Fields

You can validate fields using JavaScript. Typically, you validate the user input, identify any errors, and display the error messages.

Default Error Handling

The framework can handle and display errors using the default error component, `ui:inputDefaultError`. The following example shows how the framework handles a validation error and uses the default error component to display the error message. Here is the markup.

```
<!--c:errorHandling-->
<aura:component>
    Enter a number: <ui:inputNumber aura:id="inputCmp"/> <br/>
    <ui:button label="Submit" press="{!c.doAction}"/>
</aura:component>
```

Here is the client-side controller.

```
/*errorHandlingController.js*/
{
    doAction : function(component) {
        var inputCmp = component.find("inputCmp");
```

```
        var value = inputCmp.get("v.value");

        // Is input numeric?
        if (isNaN(value)) {
            // Set error
            inputCmp.set("v.errors", [{message:"Input not a number: "
 + value}]);
        } else {
            // Clear error
            inputCmp.set("v.errors", null);
        }
    }
}
```

When you enter a value and click **Submit**, `doAction` in the controller validates the input and displays an error message if the input is not a number. Entering a valid input clears the error. Add error messages to the input component using the `errors` attribute.

Custom Error Handling

`ui:input` and its child components can handle errors using the `onError` and `onClearErrors` events, which are wired to your custom error handlers defined in a controller. `onError` maps to a `ui:validationError` event, and `onClearErrors` maps to `ui:clearErrors`.

The following example shows how you can handle a validation error using custom error handlers and display the error message using the default error component. Here is the markup.

```
<!--c:errorHandlingCustom-->
<aura:component>
    Enter a number: <ui:inputNumber aura:id="inputCmp"
onError="{!c.handleError}" onClearErrors="{!c.handleClearError}"/>
<br/>
    <ui:button label="Submit" press="{!c.doAction}"/>
</aura:component>
```

Here is the client-side controller.

```
/*errorHandlingCustomController.js*/
{
    doAction : function(component, event) {
        var inputCmp = component.find("inputCmp");
        var value = inputCmp.get("v.value");

        // is input numeric?
```

```
        if (isNaN(value)) {
            inputCmp.set("v.errors", [{message:"Input not a number: "
+ value}]);
        } else {
            inputCmp.set("v.errors", null);
        }
    },

    handleError: function(component, event){
        /* do any custom error handling
         * logic desired here */
        // get v.errors, which is an Object[]
        var errorsArr  = event.getParam("errors");
        for (var i = 0; i < errorsArr.length; i++) {
            console.log("error " + i + ": " +
JSON.stringify(errorsArr[i]));
        }
    },

    handleClearError: function(component, event) {
        /* do any custom error handling
         * logic desired here */
    }
}
```

When you enter a value and click **Submit**, `doAction` in the controller executes. However, instead of letting the framework handle the errors, we define a custom error handler using the `onError` event in `<ui:inputNumber>`. If the validation fails, `doAction` adds an error message using the `errors` `attribute`. This automatically fires the `handleError` custom error handler.

Similarly, you can customize clearing the errors by using the `onClearErrors` event. See the `handleClearError` handler in the controller for an example.

SEE ALSO:

Handling Events with Client-Side Controllers

Component Events

Throwing and Handling Errors

The framework gives you flexibility in handling unrecoverable and recoverable app errors in JavaScript code. For example, you can throw these errors in a callback when handling an error in a server-side response.

Unrecoverable Errors

Use `throw new Error("error message here")` for unrecoverable errors, such as an error that prevents your app from starting successfully. The error message is displayed.

 Note: `$A.error()` is deprecated. Throw the native JavaScript `Error` object instead by using `throw new Error()`.

This example shows you the basics of throwing an unrecoverable error in a JavaScript controller.

```
<!--c:unrecoverableError-->
<aura:component>
    <ui:button label="throw error" press="{!c.throwError}"/>
</aura:component>
```

Here is the client-side controller source.

```
/*unrecoverableErrorController.js*/
({
    throwError : function(component, event){
        throw new Error("I can't go on. This is the end.");
    }
})
```

Recoverable Errors

To handle recoverable errors, use a component, such as `ui:message`, to tell users about the problem.

This sample shows you the basics of throwing and catching a recoverable error in a JavaScript controller.

```
<!--c:recoverableError-->
<aura:component>
    <p>Click the button to trigger the controller to throw an error.</p>

    <div aura:id="div1"></div>

    <ui:button label="Throw an Error" press="{!c.throwErrorForKicks}"/>
</aura:component>
```

Here is the client-side controller source.

```
/*recoverableErrorController.js*/
({
    throwErrorForKicks: function(cmp) {
        // this sample always throws an error to demo try/catch
        var hasPerm = false;
```

```
        try {
            if (!hasPerm) {
                throw new Error("You don't have permission to edit
this record.");
            }
        }
        catch (e) {
            $A.createComponents([
                ["ui:message",{
                    "title" : "Sample Thrown Error",
                    "severity" : "error",
                }],
                ["ui:outputText",{
                    "value" : e.message
                }]
                ],
                function(components, status){
                    if (status === "SUCCESS") {
                        var message = components[0];
                        var outputText = components[1];
                        // set the body of the ui:message to be the
ui:outputText
                        message.set("v.body", outputText);
                        var div1 = cmp.find("div1");
                        // Replace div body with the dynamic component
                        div1.set("v.body", message);
                    }
                }
            );
        }
    }
})
```

The controller code always throws an error and catches it in this example. The message in the error is displayed to the user in a dynamically created ui:message component. The body of the ui:message is a ui:outputText component containing the error text.

SEE ALSO:

Validating Fields

Dynamically Creating Components

Calling Component Methods

Use `<aura:method>` to define a method as part of a component's API. This enables you to directly call a method in a component's client-side controller instead of firing and handling a component event. Using `<aura:method>` simplifies the code needed for a parent component to call a method on a child component that it contains.

Use this syntax to call a method in JavaScript code.

```
cmp.sampleMethod(arg1, … argN);
```

`cmp` is a reference to the component. `arg1, … argN` is an optional comma-separated list of arguments passed to the method.

Let's look at an example of a component containing a button. The handler for the button calls a component method instead of firing and handling its own component event.

Here is the component source.

```
<!--c:auraMethod-->
<aura:component>
    <aura:method name="sampleMethod" action="{!c.doAction}"
access="PUBLIC"
        description="Sample method with parameters">
        <aura:attribute name="param1" type="String" default="parameter
1" />
    </aura:method>

    <ui:button label="Press Me" press="{!c.handleClick}"/>
</aura:component>
```

Here is the client-side controller.

```
/*auraMethodController.js*/
({
    handleClick : function(cmp, event) {
        console.log("in handleClick");
        // call the method declared by <aura:method> in the markup
        cmp.sampleMethod("1");
    },

    doAction : function(cmp, event) {
        var params = event.getParam('arguments');
        if (params) {
            var param1 = params.param1;
            console.log("param1: " + param1);
```

269

```
            // add your code here
        }
    },
})
```

This simple example just logs the parameter passed to the method.

The `<aura:method>` tag set name="sampleMethod" and action="{!c.doAction}" so the method is called by `cmp.sampleMethod()` and handled by `doAction()` in the controller.

 Note: If you don't specify an `action` value, the controller action defaults to the value of the method name. If we omitted action="{!c.doAction}" from the earlier example, the method would be called by `cmp.sampleMethod()` and handled by `sampleMethod()` instead of `doAction()` in the controller.

Using Inherited Methods

A sub component that extends a super component has access to any methods defined in the super component.

An interface can also include an `<aura:method>` tag. A component that implements the interface can access the method.

SEE ALSO:

aura:method

Component Events

Making API Calls

You can't make API calls from client-side code. Make API calls, including Salesforce API calls, from server-side controllers instead.

The framework uses Content Security Policy (CSP) to control the source of content that can be loaded on a page. Lightning apps are served from a different domain than Salesforce APIs so the CSP doesn't allow API calls from JavaScript code.

For information about making API calls from server-side controllers, see Making API Calls from Apex on page 304.

SEE ALSO:

Content Security Policy Overview

JavaScript Cookbook

This section includes code snippets and samples that can be used in various JavaScript files.

IN THIS SECTION:

Dynamically Creating Components

Create a component dynamically in your client-side JavaScript code by using the `$A.createComponent()` method. To create multiple components, use `$A.createComponents()`.

Detecting Data Changes

Configure a component to automatically invoke a client-side controller action when a value in one of the component's attributes changes. When the value changes, the `valueChange.evt` event is automatically fired. The `valueChange.evt` is an event with `type="VALUE"` that takes in two attributes, `value` and `index`.

Finding Components by ID

Retrieve a component by its ID in JavaScript code.

Dynamically Adding Event Handlers

You can dynamically add a handler for an event that a component fires. The component can be created dynamically on the client-side or fetched from the server at runtime.

Dynamically Showing or Hiding Markup

Use CSS to toggle markup visibility. You could use the `<aura:if>` tag to do the same thing but we recommend using CSS as it's the more standard approach.

Adding and Removing Styles

You can add or remove a CSS style on a component or element during runtime.

Which Button Was Pressed?

To find out which button was pressed in a component containing multiple buttons, use `Component.getLocalId()`.

Dynamically Creating Components

Create a component dynamically in your client-side JavaScript code by using the `$A.createComponent()` method. To create multiple components, use `$A.createComponents()`.

271

Note: Use `createComponent()` instead of the deprecated `$A.newCmp()` and `$A.newCmpAsync()` methods.

The syntax is:

```
createComponent(String type, Object attributes, function callback)
```

1. `type`—The type of component to create; for example, `"ui:button"`
2. `attributes`—A map of attributes for the component, including the local Id (`aura:id`)
3. `callback`—The callback to invoke after the component is created. The new component is passed in to the callback as a parameter

Let's add a dynamically created button to this sample component.

```
<!--c:createComponent-->
<aura:component>
    <aura:handler name="init" value="{!this}" action="{!c.doInit}"/>

    <p>Dynamically created button</p>
    {!v.body}

</aura:component>
```

The client-side controller calls `$A.createComponent()` to create the button with a local ID and a handler for the `press` event. The button is appended to the `body` of `c:createComponent`.

```
/*createComponentController.js*/
({
    doInit : function(cmp) {
        $A.createComponent(
            "ui:button",
            {
                "aura:id": "findableAuraId",
                "label": "Press Me",
                "press": cmp.getReference("c.handlePress")
            },
            function(newButton){
                //Add the new button to the body array
                if (cmp.isValid()) {
                    var body = cmp.get("v.body");
                    body.push(newButton);
                    cmp.set("v.body", body);
                }
            }
```

```
        );
    },

    handlePress : function(cmp) {
        console.log("button pressed");
    }
})
```

📝 Note: c:createComponent contains a {!v.body} expression. When you use cmp.set("v.body", ...) to set the component body, you must explicitly include {!v.body} in your component markup.

To retrieve the new button you created, use body[0].

```
var newbody = cmp.get("v.body");
var newCmp = newbody[0].find("findableAuraId");
```

Creating Nested Components

To dynamically create a component in the body of another component, use $A.createComponents() to create the components. In the function callback, nest the components by setting the inner component in the body of the outer component. This example creates a ui:outputText component in the body of a ui:message component.

```
$A.createComponents([
    ["ui:message",{
        "title" : "Sample Thrown Error",
        "severity" : "error",
    }],
    ["ui:outputText",{
        "value" : e.message
    }]
    ],
    function(components, status){
        if (status === "SUCCESS") {
            var message = components[0];
            var outputText = components[1];
            // set the body of the ui:message to be the ui:outputText

            message.set("v.body", outputText);
        }
    }
);
```

Destroying Dynamically Created Components

After a component that is declared in markup is no longer in use, the framework automatically destroys it and frees up its memory.

If you create a component dynamically in JavaScript and that component isn't added to a facet (`v.body` or another attribute of type `Aura.Component[]`), you have to destroy it manually using `Component.destroy()` to avoid memory leaks.

Avoiding a Server Trip

The `createComponent()` and `createComponents()` methods supports both client-side and server-side component creation. If no server-side dependencies are found, the methods are executed client-side.

A server-side controller is not a server-side dependency for component creation as controller actions are only called after the component has been created.

A component with server-side dependencies is created on the server. If there are no server dependencies and the definition already exists on the client via preloading or declared dependencies, no server call is made.

 Tip: There's no limit in component creation on the client side. You can create up to 10,000 components in one server request. If you hit this limit, ensure that you're creating components on the client side in markup or in JavaScript using `$A.createComponent()` or `$A.createComponents()`. To avoid a trip to the server for component creation in JavaScript code, add an `<aura:dependency>` tag for the component in the markup to explicitly tell the framework about the dependency.

The framework automatically tracks dependencies between definitions, such as components. However, some dependencies aren't easily discoverable by the framework; for example, if you dynamically create a component that isn't directly referenced in the component's markup. To tell the framework about such a dynamic dependency, use the `<aura:dependency>` tag. This ensures that the component and its dependencies are sent to the client, when needed.

The top-level component determines whether a server request is necessary for component creation.

> **Note:** Creating components where the top-level components don't have server dependencies but nested inner components do is not currently supported.

SEE ALSO:

Reference Doc App

aura:dependency

Invoking Actions on Component Initialization

Dynamically Adding Event Handlers

Detecting Data Changes

Configure a component to automatically invoke a client-side controller action when a value in one of the component's attributes changes. When the value changes, the `valueChange.evt` event is automatically fired. The `valueChange.evt` is an event with `type="VALUE"` that takes in two attributes, `value` and `index`.

In the component, define a handler with `name="change"`.

```
<aura:handler name="change" value="{!v.items}"
action="{!c.itemsChange}"/>
```

A component can have multiple `<aura:handler name="change">` tags to detect changes to different attributes.

In the controller, define the action for the handler.

```
({
    itemsChange: function(cmp, evt) {
        var v = evt.getParam("value");
        if (v === cmp.get("v.items")) {
        //do something
        }
    }
})
```

When a change occurs to a value that is represented by the `change` handler, the framework handles the firing of the event and rerendering of the component. For more information, see #ref_aura_valueChange.

SEE ALSO:

Invoking Actions on Component Initialization

Finding Components by ID

Retrieve a component by its ID in JavaScript code.

Use `aura:id` to add a local ID of `button1` to the `ui:button` component.

```
<ui:button aura:id="button1" label="button1"/>
```

You can find the component by calling `cmp.find("button1")`, where `cmp` is a reference to the component containing the button. The `find()` function has one parameter, which is the local ID of a component within the markup.

`find()` returns different types depending on the result.

- If the local ID is unique, `find()` returns the component.
- If there are multiple components with the same local ID, `find()` returns an array of the components.
- If there is no matching local ID, `find()` returns `undefined`.

SEE ALSO:

Component IDs

Value Providers

Dynamically Adding Event Handlers

You can dynamically add a handler for an event that a component fires. The component can be created dynamically on the client-side or fetched from the server at runtime.

This sample code adds an event handler to instances of `c:sampleComponent`.

```
addNewHandler : function(cmp, event) {
    var cmpArr = cmp.find({ instancesOf : "c:sampleComponent" });
    for (var i = 0; i < cmpArr.length; i++) {
        var outputCmpArr = cmpArr[i];
        outputCmpArr.addHandler("someAction", cmp, "c.someAction");
    }
}
```

You can also add an event handler to a component that is created dynamically in the callback function of `$A.createComponent()`. For more information, see Dynamically Creating Components.

`addHandler()` adds an event handler to a component.

Note that you can't force a component to start firing events that it doesn't fire. `c.someAction` can be an action in a controller in the component's hierarchy. `someAction` and `cmp` refers to the event name and value provider respectively. `someAction` must match the `name` attribute value in the `aura:registerEvent` or `aura:handler` tag. Refer to the JavaScript API reference for a full list of methods and arguments.

SEE ALSO:

Handling Events with Client-Side Controllers

Creating Server-Side Logic with Controllers

Client-Side Rendering to the DOM

Dynamically Showing or Hiding Markup

Use CSS to toggle markup visibility. You could use the `<aura:if>` tag to do the same thing but we recommend using CSS as it's the more standard approach.

This example uses `$A.util.toggleClass(cmp, 'class')` to toggle visibility of markup.

```
<!--c:toggleCss-->
<aura:component>
    <ui:button label="Toggle" press="{!c.toggle}"/>
    <p aura:id="text">Now you see me</p>
</aura:component>
```

```
/*toggleCssController.js*/
({
    toggle : function(component, event, helper) {
        var toggleText = component.find("text");
        $A.util.toggleClass(toggleText, "toggle");
    }
})
```

```
/*toggleCss.css*/
.THIS.toggle {
    display: none;
}
```

Click the **Toggle** button to hide or show the text by toggling the CSS class.

SEE ALSO:

Handling Events with Client-Side Controllers

Component Attributes

Adding and Removing Styles

Adding and Removing Styles

You can add or remove a CSS style on a component or element during runtime.

To retrieve the class name on a component, use `component.find('myCmp').get('v.class')`, where `myCmp` is the `aura:id` attribute value.

To append and remove CSS classes from a component or element, use the `$A.util.addClass(cmpTarget, 'class')` and `$A.util.removeClass(cmpTarget, 'class')` methods.

Component source

```
<aura:component>
    <div aura:id="changeIt">Change Me!</div><br />
    <ui:button press="{!c.applyCSS}" label="Add Style" />
    <ui:button press="{!c.removeCSS}" label="Remove Style" />
</aura:component>
```

CSS source

```
.THIS.changeMe {
    background-color:yellow;
    width:200px;
}
```

Client-side controller source

```
{
    applyCSS: function(cmp, event) {
        var cmpTarget = cmp.find('changeIt');
        $A.util.addClass(cmpTarget, 'changeMe');
    },

    removeCSS: function(cmp, event) {
        var cmpTarget = cmp.find('changeIt');
        $A.util.removeClass(cmpTarget, 'changeMe');
```

```
        }
    }
}
```

The buttons in this demo are wired to controller actions that append or remove the CSS styles. To append a CSS style to a component, use $A.util.addClass(cmpTarget, 'class'). Similarly, remove the class by using $A.util.removeClass(cmpTarget, 'class') in your controller. cmp.find() locates the component using the local ID, denoted by aura:id="changeIt" in this demo.

Toggling a Class

To toggle a class, use $A.util.toggleClass(cmp, 'class'), which adds or removes the class.

The cmp parameter can be component or a DOM element.

 Note: We recommend using a component instead of a DOM element. If the utility function is not used inside afterRender() or rerender(), passing in cmp.getElement() might result in your class not being applied when the components are rerendered. For more information, see Events Fired During the Rendering Lifecycle on page 192.

To hide or show markup dynamically, see Dynamically Showing or Hiding Markup on page 277.

To conditionally set a class for an array of components, pass in the array to $A.util.toggleClass().

```
mapClasses: function(arr, cssClass) {
    for(var cmp in arr) {
        $A.util.toggleClass(arr[cmp], cssClass);
    }
}
```

SEE ALSO:

Handling Events with Client-Side Controllers

CSS in Components

Component Bundles

Which Button Was Pressed?

To find out which button was pressed in a component containing multiple buttons, use Component.getLocalId().

Let's look at a component that contains multiple buttons. Each button has a unique local ID, set by an
`aura:id` attribute.

```
<!--c:buttonPressed-->
<aura:component >
    <aura:attribute name="whichButton" type="String" />

    <p>You clicked: {!v.whichButton}</p>

    <ui:button aura:id="button1" label="Click me"
press="{!c.nameThatButton}"/>
    <ui:button aura:id="button2" label="Click me too"
press="{!c.nameThatButton}"/>
</aura:component>
```

Use `event.getSource()` in the client-side controller to get the button component that was clicked.
Call `getLocalId()` to get the `aura:id` of the clicked button.

```
/* buttonPressedController.js */
({
    nameThatButton : function(cmp, event, helper) {
        var whichOne = event.getSource().getLocalId();
        console.log(whichOne);
        cmp.set("v.whichButton", whichOne);
    }
})
```

SEE ALSO:

Component IDs

Finding Components by ID

Using Apex

Use Apex to write server-side code, such as controllers and test classes.

Server-side controllers handle requests from client-side controllers. For example, a client-side controller
might handle an event and call a server-side controller action to persist a record. A server-side controller
can also load your record data.

IN THIS SECTION:

Creating Server-Side Logic with Controllers

The framework supports client-side and server-side controllers. An event is always wired to a client-side controller action, which can in turn call a server-side controller action. For example, a client-side controller might handle an event and call a server-side controller action to persist a record.

Creating Components

The `Cmp.<myNamespace>.<myComponent>` syntax to reference a component in Apex is deprecated. Use `$A.createComponent()` in client-side JavaScript code instead.

Working with Salesforce Records

It's easy to work with your Salesforce records in Apex.

Testing Your Apex Code

Before you can upload a managed package, you must write and execute tests for your Apex code to meet minimum code coverage requirements. Also, all tests must run without errors when you upload your package to AppExchange.

Making API Calls from Apex

Make API calls from an Apex controller. You can't make API calls from JavaScript code.

Creating Server-Side Logic with Controllers

The framework supports client-side and server-side controllers. An event is always wired to a client-side controller action, which can in turn call a server-side controller action. For example, a client-side controller might handle an event and call a server-side controller action to persist a record.

Server-side actions need to make a round trip, from the client to the server and back again, so they are usually completed more slowly than client-side actions.

For more details on the process of calling a server-side action, see Calling a Server-Side Action on page 285.

IN THIS SECTION:

Apex Server-Side Controller Overview

Create a server-side controller in Apex and use the `@AuraEnabled` annotation to enable client- and server-side access to the controller method.

Creating an Apex Server-Side Controller

Use the Developer Console to create an Apex server-side controller.

Returning Errors from an Apex Server-Side Controller

Create and throw a `System.AuraHandledException` from your server-side controller to return a custom error message.

Calling a Server-Side Action

Call a server-side controller action from a client-side controller. In the client-side controller, you set a callback, which is called after the server-side action is completed. A server-side action can return any object containing serializable JSON data.

Queueing of Server-Side Actions

The framework queues up actions before sending them to the server. This mechanism is largely transparent to you when you're writing code but it enables the framework to minimize network traffic by batching multiple actions into one request.

Abortable Actions

Mark an action as abortable to make it potentially abortable while it's queued to be sent to the server. An abortable action in the queue is not sent to the server if the component that created the action is no longer valid, that is `cmp.isValid() == false`. A component is automatically destroyed and marked invalid by the framework when it is unrendered.

Storable Actions

Mark an action as storable to have its response stored in the client-side cache by the framework. Caching can be useful if you want your app to be functional for devices that temporarily don't have a network connection.

Apex Server-Side Controller Overview

Create a server-side controller in Apex and use the `@AuraEnabled` annotation to enable client- and server-side access to the controller method.

Only methods that you have explicitly annotated with `@AuraEnabled` are exposed.

 Tip: Don't store component state in your controller. Store it in a component's attribute instead.

This Apex controller contains a `serverEcho` action that prepends a string to the value passed in.

```
public with sharing class SimpleServerSideController {

    //Use @AuraEnabled to enable client- and server-side access to the
method
    @AuraEnabled
    public static String serverEcho(String firstName) {
        return ('Hello from the server, ' + firstName);
```

```
    }
}
```

In addition to using the `@AuraEnabled` annotation, your Apex controller must follow these requirements.

- Methods must be `static` and marked `public` or `global`. Non-static methods are not supported.
- If a method returns an object, instance methods that retrieve the value of the object's instance field must be public.

For more information, see Understanding Classes in the *Apex Code Developer's Guide*.

SEE ALSO:

Calling a Server-Side Action

Creating an Apex Server-Side Controller

Creating an Apex Server-Side Controller

Use the Developer Console to create an Apex server-side controller.

1. Open the Developer Console.
2. Click **File** > **New** > **Apex Class**.
3. Enter a name for your server-side controller.
4. Click **OK**.
5. Enter a method for each server-side action in the body of the class.

     Note: Add the `@AuraEnabled` annotation to any methods, including getters and setters, that you wish to expose on the client- or server-side. This means that you only expose methods that you have explicitly annotated.

6. Click **File** > **Save**.
7. Open the component that you want to wire to the new controller class.
8. Add a `controller` system attribute to the `<aura:component>` tag to wire the component to the controller. For example:

```
<aura:component controller="SimpleServerSideController" >
```

SEE ALSO:

Salesforce Help: Open the Developer Console

Returning Errors from an Apex Server-Side Controller

Create and throw a `System.AuraHandledException` from your server-side controller to return a custom error message.

Errors happen. Sometimes they're expected, such as invalid input from a user, or a duplicate record in a database. Sometimes they're unexpected, such as... Well, if you've been programming for any length of time, you know that the range of unexpected errors is nearly infinite.

When your server-side controller code experiences an error, two things can happen. You can catch it there and handle it in Apex. Otherwise, the error is passed back in the controller's response.

If you handle the error Apex, you again have two ways you can go. You can process the error, perhaps recovering from it, and return a normal response to the client. Or, you can create and throw an `AuraHandledException`.

The benefit of throwing `AuraHandledException`, instead of letting a system exception be returned, is that you have a chance to handle the exception more gracefully in your client code. System exceptions have important details stripped out for security purposes, and result in the dreaded "An internal server error has occurred..." message. Nobody likes that. When you use an `AuraHandledException` you have an opportunity to add some detail back into the response returned to your client-side code. More importantly, you can choose a better message to show your users.

Here's an example of creating and throwing an `AuraHandledException` in response to bad input. However, the real benefit of using `AuraHandledException` comes when you use it in response to a system exception. For example, throw an `AuraHandledException` in response to catching a DML exception, instead of allowing that to propagate down to your client component code.

```
public with sharing class SimpleErrorController {

    static final List<String> BAD_WORDS = new List<String> {
        'bad',
        'words',
        'here'
    };


    @AuraEnabled
    public static String helloOrThrowAnError(String name) {

        // Make sure we're not seeing something naughty
        for(String badWordStem : BAD_WORDS) {
            if(name.containsIgnoreCase(badWordStem)) {
                // How rude! Gracefully return an error...
                throw new AuraHandledException('NSFW name detected.');
```

```
            }
        }

        // No bad word found, so...
        return ('Hello ' + name + '!');
    }

}
```

Calling a Server-Side Action

Call a server-side controller action from a client-side controller. In the client-side controller, you set a callback, which is called after the server-side action is completed. A server-side action can return any object containing serializable JSON data.

A client-side controller is a JavaScript object in object-literal notation containing name-value pairs. Each name corresponds to a client-side action. Its value is the function code associated with the action.

Let's say that you want to trigger a server-call from a component. The following component contains a button that's wired to a client-side controller `echo` action. `SimpleServerSideController` contains a method that returns a string passed in from the client-side controller.

```
<aura:component controller="SimpleServerSideController">
    <aura:attribute name="firstName" type="String" default="world"/>
    <ui:button label="Call server" press="{!c.echo}"/>
</aura:component>
```

The following client-side controller includes an `echo` action that executes a `serverEcho` method on a server-side controller. The client-side controller sets a callback action that is invoked after the server-side action returns. In this case, the callback function alerts the user with the value returned from the server. `action.setParams({ firstName : cmp.get("v.firstName") });` retrieves the `firstName` attribute from the component and sets the value of the `firstName` argument on the server-side controller's `serverEcho` method.

```
({
    "echo" : function(cmp) {
        // create a one-time use instance of the serverEcho action
        // in the server-side controller
        var action = cmp.get("c.serverEcho");
        action.setParams({ firstName : cmp.get("v.firstName") });

        // Create a callback that is executed after
        // the server-side action returns
```

```
        action.setCallback(this, function(response) {
            var state = response.getState();
            // This callback doesn't reference cmp. If it did,
            // you should run an isValid() check
            //if (cmp.isValid() && state === "SUCCESS") {
            if (state === "SUCCESS") {
                // Alert the user with the value returned
                // from the server
                alert("From server: " + response.getReturnValue());

                // You would typically fire a event here to trigger
                // client-side notification that the server-side
                // action is complete
            }
            //else if (cmp.isValid() && state === "INCOMPLETE") {
            else if (state === "INCOMPLETE") {
                // do something
            }
            //else if (cmp.isValid() && state === "ERROR") {
            else if (state === "ERROR") {
                var errors = response.getError();
                if (errors) {
                    if (errors[0] && errors[0].message) {
                        console.log("Error message: " +
                                errors[0].message);
                    }
                } else {
                    console.log("Unknown error");
                }
            }
        });

        // optionally set storable, abortable, background flag here

        // A client-side action could cause multiple events,
        // which could trigger other events and
        // other server-side action calls.
        // $A.enqueueAction adds the server-side action to the queue.

        $A.enqueueAction(action);
    }
})
```

In the client-side controller, we use the value provider of `c` to invoke a server-side controller action. We also use the `c` syntx in markup to invoke a client-side controller action. The `cmp.get("c.serverEcho")` call indicates that we are calling the `serverEcho` method in the server-side controller. The method name in the server-side controller must match everything after the `c.` in the client-side call.

 Tip: Use unique names for client-side and server-side actions in a component. A JavaScript function (client-side action) with the same name as a server-side action (Apex method) can lead to hard-to-debug issues.

Use `$A.enqueueAction(action)` to add the server-side controller action to the queue of actions to be executed. All actions that are enqueued will run at the end of the event loop. Rather than sending a separate request for each individual action, the framework processes the event chain and batches the actions in the queue into one request. The actions are asynchronous and have callbacks.

 Note: Always add an `isValid()` check if you reference a component in asynchronous code, such as a callback or a timeout. If you navigate elsewhere in the UI while asynchronous code is executing, the framework unrenders and destroys the component that made the asynchronous request. You can still have a reference to that component, but it is no longer valid. Add an `isValid()` call to check that the component is still valid before processing the results of the asynchronous request.

 Tip: If your action is not executing, make sure that you're not executing code outside the framework's normal rerendering lifecycle. For example, if you use `window.setTimeout()` in an event handler to execute some logic after a time delay, wrap your code in `$A.getCallback()`. You don't need to use `$A.getCallback()` if your code is executed as part of the framework's call stack; for example, your code is handling an event or in the callback for a server-side controller action.

Action States

The possible action states are:

NEW
The action was created but is not in progress yet

RUNNING
The action is in progress

SUCCESS
The action executed successfully

ERROR
The server returned an error

INCOMPLETE

The server didn't return a response. The server might be down or the client might be offline. The framework guarantees that an action's callback is always invoked as long as the component is valid. If the socket to the server is never successfully opened, or closes abruptly, or any other network error occurs, the XHR resolves and the callback is invoked with state equal to INCOMPLETE.

ABORTED

The action was aborted

 Note: setCallback() has a third parameter that registers the action state that invokes the callback. If you don't specify the third argument for setCallback(), it defaults to registering the SUCCESS and ERROR states. To set a callback for another state, such as ABORTED, you can call setCallback() multiple times with the action state set explicitly in the third argument. For example:

```
action.setCallback(this, function(response) { ...}, "ABORTED");
```

SEE ALSO:

Handling Events with Client-Side Controllers

Queueing of Server-Side Actions

Queueing of Server-Side Actions

The framework queues up actions before sending them to the server. This mechanism is largely transparent to you when you're writing code but it enables the framework to minimize network traffic by batching multiple actions into one request.

Event processing can generate a tree of events if an event handler fires more events. The framework processes the event tree and adds every action that needs to be executed on the server to a queue.

When the tree of events and all the client-side actions are processed, the framework batches actions from the queue into a message before sending it to the server. A message is essentially a wrapper around a list of actions.

Tip: If your action is not executing, make sure that you're not executing code outside the framework's normal rerendering lifecycle. For example, if you use window.setTimeout() in an event handler to execute some logic after a time delay, wrap your code in $A.getCallback().

SEE ALSO:

Modifying Components Outside the Framework Lifecycle

Abortable Actions

Mark an action as abortable to make it potentially abortable while it's queued to be sent to the server. An abortable action in the queue is not sent to the server if the component that created the action is no longer valid, that is `cmp.isValid() == false`. A component is automatically destroyed and marked invalid by the framework when it is unrendered.

 Note: We recommend that you only use abortable actions for read-only operations as they are not guaranteed to be sent to the server.

An abortable action is sent to the server and executed normally unless the component that created the action is invalid before the action is sent to the server. If the component that created the action is invalid, the action state is set to `ABORTED`.

A non-abortable action is always sent to the server and can't be aborted in the queue.

If an action response returns from the server and the associated component is now invalid, the logic has been executed on the server but the action state is set to `ABORTED`. This is true whether or not the action is marked as abortable. If the action state is set to `ABORTED`, only the callback logic associated with the `ABORTED` state (`action.getState() === "ABORTED"`) will be executed. This enables components to optionally log a message or clean up if they had an aborted action.

Marking an Action as Abortable

Mark a server-side action as abortable by using the `setAbortable()` method on the `Action` object in JavaScript. For example:

```
var action = cmp.get("c.serverEcho");
action.setAbortable();
```

`setCallback()` has a third parameter that registers the action state that invokes the callback. If you don't specify the third argument for `setCallback()`, it defaults to registering the `SUCCESS` and `ERROR` states. To check for aborted actions in your callback and take appropriate action, such as logging the aborted action, call `setCallback()` with the `ABORTED` state set explicitly in the third argument. For example:

```
// Process default action states
action.setCallback(this, function(response) {
    var state = response.getState();
    if (state === "SUCCESS") {
        // Alert the user with the value returned from the server
        alert("From server: " + response.getReturnValue());
    }
```

```
        // process other action states
    });
    // Explicitly register callback for ABORTED
    action.setCallback(this,
        function(response) {
            alert("The action was aborted");
        },
        "ABORTED"
    );
```

Rapid Clicking

Imagine a navigation menu where each action is a potentially slow request to the server. A user may click on several navigation items quickly so that none of the server responses return before the subsequent click. If all the actions are marked as abortable, none of the callbacks will be called except for the last click. This improves user experience by avoiding flickering due to sequential rendering of multiple server responses.

SEE ALSO:

Creating Server-Side Logic with Controllers

Queueing of Server-Side Actions

Calling a Server-Side Action

Storable Actions

Mark an action as storable to have its response stored in the client-side cache by the framework. Caching can be useful if you want your app to be functional for devices that temporarily don't have a network connection.

⚠ Warning: A storable action might result in no call to the server. Never mark as storable an action that updates or deletes data.

Successful actions, for which `getState()` in the JavaScript callback returns `SUCCESS`, are stored.

If a storable action is aborted after it's been sent but not yet returned from the server, its return value is still added to storage but the action callback is not called.

The action response of a storable action is saved in an internal framework-provided storage named `actions`. This stored response is returned on subsequent calls to the same server-side action instead of the response from the server-side controller, as long as the stored response hasn't expired.

If the stored response has reached its expiration time, a new response is retrieved from the server-side controller and is stored in the `actions` storage for subsequent calls.

Marking Storable Actions

To mark a server-side action as storable, call `setStorable()` on the action in JavaScript code, as follows.

```
a.setStorable();
```

Note: Storable actions are always implicitly marked as abortable too.

The `setStorable` function takes an optional parameter, which is a configuration map of key-value pairs representing the storage options and values to set. You can only set the following property:

ignoreExisting
   Set to `true` to refresh the stored item with a newly retrieved value, regardless of whether the item has expired or not. The default value is `false`.

To set the storage options for the action response, pass this configuration map into `setStorable`.

Refreshing an Action Response for Every Request

If a storable action returns dynamic content from the server, set the refresh interval to `0` to ensure that the data is refreshed from the server. If an action response is already cached, the cached response is displayed while the server roundtrip is happening.

To ignore existing stored responses, set:

```
a.setStorable({
    "ignoreExisting": "true"
});
```

Example

This example shows how to use `setStorable()` to store the server-side action response in a client-side cache. The markup includes a button that triggers the `runActionAtServerAndStore` client-side controller action. This client-side action calls a `fetchDataRecord` server-side action. Next, the action is marked as storable and is run. The server-side action return value is obtained in the callback.

This component markup initializes the actions storage and contains a button.

```
<aura:component render="client" extensible="true"
```

```
controller="java://org.auraframework.impl.java.controller.AuraStorageTestController"

 implements="auraStorage:refreshObserver">

    <auraStorage:init debugLoggingEnabled="true"
                      name="actions"
                      secure="true"
                      persistent="false"
                      clearStorageOnInit="true"
                      defaultExpiration="50"
                      defaultAutoRefreshInterval="60" />

    <ui:button label="Run action at Server and mark as storable"
      press="{!c.runActionAtServerAndStore}"
      aura:id="ForceActionAtServer"/>

</aura:component>
```

Here is the action in the component's JavaScript client-side controller.

```
runActionAtServerAndStore:function(cmp, evt, helper){
    // Get server-side action
    var action = cmp.get("c.fetchDataRecord");

    action.setCallback(cmp, function(response){
        var returnValue = response.getReturnValue();
    });

    // Set server-side action as storable
    action.setStorable();

    // Run server-side action
    $A.enqueueAction(action);
},
```

Creating Components

The `Cmp.<myNamespace>.<myComponent>` syntax to reference a component in Apex is deprecated. Use `$A.createComponent()` in client-side JavaScript code instead.

SEE ALSO:

Dynamically Creating Components

Working with Salesforce Records

It's easy to work with your Salesforce records in Apex.

The term sObject refers to any object that can be stored in Force.com. This could be a standard object, such as Account, or a custom object that you create, such as a Merchandise object.

An sObject variable represents a row of data, also known as a record. To work with an object in Apex, declare it using the SOAP API name of the object. For example:

```
Account a = new Account();
MyCustomObject__c co = new MyCustomObject__c();
```

For more information on working on records with Apex, see Working with Data in Apex.

This example controller persists an updated Account record. Note that the update method has the @AuraEnabled annotation, which enables it to be called as a server-side controller action.

```
public with sharing class AccountController {

    @AuraEnabled
    public static void updateAnnualRevenue(String accountId, Decimal
annualRevenue) {
        Account acct = [SELECT Id, Name, BillingCity FROM Account WHERE
 Id = :accountId];
        acct.AnnualRevenue = annualRevenue;

        // Perform isAccessible() and isUpdateable() checks here
        update acct;
    }
}
```

For an example of calling Apex code from JavaScript code, see the Quick Start on page 7.

Loading Record Data from a Standard Object

Load records from a standard object in a server-side controller. The following server-side controller has methods that return a list of opportunity records and an individual opportunity record.

```
public with sharing class OpportunityController {

    @AuraEnabled
    public static List<Opportunity> getOpportunities() {
        List<Opportunity> opportunities =
                [SELECT Id, Name, CloseDate FROM Opportunity];
```

```
        return opportunities;
    }

    @AuraEnabled
    public static Opportunity getOpportunity(Id id) {
        Opportunity opportunity = [
                SELECT Id, Account.Name, Name, CloseDate,
                        Owner.Name, Amount, Description, StageName
            FROM Opportunity
            WHERE Id = :id
        ];

        // Perform isAccessible() check here
        return opportunity;
    }
}
```

This example component uses the previous server-side controller to display a list of opportunity records when you press a button.

```
<aura:component controller="OpportunityController">
    <aura:attribute name="opportunities" type="Opportunity[]"/>

    <ui:button label="Get Opportunities" press="{!c.getOpps}"/>
    <aura:iteration var="opportunity" items="{!v.opportunities}">
     <p>{!opportunity.Name} : {!opportunity.CloseDate}</p>
    </aura:iteration>
</aura:component>
```

When you press the button, the following client-side controller calls the `getOpportunities()` server-side controller and sets the `opportunities` attribute on the component. For more information about calling server-side controller methods, see Calling a Server-Side Action on page 285.

```
({
    getOpps: function(cmp){
        var action = cmp.get("c.getOpportunities");
        action.setCallback(this, function(response){
            var state = response.getState();
            if (state === "SUCCESS") {
                cmp.set("v.opportunities", response.getReturnValue());


            }
        });
    $A.enqueueAction(action);
```

```
    }
})
```

📝 Note: To load record data during component initialization, use the `init` handler.

Loading Record Data from a Custom Object

Load record data using an Apex controller and setting the data on a component attribute. This server-side controller returns records on a custom object `myObj__c`.

```
public with sharing class MyObjController {

    @AuraEnabled
    public static List<MyObj__c> getMyObjects() {

        // Perform isAccessible() checks here
        return [SELECT Id, Name, myField__c FROM MyObj__c];
    }
}
```

This example component uses the previous controller to display a list of records from the `myObj__c` custom object.

```
<aura:component controller="MyObjController"/>
<aura:attribute name="myObjects" type="namespace.MyObj__c[]"/>
<aura:iteration items="{!v.myObjects}" var="obj">
    {!obj.Name}, {!obj.namespace__myField__c}
</aura:iteration>
```

This client-side controller sets the `myObjects` component attribute with the record data by calling the `getMyObjects()` method in the server-side controller. This step can also be done during component initialization using the `init` handler.

```
getMyObjects: function(cmp){
    var action = cmp.get("c.getMyObjects");
    action.setCallback(this, function(response){
        var state = response.getState();
        if (state === "SUCCESS") {
            cmp.set("v.myObjects", response.getReturnValue());
        }
    });
    $A.enqueueAction(action);
}
```

For an example on loading and updating records using controllers, see the Quick Start on page 7.

IN THIS SECTION:

CRUD and Field-Level Security (FLS)

In addition to the Content Security Policy, Lightning Components imposes CRUD and field-level security to ensure component security.

Saving Records

You can take advantage of the built-in create and edit record pages in Salesforce1 to create or edit records via a Lightning component.

Deleting Records

You can delete records via a Lightning component to remove them from both the view and database.

SEE ALSO:

CRUD and Field-Level Security (FLS)

CRUD and Field-Level Security (FLS)

In addition to the Content Security Policy, Lightning Components imposes CRUD and field-level security to ensure component security.

Lightning components don't automatically enforce CRUD and FLS when you reference objects or retrieve the objects from an Apex controller. This means that the framework continues to display records and fields for which users don't have CRUD access and FLS visibility. You must manually enforce CRUD and FLS in your Apex controllers. For example, including the `with sharing` keyword in an Apex controller ensures that users see only the records they have access to in a Lightning component. Additionally, you must explicitly check for `isAccessible()`, `isCreateable()`, `isDeletable()`, and `isUpdateable()` prior to performing operations on records or objects.

This example shows the recommended way to perform an operation on a custom expense object.

```
public with sharing class ExpenseController {

    // ns refers to namespace; leave out ns__ if not needed
    // This method is vulnerable.
    @AuraEnabled
    public static List<ns__Expense__c> get_UNSAFE_Expenses() {
        return [SELECT Id, Name, ns__Amount__c, ns__Client__c,
ns__Date__c,
            ns__Reimbursed__c, CreatedDate FROM ns__Expense__c];
```

```
    }

    // This method is recommended.
    @AuraEnabled
    public static List<ns__Expense__c> getExpenses() {
        String [] expenseAccessFields = new String [] {'Id',
                                                       'Name',
                                                       'ns__Amount__c',

                                                       'ns__Client__c',

                                                       'ns__Date__c',

'ns__Reimbursed__c',
                                                       'CreatedDate'
                                                       };


    // Obtain the field name/token map for the Expense object
    Map<String,Schema.SObjectField> m =
Schema.SObjectType.ns__Expense__c.fields.getMap();

    for (String fieldToCheck : expenseAccessFields) {

        // Check if the user has access to view field
        if (!m.get(fieldToCheck).getDescribe().isAccessible()) {

            // Pass error to client
            throw new System.NoAccessException()

            // Suppress editor logs
            return null;
        }
    }

    // Query the object safely
    return [SELECT Id, Name, ns__Amount__c, ns__Client__c, ns__Date__c,

           ns__Reimbursed__c, CreatedDate FROM ns__Expense__c];


    }
}
```

Note: For more information, see the articles on Enforcing CRUD and FLS and Lightning Security.

Saving Records

You can take advantage of the built-in create and edit record pages in Salesforce1 to create or edit records via a Lightning component.

The following component contains a button that calls a client-side controller to display the edit record page.

```
<aura:component>
    <ui:button label="Edit Record" press="{!c.edit}"/>
</aura:component>
```

The client-side controller fires the force:recordEdit event, which displays the edit record page for a given contact ID. For this event to be handled correctly, the component must be included in Salesforce1.

```
edit : function(component, event, helper) {
    var editRecordEvent = $A.get("e.force:editRecord");
    editRecordEvent.setParams({
        "recordId": component.get("v.contact.Id")
    });
    editRecordEvent.fire();
}
```

Records updated using the force:recordEdit event are persisted by default.

Saving Records using a Lightning Component

Alternatively, you might have a Lightning component that provides a custom form for users to add a record. To save the new record, wire up a client-side controller to an Apex controller. The following list shows how you can persist a record via a component and Apex controller.

 Note: If you create a custom form to handle record updates, you must provide your own field validation.

Create an Apex controller to save your updates with the upsert operation. The following example is an Apex controller for upserting record data.

```
@AuraEnabled
public static Expense__c saveExpense(Expense__c expense) {
    // Perform isUpdateable() check here
    upsert expense;
```

```
        return expense;
}
```

Call a client-side controller from your component. For example, `<ui:button label="Submit" press="{!c.createExpense}"/>`.

In your client-side controller, provide any field validation and pass the record data to a helper function.

```
createExpense : function(component, event, helper) {
    // Validate form fields
    // Pass form data to a helper function
    var newExpense = component.get("v.newExpense");
    helper.createExpense(component, newExpense);
}
```

In your component helper, get an instance of the server-side controller and set a callback. The following example upserts a record on a custom object. Recall that `setParams()` sets the value of the `expense` argument on the server-side controller's `saveExpense()` method.

```
createExpense: function(component, expense) {
    //Save the expense and update the view
    this.upsertExpense(component, expense, function(a) {
        var expenses = component.get("v.expenses");
        expenses.push(a.getReturnValue());
        component.set("v.expenses", expenses);
    });
},
upsertExpense : function(component, expense, callback) {
  var action = component.get("c.saveExpense");
  action.setParams({
      "expense": expense
  });
  if (callback) {
      action.setCallback(this, callback);
  }
  $A.enqueueAction(action);
}
```

SEE ALSO:

CRUD and Field-Level Security (FLS)

Deleting Records

You can delete records via a Lightning component to remove them from both the view and database.

Create an Apex controller to delete a specified record with the `delete` operation. The following Apex controller deletes an expense object record.

```
@AuraEnabled
public static Expense__c deleteExpense(Expense__c expense) {
    // Perform isDeletable() check here
    delete expense;
    return expense;
}
```

Depending on how your components are set up, you might need to create an event to tell another component that a record has been deleted. For example, you have a component that contains a sub-component that is iterated over to display the records. Your sub-component contains a button (1), which when pressed fires an event that's handled by the container component (2), which deletes the record that's clicked on.

```
<aura:registerEvent name="deleteExpenseItem"
type="c:deleteExpenseItem"/>
<ui:button label="Delete" press="{!c.delete}"/>
```

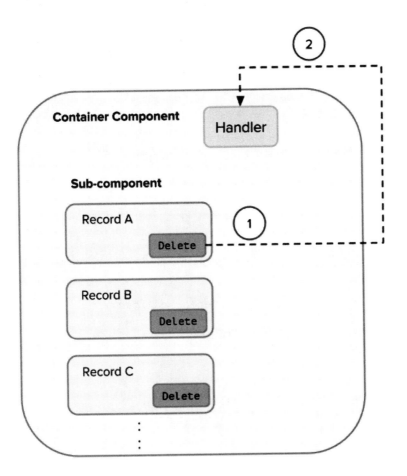

Create a component event to capture and pass the record that's to be deleted. Name the event `deleteExpenseItem`.

```
<aura:event type="COMPONENT">
    <aura:attribute name="expense" type="Expense__c"/>
</aura:event>
```

Then, pass in the record to be deleted and fire the event in your client-side controller.

```
delete : function(component, evt, helper) {
    var expense = component.get("v.expense");
    var deleteEvent = component.getEvent("deleteExpenseItem");
    deleteEvent.setParams({ "expense": expense }).fire();
}
```

In the container component, include a handler for the event. In this example, `c:expenseList` is the sub-component that displays records.

```
<aura:handler name="deleteExpenseItem" event="c:deleteExpenseItem"
action="c:deleteEvent"/>
<aura:iteration items="{!v.expenses}" var="expense">
    <c:expenseList expense="{!expense}"/>
</aura:iteration>
```

And handle the event in the client-side controller of the container component.

```
deleteEvent : function(component, event, helper) {
    // Call the helper function to delete record and update view
    helper.deleteExpense(component, event.getParam("expense"));
}
```

Finally, in the helper function of the container component, call your Apex controller to delete the record and update the view.

```
deleteExpense : function(component, expense, callback) {
    // Call the Apex controller and update the view in the callback
    var action = component.get("c.deleteExpense");
    action.setParams({
        "expense": expense
    });
    action.setCallback(this, function(response) {
        var state = response.getState();
        if (state === "SUCCESS") {
            // Remove only the deleted expense from view
            var expenses = component.get("v.expenses");
            var items = [];
            for (i = 0; i < expenses.length; i++) {
                if(expenses[i]!==expense) {
                    items.push(expenses[i]);
                }
            }
            component.set("v.expenses", items);
            // Other client-side logic
        }
    });
    $A.enqueueAction(action);
}
```

The helper function calls the Apex controller to delete the record in the database. In the callback function, `component.set("v.expenses", items)` updates the view with the updated array of records.

SEE ALSO:

CRUD and Field-Level Security (FLS)

Create a Standalone Lightning App

Component Events

Calling a Server-Side Action

Testing Your Apex Code

Before you can upload a managed package, you must write and execute tests for your Apex code to meet minimum code coverage requirements. Also, all tests must run without errors when you upload your package to AppExchange.

To package your application and components that depend on Apex code, the following must be true.

- At least 75% of your Apex code must be covered by unit tests, and all of those tests must complete successfully.

  Note the following.

  - When deploying Apex to a production organization, each unit test in your organization namespace is executed by default.
  - Calls to `System.debug` are not counted as part of Apex code coverage.
  - Test methods and test classes are not counted as part of Apex code coverage.
  - While only 75% of your Apex code must be covered by tests, your focus shouldn't be on the percentage of code that is covered. Instead, you should make sure that every use case of your application is covered, including positive and negative cases, as well as bulk and single records. This should lead to 75% or more of your code being covered by unit tests.

- Every trigger must have some test coverage.

- All classes and triggers must compile successfully.

This sample shows an Apex test class that is used with the controller class in the expense tracker app available at Create a Standalone Lightning App on page 9.

```
@isTest
class TestExpenseController {
    static testMethod void test() {
        //Create new expense and insert it into the database
```

```
        Expense__c exp = new Expense__c(name='My New Expense',
                          amount__c=20, client__c='ABC',
                          reimbursed__c=false, date__c=null);
        ExpenseController.saveExpense(exp);

        //Assert the name field and saved expense
        System.assertEquals('My New Expense',
                        ExpenseController.getExpenses()[0].Name,
                        'Name does not match');
        System.assertEquals(exp, ExpenseController.saveExpense(exp));

    }
}
```

📝 Note: Apex classes must be manually added to your package.

For more information on distributing Apex code, see the *Apex Code Developer's Guide*.

SEE ALSO:

Distributing Applications and Components

Making API Calls from Apex

Make API calls from an Apex controller. You can't make API calls from JavaScript code.

For information about making API calls from Apex, see the *Force.com Apex Code Developer's Guide*.

Controlling Access

The framework enables you to control access to your applications, attributes, components, events, interfaces, and methods via the `access` system attribute. The `access` system attribute indicates whether the resource can be used outside of its own namespace.

Use the `access` system attribute on these tags:

- `<aura:application>`
- `<aura:attribute>`
- `<aura:component>`
- `<aura:event>`
- `<aura:interface>`

- `<aura:method>`

Access Values

You can specify these values for the `access` system attribute.

private
> Available within the component, app, interface, or event and can't be referenced externally. This value can only be used for `aura:attribute`.

public
> Available within the same namespace. This is the default access value.

global
> Available in all namespaces.

> Note: Mark your resources, such as a component, with `access="global"` to make the resource usable outside of your own org; for example, if you want a component to be usable in an installed package or by a Lightning App Builder user or a Community Builder user in another org.

Example

This sample component has global access.

```
<aura:component access="global">
    ...
</aura:component>
```

Access Violations

If your code accesses a resource, such as a component or attribute, that doesn't have an `access` system attribute allowing you to access it, the code doesn't execute or returns `undefined`. You also see an error message in your browser console if you enabled debug mode. Access check enforcement is a critical update in this release. If you don't update it, you continue to see warning messages in the browser console instead of errors.

> Note: Access check failures for `<aura:event>` and `<aura:method>` aren't enforced yet. They show up as warnings in your browser console if you've enabled debug mode. The framework will enforce the `<aura:event>` and `<aura:method>` access checks more strictly in a later release so you shouldn't ignore them.

Anatomy of an Access Check Error Message

This is a sample access check error message for an access violation.

```
Access  Check  Failed !
ComponentService.getDef():'markup://c:targetComponent' is not visible
 to 'undefined'.
```

An error message has four parts:

1. The context (who is trying to access the resource). In our example, this is `undefined`.

2. The target (the resource being accessed). In our example, this is
   `markup://c:targetComponent`.

3. The type of failure. In our example, this is `not visible`.

4. The code that triggered the failure. This is usually a class method. In our example, this is
   `ComponentService.getDef()`, which means that the target definition (component) was
   not accessible. A definition describes metadata for a resource, such as a component.

Fixing Access Check Errors

You can fix access check errors using one or more of these techniques.

- Add appropriate `access` system attributes to the resources that you own.

- Remove references in your code to resources that aren't available.

- Ensure that the attribute that you're accessing exists and you're using the correct case-sensitive spelling.

  Accessing an undefined attribute or a private attribute triggers the same access violation message
  because the access context doesn't know whether the attribute is undefined or private.

- Use `$A.getCallback()` to wrap code that accesses a component outside the normal rerendering
  lifecycle, such as in a `setTimeout()` or `setInterval()` call or in an ES6 Promise.

  `$A.getCallback()` preserves the current execution context and grants the correct access level
  to the asynchronous code. Otherwise, the framework loses context and allows access only to global
  resources.

Activate the Critical Update

We recommend that you test this update in a sandbox or Developer Edition org to verify correct behavior
before enabling it in your production org.

To activate this critical update:

1. From Setup, enter *Critical Updates* in the Quick Find box, and then select **Critical Updates**.

2. For "Enforce Lightning Components Access Checks", click **Activate**.

IN THIS SECTION:

Application Access Control

The `access` attribute on the `aura:application` tag controls whether the app can be used outside of the app's namespace.

Interface Access Control

The `access` attribute on the `aura:interface` tag controls whether the interface can be used outside of the interface's namespace.

Component Access Control

The `access` attribute on the `aura:component` tag controls whether the component can be used outside of the component's namespace.

Attribute Access Control

The `access` attribute on the `aura:attribute` tag controls whether the attribute can be used outside of the attribute's namespace.

Event Access Control

The `access` attribute on the `aura:event` tag controls whether the event can be used outside of the event's namespace.

SEE ALSO:

Enable Debug Mode for Lightning Components

Application Access Control

The `access` attribute on the `aura:application` tag controls whether the app can be used outside of the app's namespace.

Possible values are listed below.

Modifier	Description
`public`	Available within the same namespace. This is the default access value.
`global`	Available in all namespaces.

Interface Access Control

The `access` attribute on the `aura:interface` tag controls whether the interface can be used outside of the interface's namespace.

Possible values are listed below.

Modifier	Description
public	Available within the same namespace. This is the default access value.
global	Available in all namespaces.

A component can implement an interface using the `implements` attribute on the `aura:component` tag.

Component Access Control

The `access` attribute on the `aura:component` tag controls whether the component can be used outside of the component's namespace.

Possible values are listed below.

Modifier	Description
public	Available within the same namespace. This is the default access value.
global	Available in all namespaces.

Note: Components aren't directly addressable via a URL. To check your component output, embed your component in a `.app` resource.

Attribute Access Control

The `access` attribute on the `aura:attribute` tag controls whether the attribute can be used outside of the attribute's namespace.

Possible values are listed below.

Access	Description
private	Available within the component, app, interface, or event and can't be referenced externally.
	Note: Accessing a private attribute returns undefined unless you reference it from the component in which it's declared. You can't access a private attribute from a sub-component that extends the component containing the private attribute.
public	Available within the same namespace. This is the default access value.
global	Available in all namespaces.

Event Access Control

The access attribute on the aura:event tag controls whether the event can be used outside of the event's namespace.

Possible values are listed below.

Modifier	Description
public	Available within the same namespace. This is the default access value.
global	Available in all namespaces.

Using Object-Oriented Development

The framework provides the basic constructs of inheritance and encapsulation from object-oriented programming and applies them to presentation layer development.

For example, components are encapsulated and their internals stay private. Consumers of the component can access the public shape (attributes and registered events) of the component, but can't access other implementation details in the component bundle. This strong separation gives component authors freedom to change the internal implementation details and insulates component consumers from those changes.

You can extend a component, app, or interface, or you can implement a component interface.

What is Inherited?

This topic lists what is inherited when you extend a definition, such as a component.

When a component contains another component, we refer in the documentation to parent and child components in the containment hierarchy. When a component extends another component, we refer to sub and super components in the inheritance hierarchy.

Component Attributes

A sub component that extends a super component inherits the attributes of the super component. Use `<aura:set>` in the markup of a sub component to set the value of an attribute inherited from a super component.

Events

A sub component that extends a super component can handle events fired by the super component. The sub component automatically inherits the event handlers from the super component.

The super and sub component can handle the same event in different ways by adding an `<aura:handler>` tag to the sub component. The framework doesn't guarantee the order of event handling.

Helpers

A sub component's helper inherits the methods from the helper of its super component. A sub component can override a super component's helper method by defining a method with the same name as an inherited method.

Controllers

A sub component that extends a super component can call actions in the super component's client-side controller. For example, if the super component has an action called `doSomething`, the sub component can directly call the action using the `{!c.doSomething}` syntax.

> ✏️ Note: We don't recommend using inheritance of client-side controllers as this feature may be deprecated in the future to preserve better component encapsulation. We recommend that you put common code in a helper instead.

SEE ALSO:

Component Attributes

Communicating with Events

Sharing JavaScript Code in a Component Bundle

Handling Events with Client-Side Controllers

aura:set

Inherited Component Attributes

A sub component that extends a super component inherits the attributes of the super component.

Attribute values are identical at any level of extension. There is an exception to this rule for the body attribute, which we'll look at more closely soon.

Let's start with a simple example. c:super has a description attribute with a value of "Default description",

```
<!--c:super-->
<aura:component extensible="true">
    <aura:attribute name="description" type="String" default="Default
 description" />

    <p>super.cmp description: {!v.description}</p>

    {!v.body}
</aura:component>
```

Don't worry about the {!v.body} expression for now. We'll explain that when we talk about the body attribute.

c:sub extends c:super by setting extends="c:super" in its <aura:component> tag.

```
<!--c:sub-->
<aura:component extends="c:super">
    <p>sub.cmp description: {!v.description}</p>
</aura:component
```

Note that `sub.cmp` has access to the inherited `description` attribute and it has the same value in `sub.cmp` and `super.cmp`.

Use `<aura:set>` in the markup of a sub component to set the value of an inherited attribute.

Inherited **body** Attribute

Every component inherits the `body` attribute from `<aura:component>`. The inheritance behavior of `body` is different than other attributes. It can have different values at each level of component extension to enable different output from each component in the inheritance chain. This will be clearer when we look at an example.

Any free markup that is not enclosed in another tag is assumed to be part of the `body`. It's equivalent to wrapping that free markup inside `<aura:set attribute="body">`.

The default renderer for a component iterates through its `body` attribute, renders everything, and passes the rendered data to its super component. The super component can output the data passed to it by including `{!v.body}` in its markup. If there is no super component, you've hit the root component and the data is inserted into `document.body`.

Let's look at a simple example to understand how the `body` attribute behaves at different levels of component extension. We have three components.

`c:superBody` is the super component. It inherently extends `<aura:component>`.

```
<!--c:superBody-->
<aura:component extensible="true">
    Parent body: {!v.body}
</aura:component>
```

At this point, `c:superBody` doesn't output anything for `{!v.body}` as it's just a placeholder for data that will be passed in by a component that extends `c:superBody`.

`c:subBody` extends `c:superBody` by setting `extends="c:superBody"` in its `<aura:component>` tag.

```
<!--c:subBody-->
<aura:component extends="c:superBody">
    Child body: {!v.body}
</aura:component>
```

`c:subBody` outputs:

```
Parent body: Child body:
```

In other words, `c:subBody` sets the value for `{!v.body}` in its super component, `c:superBody`.

`c:containerBody` contains a reference to `c:subBody`.

```
<!--c:containerBody-->
<aura:component>
    <c:subBody>
        Body value
    </c:subBody>
</aura:component>
```

In `c:containerBody`, we set the `body` attribute of `c:subBody` to Body value.
`c:containerBody` outputs:

```
Parent body: Child body: Body value
```

SEE ALSO:

aura:set

Component Body

Component Markup

Abstract Components

Object-oriented languages, such as Java, support the concept of an abstract class that provides a partial implementation for an object but leaves the remaining implementation to concrete sub-classes. An abstract class in Java can't be instantiated directly, but a non-abstract subclass can.

Similarly, the Lightning Component framework supports the concept of abstract components that have a partial implementation but leave the remaining implementation to concrete sub-components.

To use an abstract component, you must extend it and fill out the remaining implementation. An abstract component can't be used directly in markup.

The `<aura:component>` tag has a boolean `abstract` attribute. Set `abstract="true"` to make the component abstract.

SEE ALSO:

Interfaces

313

Interfaces

Object-oriented languages, such as Java, support the concept of an interface that defines a set of method signatures. A class that implements the interface must provide the method implementations. An interface in Java can't be instantiated directly, but a class that implements the interface can.

Similarly, the Lightning Component framework supports the concept of interfaces that define a component's shape by defining its attributes.

An interface starts with the `<aura:interface>` tag. It can only contain these tags:

* `<aura:attribute>` tags to define the interface's attributes.
* `<aura:registerEvent>` tags to define the events that it may fire.

You can't use markup, renderers, controllers, or anything else in an interface.

To use an interface, you must implement it. An interface can't be used directly in markup otherwise. Set the `implements` system attribute in the `<aura:component>` tag to the name of the interface that you are implementing. For example:

```
<aura:component implements="mynamespace:myinterface" >
```

A component can implement an interface and extend another component.

```
<aura:component extends="ns1:cmp1" implements="ns2:intf1" >
```

An interface can extend multiple interfaces using a comma-separated list.

```
<aura:interface extends="ns:intf1,ns:int2" >
```

 Note: Use `<aura:set>` in a sub component to set the value of any attribute that is inherited from the super component. This usage works for components and abstract components, but it doesn't work for interfaces. To set the value of an attribute inherited from an interface, redefine the attribute in the sub component using `<aura:attribute>` and set the value in its default attribute.

Since there are fewer restrictions on the content of abstract components, they are more common than interfaces. A component can implement multiple interfaces but can only extend one abstract component, so interfaces can be more useful for some design patterns.

SEE ALSO:

Setting Attributes Inherited from an Interface

Abstract Components

Marker Interfaces

You can use an interface as a marker interface that is implemented by a set of components that you want to easily identify for specific usage in your app.

In JavaScript, you can determine if a component implements an interface by using `myCmp.isInstanceOf("mynamespace:myinterface")`.

Inheritance Rules

This table describes the inheritance rules for various elements.

Element	extends	implements	Default Base Element
component	one extensible component	multiple interfaces	`<aura:component>`
app	one extensible app	N/A	`<aura:application>`
interface	multiple interfaces using a comma-separated list (extends="ns:intf1,ns:int2")	N/A	N/A

SEE ALSO:

Interfaces

Caching with Storage Service

The Storage Service provides a powerful, simple-to-use caching infrastructure that enhances the user experience on the client. Client applications can benefit from caching data to reduce response times of pages by storing and accessing data locally rather than requesting data from the server. Caching is especially beneficial for high-performance, mostly connected applications operating over high latency connections, such as 3G networks.

The advantage of using the Storage Service instead of other caching infrastructures, such as Apple local storage for iOS devices, is that the Storage Service offers several types of storage through adapters. Storage can be persistent and secure. With persistent storage, cached data is preserved between user sessions in the browser. With secure storage, cached data is encrypted.

Storage Adapter Name	Persistent	Secure
SmartStore	true	true
IndexedDB	true	false
MemoryAdapter	false	true

SmartStore

(Persistent and secure) Provides a caching service that is only available for apps built with the Salesforce Mobile SDK. The Salesforce Mobile SDK enables developing mobile applications that integrate with Salesforce. You can use SmartStore with these mobile applications for caching data.

IndexedDB

(Persistent but not secure) Provides access to an API for client-side storage and search of structured data. For more information, see the Indexed Database API.

MemoryAdapter

(Not persistent but secure) Provides access to the JavaScript main memory space for caching data. The stored cache persists only per browser page. Browsing to a new page resets the cache.

The Storage Service selects a storage adapter on your behalf that matches the persistent and secure options you specify when initializing the service. For example, if you request a persistent and insecure storage service, the Storage Service returns the IndexedDB storage.

When you initialize storage, you can set certain options, such as the name, maximum cache size, and the default expiration time.

Server-side actions storage is the only currently supported type of storage. Storage for server-side actions caches action response values. The storage name must be `actions`.

SEE ALSO:

Creating Server-Side Logic with Controllers

Storable Actions

Initializing Storage Service

Initializing Storage Service

Initialize storage in your app's template for caching server-side action response values.

Initialize in Markup

This example uses a template to initialize storage for server-side action response values. The template contains an `<auraStorage:init>` tag that specifies storage initialization properties.

```
<aura:component isTemplate="true" extends="aura:template">
    <aura:set attribute="auraPreInitBlock">
        <!-- Note that the maxSize attribute in <auraStorage:init> is
 in KB -->
        <auraStorage:init name="actions" persistent="false"
secure="false"
            maxSize="1024" version="1.0"/>
    </aura:set>
</aura:component>
```

When you initialize storage, you can set certain options, such as the name, maximum cache size, and the default expiration time.

Server-side actions storage is the only currently supported type of storage. Storage for server-side actions caches action response values. The storage name must be `actions`.

The expiration time for an item in storage specifies the duration after which an item should be replaced with a fresh copy. The refresh interval takes effect only if the item hasn't expired yet and applies to the actions storage only. In that case, if the refresh interval for an item has passed, the item gets refreshed after the same action is called. If stored items have reached their expiration times or have exceeded their refresh intervals, they're replaced only after a call is made to access them and if the client is online.

SEE ALSO:

Storable Actions

Using the AppCache

Application cache (AppCache) speeds up app response time and reduces server load by only downloading resources that have changed. It improves page loads affected by limited browser cache persistence on some devices.

AppCache can be useful if you're developing apps for mobile devices, which sometimes have very limited browser cache. Apps built for desktop clients may not benefit from the AppCache. The framework supports AppCache for WebKit-based browsers, such as Chrome and Safari.

 Note: See an introduction to AppCache for more information.

IN THIS SECTION:

Enabling the AppCache

The framework disables the use of AppCache by default.

Loading Resources with AppCache

A cache manifest file is a simple text file that defines the Web resources to be cached offline in the AppCache.

SEE ALSO:

aura:application

Enabling the AppCache

The framework disables the use of AppCache by default.

To enable AppCache in your application, set the `useAppcache="true"` system attribute in the `aura:application` tag. We recommend disabling AppCache during initial development while your app's resources are still changing. Enable AppCache when you are finished developing the app and before you start using it in production to see whether AppCache improves the app's response time.

Loading Resources with AppCache

A cache manifest file is a simple text file that defines the Web resources to be cached offline in the AppCache.

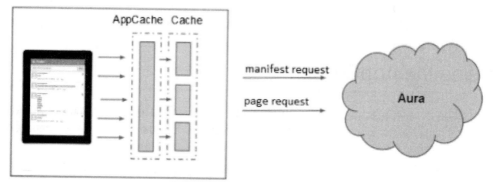

The cache manifest is auto-generated for you at runtime if you have enabled AppCache in your application. If there are any changes to the resources, the framework updates the timestamp to trigger a refetch of all resources. Fetching resources only when necessary reduces server trips for users.

When a browser initially requests an app, a link to the manifest file is included in the response.

```
<html manifest="/path/to/app.manifest">
```

The manifest path includes the mode and app name of the app that's currently running. This manifest file lists framework resources as well as your JavaScript code and CSS, which are cached after they're downloaded for the first time. A hash in the URL ensures that you always have the latest resources.

 Note: You'll see different resources depending on which mode you're running in. For example, `aura_prod.js` is available in `PROD` mode and `aura_proddebug.js` is available in `PRODDEBUG` mode.

Distributing Applications and Components

As an ISV or Salesforce partner, you can package and distribute applications and components to other Salesforce users and organizations, including those outside your company.

Publish applications and components to and install them from AppExchange. When adding an application or component to a package, all definition bundles referenced by the application or component are automatically included, such as other components, events, and interfaces. Custom fields, custom objects, list views, page layouts, and Apex classes referenced by the application or component are also included. However, when you add a custom object to a package, the application and other definition bundles that reference that custom object must be explicitly added to the package.

A managed package ensures that your application and other resources are fully upgradeable. To create and work with managed packages, you must use a Developer Edition organization and register a namespace prefix. A managed package includes your namespace prefix in the component names and prevents naming conflicts in an installer's organization. An organization can create a single managed package that can be downloaded and installed by other organizations. After installation from a managed package, the application or component names are locked, but the following attributes are editable.

- API Version
- Description
- Label
- Language
- Markup

Any Apex that is included as part of your definition bundle must have at least 75% cumulative test coverage. When you upload your package to AppExchange, all tests are run to ensure that they run without errors. The tests are also run when the package is installed.

For more information on packaging and distributing, see the *ISVforce Guide*.

SEE ALSO:

Testing Your Apex Code

CHAPTER 7   Debugging

In this chapter ...

- Enable Debug Mode for Lightning Components
- Salesforce Lightning Inspector Chrome Extension
- Log Messages
- Warning Messages

There are a few basic tools and techniques that can help you to debug applications.

Use Chrome DevTools to debug your client-side code.

- To open DevTools on Windows and Linux, press Control-Shift-I in your Google Chrome browser. On Mac, press Option-Command-I.

- To quickly find which line of code is failing, enable the **Pause on all exceptions** option before running your code.

To learn more about debugging JavaScript on Google Chrome, refer to the Google Chrome's DevTools website.

Enable Debug Mode for Lightning Components

Enable debug mode to make it easier to debug JavaScript code in your Lightning components.

There are two modes: production and debug. By default, the Lightning Component framework runs in production mode. This mode is optimized for performance. It uses the Google Closure Compiler to optimize and minimize the size of the JavaScript code. The method names and code are heavily obfuscated.

When you enable debug mode, the framework doesn't use Google Closure Compiler so the JavaScript code isn't minimized and is easier to read and debug.

To enable debug mode for your org:

1. From Setup, enter `Lightning Components` in the `Quick Find` box, then select **Lightning Components**.

2. Select the `Enable Debug Mode` checkbox.

3. Click **Save**.

EDITIONS

Available in: Salesforce Classic and Lightning Experience

Available for use in: **Contact Manager, Group, Professional, Enterprise, Performance, Unlimited,** and **Developer** Editions

Create Lightning components using the UI in **Enterprise, Performance, Unlimited, Developer** Editions or a sandbox.

Salesforce Lightning Inspector Chrome Extension

The Salesforce Lightning Inspector is a Google Chrome DevTools extension that enables you to navigate the component tree, inspect component attributes, and profile component performance. The extension also helps you to understand the sequence of event firing and handling.

The extension helps you to:

- Navigate the component tree in your app, inspect components and their associated DOM elements.
- Identify performance bottlenecks by looking at a graph of component creation time.
- Debug server interactions faster by monitoring and modifying responses.
- Test the fault tolerance of your app by simulating error conditions or dropped action responses.
- Track the sequence of event firing and handling for one or more actions.

This documentation assumes that you are familiar with Google Chrome DevTools.

IN THIS SECTION:

Install Salesforce Lightning Inspector
Install the Google Chrome DevTools extension to help you debug and profile component performance.

Use Salesforce Lightning Inspector
The Chrome extension adds a Lightning tab to the DevTools menu. Use it to inspect different aspects of your app.

Install Salesforce Lightning Inspector

Install the Google Chrome DevTools extension to help you debug and profile component performance.

1. In Google Chrome, navigate to the Salesforce Lightning Inspector extension page on the Chrome Web Store.
2. Click the **Add to Chrome** button.

Use Salesforce Lightning Inspector

The Chrome extension adds a Lightning tab to the DevTools menu. Use it to inspect different aspects of your app.

1. Navigate to a Lightning app (the URL should end with .app). For this doc, we're using Lightning Experience (one.app).
2. Open the Chrome DevTools (**More tools** > **Developer tools** in the Chrome control menu). You should see a Lightning tab in the DevTools menu.

There are several sub tabs available to inspect different aspects of your app.

IN THIS SECTION:

Component Tree Tab
This tab shows the component markup including the tree of nested components.

Performance Tab
This tab shows a flame graph of the creation time for your components. Look at longer and deeper portions of the graph for potential performance bottlenecks.

Transactions Tab

This tab shows transactions. Some apps delivered by Salesforce include transaction markers that enable you to see fine-grained metrics for actions within those transactions. You can't create your own transactions currently.

Event Log Tab

This tab shows all the events fired. The event graph helps you to understand the sequence of events and handlers for one or more actions.

Actions Tab

This tab shows the server-side actions executed. The list automatically refreshes when the page updates.

Storage Tab

This tab shows the client-side storage for Lightning applications. Actions marked as storable are stored in the `actions` store. Use this tab to analyze storage in Salesforce1 and Lightning Experience.

Component Tree Tab

This tab shows the component markup including the tree of nested components.

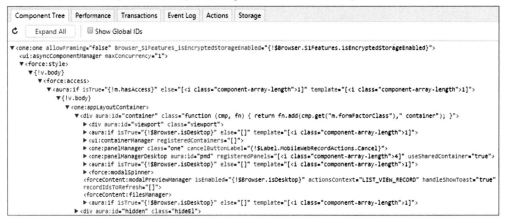

Collapse or Expand Markup

Expand or collapse the component hierarchy by clicking a triangle at the start of a line.

Refresh the Data

The component tree is expensive to serialize, and doesn't respond to component updates. You must manually update the tree when necessary by scrolling to the top of the panel and clicking the Refresh ⟳ icon.

See More Details for a Component

Click a node to see a sidebar with more details for that selected component. While you must manually refresh the component tree, the component details in the sidebar are automatically refreshed.

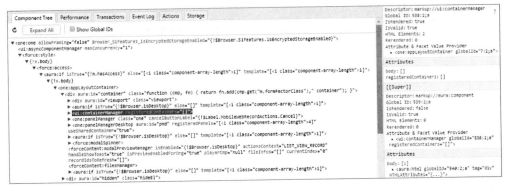

The sidebar contains these sections:

Top Panel

- **Descriptor**—Description of a component in a format of `prefix://namespace:name`

- **Global ID**—The unique identifier for the component for the lifetime of the application

- **IsRendered**—A component can be present in the component tree but not rendered in the app. The component is rendered when it's included in `v.body` or in an expression, such as `{!v.myCmp}`.

- **IsValid**—When a component is destroyed, it becomes invalid. While you can still hold a reference to an invalid component, it should not be used.

- **HTML Elements**—The count of HTML elements for the component (including children components)

- **Rerendered**—The number of times the component has been rerendered since you opened the Inspector. Changing properties on a component makes it dirty, which triggers a rerender. Rerendering can be an expensive operation, and you generally want to avoid it, if possible.

- **Attribute & Facet Value Provider**—The attribute value provider and facet value provider are usually the same component. If so, they are consolidated into one entry.

  The attribute value provider is the component that provides attribute values for expressions. In the following example, the name attribute of `<c:myComponent>` gets its value from the `avpName` attribute of its attribute value provider.

  ```
  <c:myComponent name="{!v.avpName}" />
  ```

  The facet value provider is the value provider for facet attributes (attributes of type `Aura.Component[]`). The facet value provider can be different than the attribute value provider for the component. We won't get into that here as it's complicated! However, it's important to know that if you have expressions in facets, the expressions use the facet value provider instead of the attribute value provider.

Attributes

Shows the attribute values for a component. Use `v.attributeName` when you reference an attribute in an expression or code.

[[Super]]

When a component extends another component, the sub component creates an instance of the super component during its creation. Each of these super components has their own set of properties. `IsRendered` is `false` for any super component instances as only the most specific component (the concrete sub component) is rendered. While a super component has its own attributes section, the super component only has a `body` attribute. All other attribute values are shared in the extension hierarchy.

Model

Some components you see might have a Model section. Models are a deprecated feature and they are included simply for debugging purposes. Don't reference models or your code will break.

Get a Reference to a Component in the Console

Click a component reference anywhere in the Inspector to generate a `$auraTemp` variable that points at that component. You can explore the component further by referring to `$auraTemp` in the Console tab.

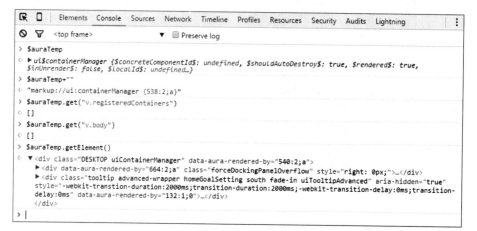

These commands are useful to explore the component contents using the `$auraTemp` variable.

`$auraTemp+""`

Returns the component descriptor.

`$auraTemp.get("v.attributeName")`

Returns the value for the *attributeName* attribute.

`$auraTemp.getElement()`

Returns the corresponding DOM element.

`inspect($auraTemp.getElement())`

Opens the Elements tab and inspects the DOM element for the component.

Performance Tab

This tab shows a flame graph of the creation time for your components. Look at longer and deeper portions of the graph for potential performance bottlenecks.

Record Performance Data

Use the Record ●, Clear ⊘, and Show current collected ıl.ıl buttons to gather performance data about specific user actions or collections of user actions.

1. To start gathering performance data, press ●.

2. Take one or more actions in the app.

3. To stop gathering performance data, press ●.

The flame graph for your actions displays. To see the graph before you stop recording, press the ıl.ıl button.

See More Performance Details for a Component

Hover over a component in the flame graph to see more detailed information about that component in the bottom-left corner. This information includes the component complexity and timing information, and can help to diagnose performance issues.

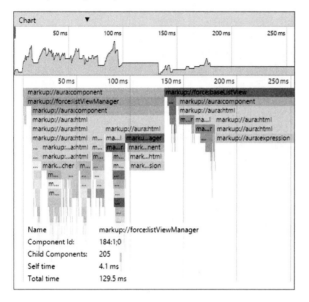

Narrow the Timeline

Drag the vertical handles on the timeline to select a time window to focus on. Zoom in on a smaller time window to inspect component creation time for potential performance hot spots.

Transactions Tab

This tab shows transactions. Some apps delivered by Salesforce include transaction markers that enable you to see fine-grained metrics for actions within those transactions. You can't create your own transactions currently.

See More Transaction Details

Click the ID of a transaction to see more data in the Chrome DevTools Console. Open the Console tab to dig into the details.

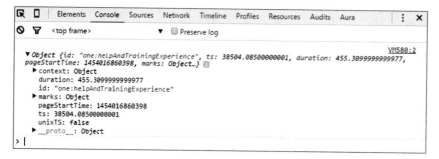

Event Log Tab

This tab shows all the events fired. The event graph helps you to understand the sequence of events and handlers for one or more actions.

Component Tree	Performance	Transactions	Event Log	Actions	Storage

▶ ui:scrollerRefreshed
CMP

▶ ui:carouselPageEvent
CMP

▶ ui:notify
CMP

▶ aura:methodCall
CMP

▶ aura:methodCall
CMP

▶ ui:notify
CMP

Record Events

Use the Toggle recording ● and Clear ⊘ buttons to capture specific user actions or collections of user actions.

1. To start gathering event data, press ●.

2. Take one or more actions in the app.

3. To stop gathering event data, press ●.

View Event Details

Expand an event to see more details.

```
▼ ui:dataChanged
  CMP
  Parameters   +{...}

  Caller       function(component, event, helper) {

                   var evtName = event.getName();
                   var params = event.getParams();
                   var evt = component.getEvent(evtName);
                   if (params) {
                       evt.setParams(params);
                   }
                   evt.fire();
               }

  Source       <force:objectHomeDataProvider globalId="3:12056;a" columns="[]" items="[]" currentPage="1" endIndex="-1"
               pageCount="0" pageSize="50" startIndex="-1" totalItems="0" sortBy="" layoutType="SEARCH" filterName="Recent"
               scope="Opportunity" enableRowActions="false" filteredByLabels="[]" orderedByLabels="[]" emptyContentLabels="
               [2]" lastUpdated="2016-02-01T21:06:26.919Z" canLoadMore="false">

  Duration     10.0250ms

  Handled By   <force:objectHomeListView globalId="1:12056;a" scope="Opportunity" filterName="Recent" dir="ltr"
               actionable="true" ariaDescribedBy="" value="null" visible="true" dataProvider="[1]" emptyContent="[1]"
               selectionHeader="[]" selectionColumn="[]" headerColumns="[]" columns="[]" keyboardNavigation="false" items="
               []" sortBy="" pageSize="50" totalItems="0" layoutType="SEARCH" retryAction="[]" deviceMode="online"
               scrollerPlugin="ActionBar,FixedHeader" hasData="true" doneRendering="true" stencilCols="5" stencilRows="10"
               infiniteLoading="true" recordLayout="[1]" useRowHeaders="true" enableResizableColumns="true"
               resizableColumnsConfig="{...}" displayType="grid" emptyContentLabels="[2]" columnWidths="[6]">
                   c.handleDataChange
```

Filter the List of Events

By default, both application and component events are shown. You can hide or show both types of events by toggling the **App Events** and **Cmp Events** buttons.

Enter a search string in the `Filter` field to match any substring.

Invert the filter by starting the search string with `!`. For example, `!aura` returns all events that don't contain the string `aura`.

Show Unhandled Events

Show events that are fired but are not handled. Unhandled events aren't listed by default but can be useful to see during development.

View Graph of Events

Expand an event to see more details. Click the **Toggle Grid** button to generate a network graph showing the events fired before and after this event, and the components handling those events. Event-driven programming can be confusing when a cacophony of events explode. The event graph helps you to join the dots and understand the sequence of events and handlers.

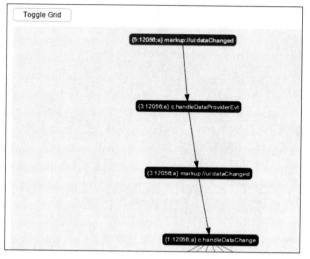

The graph is color coded.

- **Black**—The current event
- **Maroon**—A controller action
- **Blue**—Another event fired before or after the current event

SEE ALSO:

Communicating with Events

Actions Tab

This tab shows the server-side actions executed. The list automatically refreshes when the page updates.

Filter the List of Actions

To filter the list of actions, toggle the buttons related to the different action types or states.

- **Storable**—Storable actions whose responses can be cached.
- **Cached**—Storable actions whose responses are cached. Toggle this button off to show cache misses and non-storable actions. This information can be valuable if you're investigating performance bottlenecks.
- **Background**—Not supported for Lightning components. Available in the open-source Aura framework.
- **Success**—Actions that were executed successfully.
- **Incomplete**—Actions with no server response. The server might be down or the client might be offline.
- **Error**—Actions that returned a server error.
- **Aborted**—Actions that were aborted.

Enter a search string in the `Filter` field to match any substring.

Invert the filter by starting the search string with `!`. For example, `!aura` returns all actions that don't contain the string `aura` and filters out many framework-level actions.

IN THIS SECTION:

Manually Override Server Responses

The Overrides panel on the right side of the Actions tab lets you manually tweak the server responses and investigate the fault tolerance of your app.

SEE ALSO:

Calling a Server-Side Action

Manually Override Server Responses

The Overrides panel on the right side of the Actions tab lets you manually tweak the server responses and investigate the fault tolerance of your app.

Drag an action from the list on the left side to the PENDING OVERRIDES section.

The next time the same action is enqueued to be sent to the server, the framework won't send it. Instead, the framework mocks the response based on the override option that you choose. Here are the override options.

- Override the Result

- Error Response Next Time
- Drop the Action

Note: The same action means an action with the same name. The action parameters don't have to be identical.

IN THIS SECTION:

Modify an Action Response

Modify an action response in the Salesforce Lightning Inspector by changing one of the JSON object values and see how the UI is affected. The server returns a JSON object when you call a server-side action.

Set an Error Response

Your app should degrade gracefully when an error occurs so that users understand what happened or know how to proceed. Use the Salesforce Lightning Inspector to simulate an error condition and see how the user experience is affected.

Drop an Action Response

Your app should degrade gracefully when a server-side action times out or the response is dropped. Use the Salesforce Lightning Inspector to simulate a dropped action response and see how the user experience is affected.

Modify an Action Response

Modify an action response in the Salesforce Lightning Inspector by changing one of the JSON object values and see how the UI is affected. The server returns a JSON object when you call a server-side action.

1. Drag the action whose response you want to modify to the PENDING OVERRIDES section.
2. Select Override the Result in the drop-down list.
3. Select a response key to modify in the `Key` field.
4. Enter a modified value for the key in the `New Value` field.

5. Click **Save**.

6. To trigger execution of the action, refresh the page.
   The modified action response moves from the PENDING OVERRIDES section to the PROCESSED OVERRIDES section.

7. Note the UI change, if any, related to your change.

Set an Error Response

Your app should degrade gracefully when an error occurs so that users understand what happened or know how to proceed. Use the Salesforce Lightning Inspector to simulate an error condition and see how the user experience is affected.

1. Drag the action whose response you want to modify to the PENDING OVERRIDES section.

2. Select Error Response Next Time in the drop-down list.

3. Add an `Error Message`.

4. Add some text in the `Error Stack` field.

336

5. Click **Save**.

6. To trigger execution of the action, refresh the page.

   - The modified action response moves from the PENDING OVERRIDES section to the PROCESSED OVERRIDES section.

   - The action response displays in the COMPLETED section in the left panel with a `State` equals `ERROR`.

7. Note the UI change, if any, related to your change. The UI should handle errors by alerting the user or allowing them to continue using the app.

To degrade gracefully, make sure that your action response callback handles an error response (`response.getState() === "ERROR"`).

SEE ALSO:

Calling a Server-Side Action

Drop an Action Response

Your app should degrade gracefully when a server-side action times out or the response is dropped. Use the Salesforce Lightning Inspector to simulate a dropped action response and see how the user experience is affected.

1. Drag the action whose response you want to modify to the PENDING OVERRIDES section.

2. Select Drop the Action in the drop-down list.

3. To trigger execution of the action, refresh the page.

   • The modified action response moves from the PENDING OVERRIDES section to the PROCESSED OVERRIDES section.

   • The action response displays in the COMPLETED section in the left panel with a `State` equals `INCOMPLETE`.

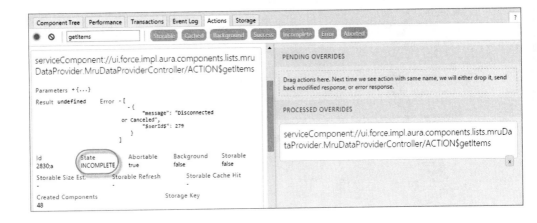

4. Note the UI change, if any, related to your change. The UI should handle the dropped action by alerting the user or allowing them to continue using the app.

   To degrade gracefully, make sure that your action response callback handles an incomplete response (`response.getState() === "INCOMPLETE"`).

SEE ALSO:

Calling a Server-Side Action

Storage Tab

This tab shows the client-side storage for Lightning applications. Actions marked as storable are stored in the `actions` store. Use this tab to analyze storage in Salesforce1 and Lightning Experience.

Component Tree	Performance	Transactions	Event Log	Actions	Storage

```
c

- {
    "actions": - {
        "Adapter": "crypto",
        "sizeEstimate": "1017.4 KB (10% of 10240 KB)",
        "Version": "37.0",
        "Items": +{...}
    },
    "objectHomeStateManager": - {
        "Adapter": "indexeddb",
        "sizeEstimate": "0.0 KB (0% of 2048 KB)",
        "Version": "1.0",
        "Items": {}
    },
    "ComponentDefStorage": - {
        "Adapter": "indexeddb",
        "sizeEstimate": "1199.7 KB (30% of 4000 KB)",
        "Version": "37.0",
        "Items": +{...}
    }
}
```

SEE ALSO:

Caching with Storage Service

Log Messages

To help debug your client-side code, you can write output to the JavaScript console of a web browser.

Use the $A.log(string[, error]) method to output a log message to the JavaScript console. The first parameter is the string to log.

The optional second parameter is an error object that can include more detail.

 Note: $A.log() doesn't output by default for Lightning components, which run in either PROD or PRODDEBUG modes. To log messages in PROD or PRODDEBUG modes, see Logging in Production Modes on page 341. Alternatively, use console.log() if your browser supports it.

For example, $A.log("This is a log message") outputs to the JavaScript console:

```
This is a log message
```

Adding $A.log("The name of the action is: " + this.getDef().getName()) in an action called openNote in a client-side controller outputs to the JavaScript console:

```
The name of the action is: openNote
```

For instructions on using the JavaScript console, refer to the instructions for your web browser.

Logging in Production Modes

To log messages in `PROD` or `PRODDEBUG` modes, write a custom logging function. You must use `$A.logger.subscribe(String level, function callback)` to subscribe to log messages at a certain severity level.

The first parameter is the severity level you're subscribing to. The valid values are:

- `ASSERT`
- `ERROR`
- `INFO`
- `WARNING`

The second parameter is the callback function that will be called when a message at the subscribed severity level is logged.

Note that `$A.log()` logs a message at the `INFO` severity level. Adding `$A.logger.subscribe("INFO", logCustom)` causes `$A.log()` to log using the custom `logCustom()` function you define.

Let's look at some sample JavaScript code in a client-side controller.

```
({
    sampleControllerAction: function(cmp) {
        // subscribe to severity levels
        $A.logger.subscribe("INFO", logCustom);
        // Following subscriptions not exercised here but shown for
completeness
        //$A.logger.subscribe("WARNING", logCustom);
        //$A.logger.subscribe("ASSERT", logCustom);
        //$A.logger.subscribe("ERROR", logCustom);

        $A.log("log one arg");
        $A.log("log two args", {message: "drat and double drat"});

        function logCustom(level, message, error) {
            console.log(getTimestamp(), "logCustom: ", arguments);
        }

        function getTimestamp() {
            return new Date().toJSON();
        }
    }
})
```

341

`$A.logger.subscribe("INFO", logCustom)` subscribes so that messages logged at the `INFO` severity level will call the `logCustom()` function. In this case, `logCustom()` simply logs the message to the console with a timestamp.

The `$A.log()` calls log messages at the `INFO` severity level, which matches the subscription and invokes the `logCustom()` callback.

Warning Messages

To help debug your client-side code, you can use the `warning()` method to write output to the JavaScript console of your web browser.

Use the `$A.warning(string)` method to write a warning message to the JavaScript console. The parameter is the message to display.

For example, `$A.warning("This is a warning message.");` outputs to the JavaScript console.

```
This is a warning message.
```

Note: `$A.warning()` doesn't output by default for Lightning components, which run in either `PROD` or `PRODDEBUG` modes. To log warning messages in `PROD` or `PRODDEBUG` modes, use `$A.logger.subscribe("WARNING", logCustom)`, where `logCustom()` is a custom function that you define. For more information, see Logging in Production Modes on page 341.

For instructions on using the JavaScript console, refer to the instructions for your web browser.

CHAPTER 8   Reference

In this chapter ...

- Reference Doc App
- Supported
  aura:attribute Types
- aura:application
- aura:dependency
- aura:event
- aura:interface
- aura:method
- aura:set

This section contains reference documentation including details of the various tags available in the framework.

Reference Doc App

The reference doc app includes reference information, including descriptions and source for the out-of-the-box components that come with the framework, as well as the JavaScript API. Access the app at:

`https://<myDomain>.lightning.force.com/auradocs/reference.app`, where `<myDomain>` is the name of your custom Salesforce domain.

Supported aura:attribute Types

`aura:attribute` describes an attribute available on an app, interface, component, or event.

Attribute Name	Type	Description
access	String	Indicates whether the attribute can be used outside of its own namespace. Possible values are `public` (default), and `global`, and `private`.
name	String	Required. The name of the attribute. For example, if you set `<aura:attribute name="isTrue" type="Boolean" />` on a component called `aura:newCmp`, you can set this attribute when you instantiate the component; for example,`<aura:newCmp isTrue="false" />`.
type	String	Required. The type of the attribute. For a list of basic types supported, see Basic Types.
default	String	The default value for the attribute, which can be overwritten as needed. When setting a default value, expressions using the `$Label`, `$Locale`, and `$Browser` global value providers are supported. Alternatively, to set a dynamic default, use an `init` event. See Invoking Actions on Component Initialization on page 262.
required	Boolean	Determines if the attribute is required. The default is `false`.
description	String	A summary of the attribute and its usage.

All `<aura:attribute>` tags have name and type values. For example:

```
<aura:attribute name="whom" type="String" />
```

 Note: Although type values are case insensitive, case sensitivity should be respected as your markup interacts with JavaScript, CSS, and Apex.

SEE ALSO:

Component Attributes

Basic Types

Here are the supported basic type values. Some of these types correspond to the wrapper objects for primitives in Java. Since the framework is written in Java, defaults, such as maximum size for a number, for these basic types are defined by the Java objects that they map to.

type	Example	Description
Boolean	`<aura:attribute name="showDetail" type="Boolean" />`	Valid values are `true` or `false`. To set a default value of `true`, add `default="true"`.
Date	`<aura:attribute name="startDate" type="Date" />`	A date corresponding to a calendar day in the format yyyy-mm-dd. The hh:mm:ss portion of the date is not stored. To include time fields, use `DateTime` instead.
DateTime	`<aura:attribute name="lastModifiedDate" type="DateTime" />`	A date corresponding to a timestamp. It includes date and time details with millisecond precision.
Decimal	`<aura:attribute name="totalPrice" type="Decimal" />`	`Decimal` values can contain fractional portions (digits to the right of the decimal). Maps to java.math.BigDecimal. `Decimal` is better than `Double` for maintaining precision for floating-point calculations. It's preferable for currency fields.

type	Example	Description

Double	`<aura:attribute`
	`name="widthInchesFractional"`
	`type="Double" />`
		`Double` values can contain fractional portions. Maps to java.lang.Double. Use `Decimal` for currency fields instead.

Integer	`<aura:attribute`
	`name="numRecords"`
	`type="Integer" />`
		`Integer` values can contain numbers with no fractional portion. Maps to java.lang.Integer, which defines its limits, such as maximum size.

Long	`<aura:attribute`
	`name="numSwissBankAccount"`
	`type="Long" />`
		`Long` values can contain numbers with no fractional portion. Maps to java.lang.Long, which defines its limits, such as maximum size.
		
		Use this data type when you need a range of values wider than those provided by `Integer`.

String	`<aura:attribute`
	`name="message"`
	`type="String" />`
		A sequence of characters.

You can use arrays for each of these basic types. For example:

```
<aura:attribute name="favoriteColors" type="String[]"
default="['red','green','blue']" />
```

Retrieving Data from an Apex Controller

To retrieve the string array from an Apex controller, bind the component to the controller. This component retrieves the string array when a button is clicked.

```
<aura:component controller="namespace.AttributeTypes">
   <aura:attribute name="favoriteColors" type="String[]" default="cyan,
 yellow, magenta"/>
    <aura:iteration items="{!v.favoriteColors}" var="s">
        {!s}
    </aura:iteration>
```

```
        <ui:button press="{!c.getString}" label="Update"/>
</aura:component>
```

Set the Apex controller to return a `List<String>` object.

```
public class AttributeTypes {
    private final String[] arrayItems;

 @AuraEnabled
    public static List<String> getStringArray() {
        String[] arrayItems = new String[]{ 'red', 'green', 'blue' };

        return arrayItems;
    }

}
```

This client-side controller retrieves the string array from the Apex controller and displays it using the `{!v.favoriteColors}` expression.

```
({
    getString : function(component, event) {
    var action = component.get("c.getStringArray");
     action.setCallback(this, function(response) {
            var state = response.getState();
            if (state === "SUCCESS") {
                var stringItems = response.getReturnValue();
                component.set("v.favoriteColors", stringItems);
            }
        });
        $A.enqueueAction(action);
    }
})
```

Object Types

An attribute can have a type corresponding to an Object.

```
<aura:attribute name="data" type="Object" />
```

For example, you may want to create an attribute of type `Object` to pass a JavaScript array as an event parameter. In the component event, declare the event parameter using `aura:attribute`.

```
<aura:event type="COMPONENT">
    <aura:attribute name="arrayAsObject" type="Object" />
<aura:event>
```

In JavaScript code, you can set the attribute of type `Object`.

```
// Set the event parameters
var event = component.getEvent(eventType);
event.setParams({
    arrayAsObject:["file1", "file2", "file3"]
});
event.fire();
```

Checking for Types

To determine a variable type, use `typeof` or a standard JavaScript method instead. The `instanceof` operator is unreliable due to the potential presence of multiple windows or frames.

SEE ALSO:

Working with Salesforce Records

Standard and Custom Object Types

An attribute can have a type corresponding to a standard or custom object. For example, this is an attribute for a standard `Account` object:

```
<aura:attribute name="acct" type="Account" />
```

This is an attribute for an `Expense__c` custom object:

```
<aura:attribute name="expense" type="Expense__c" />
```

 Note: Make your Apex class methods, getter and setter methods, available to your components by annotating them with `@AuraEnabled`.

SEE ALSO:

Working with Salesforce Records

Collection Types

Here are the supported collection type values.

type	Example	Description
type[] (Array)	```<aura:attribute name="colorPalette" type="String[]" default="['red', 'green', 'blue']" />```	An array of items of a defined type.
List	```<aura:attribute name="colorPalette" type="List" default="['red', 'green', 'blue']" />```	An ordered collection of items.
Map	```<aura:attribute name="sectionLabels" type="Map" default="{ a: 'label1', b: 'label2' }" />```	A collection that maps keys to values. A map can't contain duplicate keys. Each key can map to at most one value. Defaults to an empty object, {}. Retrieve values by using `cmp.get("v.sectionLabels")['a']`.
Set	```<aura:attribute name="collection" type="Set" default="['red', 'green', 'blue']" />```	A collection that contains no duplicate elements. The order for set items is not guaranteed. For example, `"red,green,blue"` might be returned as `"blue,green,red"`.

Checking for Types

To determine a variable type, use `typeof` or a standard JavaScript method, such as `Array.isArray()`, instead. The `instanceof` operator is unreliable due to the potential presence of multiple windows or frames.

Setting List Items

There are several ways to set items in a list. To use a client-side controller, create an attribute of type List and set the items using `component.set()`.

This example retrieves a list of numbers from a client-side controller when a button is clicked.

```
<aura:attribute name="numbers" type="List"/>
<ui:button press="{!c.getNumbers}" label="Display Numbers" />
<aura:iteration var="num" items="{!v.numbers}">
  {!num.value}
</aura:iteration>
```

```
/** Client-side Controller **/
({
  getNumbers: function(component, event, helper) {
    var numbers = [];
    for (var i = 0; i < 20; i++) {
      numbers.push({
        value: i
      });
    }
    component.set("v.numbers", numbers);
  }
})
```

To retrieve list data from a controller, use `aura:iteration`.

Setting Map Items

To add a key and value pair to a map, use the syntax `myMap['myNewKey'] = myNewValue`.

```
var myMap = cmp.get("v.sectionLabels");
myMap['c'] = 'label3';
```

The following example retrieves data from a map.

```
for (key in myMap){
    //do something
}
```

Custom Apex Class Types

An attribute can have a type corresponding to an Apex class. For example, this is an attribute for a `Color` Apex class:

```
<aura:attribute name="color" type="docSampleNamespace.Color" />
```

Using Arrays

If an attribute can contain more than one element, use an array.

This `aura:attribute` tag shows the syntax for an array of Apex objects:

```
<aura:attribute name="colorPalette" type="docSampleNamespace.Color[]"
 />
```

 Note: Make your Apex class methods, getter and setter methods, available to your components by annotating them with `@AuraEnabled`.

SEE ALSO:

Working with Salesforce Records

Framework-Specific Types

Here are the supported type values that are specific to the framework.

type	Example	Description
`Aura.Component`	N/A	A single component. We recommend using `Aura.Component[]` instead.
`Aura.Component[]`	`<aura:attribute name="detail" type="Aura.Component[]"/>` To set a default value for `type="Aura.Component[]"`,	Use this type to set blocks of markup. An attribute of type

type	Example	Description
	put the default markup in the body of `aura:attribute`. For example: ```<aura:component> <aura:attribute name="detail" type="Aura.Component[]"> <p>default paragraph1</p> </aura:attribute> Default value is: {!v.detail}</aura:component>```	`Aura.Component[]` is called a facet.

SEE ALSO:

Component Body

Component Facets

aura:application

An app is a special top-level component whose markup is in a `.app` resource.

The markup looks similar to HTML and can contain components as well as a set of supported HTML tags. The `.app` resource is a standalone entry point for the app and enables you to define the overall application layout, style sheets, and global JavaScript includes. It starts with the top-level `<aura:application>` tag, which contains optional system attributes. These system attributes tell the framework how to configure the app.

System Attribute	Type	Description
access	String	Indicates whether the app can be extended by another app outside of a namespace. Possible values are `public` (default), and `global`.

System Attribute	Type	Description
controller	String	The server-side controller class for the app. The format is `namespace.myController`.
description	String	A brief description of the app.
extends	Component	The app to be extended, if applicable. For example, `extends="namespace:yourApp"`.
extensible	Boolean	Indicates whether the app is extensible by another app. Defaults to `false`.
implements	String	A comma-separated list of interfaces that the app implements.
template	Component	The name of the template used to bootstrap the loading of the framework and the app. The default value is `aura:template`. You can customize the template by creating your own component that extends the default template. For example: `<aura:component extends="aura:template" ... >`
useAppcache	Boolean	Specifies whether to use the application cache. Valid options are `true` or `false`. Defaults to `false`.

`aura:application` also includes a `body` attribute defined in a `<aura:attribute>` tag. Attributes usually control the output or behavior of a component, but not the configuration information in system attributes.

Attribute	Type	Description
body	Component[]	The body of the app. In markup, this is everything in the body of the tag.

SEE ALSO:

Creating Apps

Using the AppCache

Application Access Control

aura:dependency

The `<aura:dependency>` tag enables you to declare dependencies that can't easily be discovered by the framework.

The framework automatically tracks dependencies between definitions, such as components. This enables the framework to automatically reload when it detects that you've changed a definition during development. However, if a component uses a client- or server-side provider that instantiates components that are not directly referenced in the component's markup, use `<aura:dependency>` in the component's markup to explicitly tell the framework about the dependency. Adding the `<aura:dependency>` tag ensures that a component and its dependencies are sent to the client, when needed.

For example, adding this tag to a component marks the `aura:placeholder` component as a dependency.

```
<aura:dependency resource="markup://aura:placeholder" />
```

The `<aura:dependency>` tag includes these system attributes.

System Attribute	Description
resource	The resource that the component depends on. For example, `resource="markup://sampleNamespace:sampleComponent"` refers to the `sampleComponent` in the `sampleNamespace` namespace.
	Use an asterisk (`*`) in the resource name for wildcard matching. For example, `resource="markup://sampleNamespace:*"` matches everything in the namespace;

System Attribute	Description
	`resource="markup://sampleNamespace:input*"` matches everything in the namespace that starts with `input`.
	Don't use an asterisk (*) in the namespace portion of the resource name. For example, `resource="markup://sample*:sampleComponent"` is not supported.
`type`	The type of resource that the component depends on. The default value is `COMPONENT`. Use `type="*"` to match all types of resources. The most commonly used values are: • `COMPONENT` • `APPLICATION` • `EVENT` Use a comma-separated list for multiple types; for example: `COMPONENT,APPLICATION`.

SEE ALSO:

Dynamically Creating Components

aura:event

An event is represented by the `aura:event` tag, which has the following attributes.

Attribute	Type	Description
`access`	String	Indicates whether the event can be extended or used outside of its own namespace. Possible values are `public` (default), and `global`.
`description`	String	A description of the event.
`extends`	Component	The event to be extended. For example, `extends="namespace:myEvent"`.

Attribute	Type	Description
type	String	Required. Possible values are COMPONENT or APPLICATION.

SEE ALSO:

Communicating with Events

Event Access Control

aura:interface

The `aura:interface` tag has the following optional attributes.

Attribute	Type	Description
access	String	Indicates whether the interface can be extended or used outside of its own namespace. Possible values are public (default), and global.
description	String	A description of the interface.
extends	Component	The comma-seperated list of interfaces to be extended. For example, extends="namespace:intfB".

SEE ALSO:

Interfaces

Interface Access Control

aura:method

Use `<aura:method>` to define a method as part of a component's API. This enables you to directly call a method in a component's client-side controller instead of firing and handling a component event. Using `<aura:method>` simplifies the code needed for a parent component to call a method on a child component that it contains.

The `<aura:method>` tag has these system attributes.

Attribute	Type	Description
name	String	The method name. Use the method name to call the method in JavaScript code. For example: `cmp.sampleMethod(param1);`
action	Expression	The client-side controller action to execute. For example: `action="{!c.sampleAction}"` `sampleAction` is an action in the client-side controller. If you don't specify an `action` value, the controller action defaults to the value of the method `name`.
access	String	The access control for the method. Valid values are: • **public**—Any component in the same namespace can call the method. This is the default access level. • **global**—Any component in any namespace can call the method.
description	String	The method description.

Declaring Parameters

An `<aura:method>` can optionally include parameters. Use an `<aura:attribute>` tag within an `<aura:method>` to declare a parameter for the method. For example:

```
<aura:method name="sampleMethod" action="{!c.doAction}" access="PUBLIC"

  description="Sample method with parameters">
    <aura:attribute name="param1" type="String" default="parameter
1"/>
    <aura:attribute name="param2" type="Object" />
</aura:method>
```

📝 Note: You don't need an `access` system attribute in the `<aura:attribute>` tag for a parameter.

357

Creating a Handler Action

This handler action shows how to access the arguments passed to the method.

```
({
    doAction : function(cmp, event) {
        var params = event.getParam('arguments');
        if (params) {
            var param1 = params.param1;
            // add your code here
        }
    }
})
```

Retrieve the arguments using `event.getParam('arguments')`. It returns an object if there are arguments or an empty array if there are no arguments.

SEE ALSO:

Calling Component Methods

Component Events

aura:set

Use `<aura:set>` in markup to set the value of an attribute inherited from a super component, event, or interface.

To learn more, see:

- Setting Attributes Inherited from a Super Component
- Setting Attributes on a Component Reference
- Setting Attributes Inherited from an Interface

Setting Attributes Inherited from a Super Component

Use `<aura:set>` in the markup of a sub component to set the value of an inherited attribute.

Let's look at an example. Here is the `c:setTagSuper` component.

```
<!--c:setTagSuper-->
<aura:component extensible="true">
    <aura:attribute name="address1" type="String" />
```

```
    setTagSuper address1: {!v.address1}<br/>
</aura:component>
```

`c:setTagSuper` outputs:

```
setTagSuper address1:
```

The `address1` attribute doesn't output any value yet as it hasn't been set.

Here is the `c:setTagSub` component that extends `c:setTagSuper`.

```
<!--c:setTagSub-->
<aura:component extends="c:setTagSuper">
    <aura:set attribute="address1" value="808 State St" />
</aura:component>
```

`c:setTagSub` outputs:

```
setTagSuper address1: 808 State St
```

`sampleSetTagExc:setTagSub` sets a value for the `address1` attribute inherited from the super component, `c:setTagSuper`.

> Warning: This usage of `<aura:set>` works for components and abstract components, but it doesn't work for interfaces. For more information, see Setting Attributes Inherited from an Interface on page 360.

If you're using a component by making a reference to it in your component, you can set the attribute value directly in the markup. For example, `c:setTagSuperRef` makes a reference to `c:setTagSuper` and sets the `address1` attribute directly without using `aura:set`.

```
<!--c:setTagSuperRef-->
<aura:component>
    <c:setTagSuper address1="1 Sesame St" />
</aura:component>
```

`c:setTagSuperRef` outputs:

```
setTagSuper address1: 1 Sesame St
```

SEE ALSO:

Component Body

Inherited Component Attributes

Setting Attributes on a Component Reference

Setting Attributes on a Component Reference

When you include another component, such as `<ui:button>`, in a component, we call that a component reference to `<ui:button>`. You can use `<aura:set>` to set an attribute on the component reference. For example, if your component includes a reference to `<ui:button>`:

```
<ui:button label="Save">
    <aura:set attribute="buttonTitle" value="Click to save the record"/>
</ui:button>
```

This is equivalent to:

```
<ui:button label="Save" buttonTitle="Click to save the record" />
```

The latter syntax without `aura:set` makes more sense in this simple example. You can also use this simpler syntax in component references to set values for attributes that are inherited from parent components.

`aura:set` is more useful when you want to set markup as the attribute value. For example, this sample specifies the markup for the `else` attribute in the `aura:if` tag.

```
<aura:component>
    <aura:attribute name="display" type="Boolean" default="true"/>
    <aura:if isTrue="{!v.display}">
        Show this if condition is true
        <aura:set attribute="else">
            <ui:button label="Save" press="{!c.saveRecord}" />
        </aura:set>
    </aura:if>
</aura:component>
```

SEE ALSO:

Setting Attributes Inherited from a Super Component

Setting Attributes Inherited from an Interface

To set the value of an attribute inherited from an interface, redefine the attribute in the component and set its default value. Let's look at an example with the `c:myIntf` interface.

```
<!--c:myIntf-->
<aura:interface>
    <aura:attribute name="myBoolean" type="Boolean" default="true" />
</aura:interface>
```

This component implements the interface and sets `myBoolean` to `false`.

```
<!--c:myIntfImpl-->
<aura:component implements="c:myIntf">
    <aura:attribute name="myBoolean" type="Boolean" default="false"
/>

    <p>myBoolean: {!v.myBoolean}</p>
</aura:component>
```

INDEX

$Browser 79, 81
$Label 79, 97
$Locale 79, 82
$Resource 85

A

Access control
    application 307
    attribute 308
    component 308
    event 309
    interface 308
    JavaScript 263
Accessibility
    audio messages 134
    buttons 133
    events 135
    help and error messages 133
    menus 135
Actions
    calling server-side 285
    queueing 288
    storable 290
Anti-patterns
    events 191
Apex
    API calls 304
    controllers 282–284
    custom objects 293
    deleting records 300
    Lightning components 292
    records 293
    saving records 298
    standard objects 293
API calls 270, 304
app design 39

Application
    attributes 352
    aura:application 352
    building and running 7
    creating 201
    layout and UI 202
    styling 221
Application cache
    browser support 317
    enabling 318
    loading 318
    overview 317
Application events
    handling 178
Application templates
    external CSS 202
    JavaScript libraries 202
application, creating 9
application, static mockup 16
Applications
    CSS 223, 227–229, 231–233, 246
    overview 202
    styling 223, 227–229, 231–233, 246
    token 227–229, 231–233, 246
Apps
    overview 202
Attribute types
    Aura.Action 351
    Aura.Component 351
    basic 345
    collection 349
    custom Apex class 351
    custom object 348
    Object 347
    standard object 348
Attribute value, setting 358

Attributes
    component reference, setting on 360
    interface, setting on 360
    JavaScript 253
    super component, setting on 358
aura:application 352
aura:attribute 344
aura:dependency 354
aura:event 355
aura:if 73, 78
aura:interface 356
aura:method 356
aura:renderIf 73
aura:set 358, 360
aura:template 202
authentication 149

B

Benefits 2
Best practices
    events 190
Body
    JavaScript 254
Bubbling 168
Buttons
    local ID 279
    pressed 279

C

Chrome extension 322
Client-side controllers 162
Community Builder
    configuring custom components 150
    creating custom layouts 151
Component
    abstract 313
    attributes 65
    aura:interface 356
    body, setting and accessing 70
    documentation 103

Component (continued)
    nest 67
    rendering lifecycle 192
    themes, vendor prefixes 226
Component attributes
    inheritance 311
Component body
    JavaScript 254
Component bundles
    configuring for Community Builder 150
    configuring for Lightning App Builder 153,
        156, 158, 225
    configuring for Lightning Experience Record
        Home pages 158
    configuring for Lightning Experience record
        pages 156
    configuring for Lightning Pages 153, 156,
        158, 225
    tips for configuring for Lightning App Builder
        158
Component definitions
    dependency 354
Component events
    handling 168
    handling dynamically 173
Component facets 72
component, creating 19, 31
component, nested 29
Components
    access control 263
    calling methods 269
    conditional markup 73
    creating 271
    CSS 223, 227–229, 231–233, 246
    HTML markup, using 63
    ID, local and global 61
    markup 51–52
    methods 356
    modifying 263
    namespace 54–56

Components *(continued)*
   overview 51
   styling 223, 227–229, 231–233, 246
   styling with CSS 63
   support level 51
   token 227–229, 231–233, 246
   unescaping HTML 63
   using 137
Conditional expressions 78
Content security policy 204
Controllers
   calling server-side actions 285
   client-side 162
   creating server-side 282–283
   server-side 284
Cookbook
   JavaScript 271
CRUD access 296
CSP 204
CSS
   external 223
   tokens 227–229, 231–233, 246
Custom labels 97
custom layouts
   creating for Community Builder 151
custom object, create 13

D

Data changes
   detecting 275
Debug
   JavaScript 322
Debugging
   Chrome extension 322
   Salesforce Lightning Inspector 322
dependency 145
Detecting
   data changes 275
Developer Console 4
Developer Edition organization, sign up 8

DOM 250
Dynamic output 77

E

Errors
   handling 266
   throwing 266
Event bubbling 168
Event handlers 276
Events
   anti-patterns 191
   application 176, 178
   aura:event 355
   best practices 190
   bubbling 168
   component 166, 173
   demo 183
   example 173, 178
   firing from non-Lightning code 189
   handling 181
   Salesforce1 197
   Salesforce1 and Lightning Experience demo 41
   Salesforce1 demo 43, 47
   system 198
Events and actions 164
Expressions
   conditional 78
   dynamic output 77
   format() 99
   functions 92
   operators 88

F

Field-level security 296
format() 99

G

globalID 79

H

Handling Input Field Errors 264
Helpers 256
HTML, unescaping 63

I

Inheritance 310, 315
Input Field Validation 264
Inspector
    Actions tab 332
    Component Tree tab 324
    drop the action 338
    error response 336
    Event Log tab 330
    install 323
    modify action response 335
    override actions 334
    Performance tab 327
    Storage tab 339
    Transactions tab 329
    use 323
Interfaces
    marker 315
Introduction 1–2

J

JavaScript
    access control 263
    API calls 270
    attribute values 253
    calling component methods 269
    component 254
    get() and set() methods 253
    libraries 251
    sharing code in bundle 256
    strict mode 205
JavaScript console 340
JavaScript cookbook 271

L

Label
    setting via parent attribute 100
Label parameters 99
Labels 97–98
Lifecycle 263
Lightning 2
Lightning App Builder
    configuring custom components 153, 156,
        158, 225
    CSS tips 225
Lightning CLI 206–213, 215–216, 218, 220
Lightning components
    Lightning Experience 140
    Salesforce1 139
Lightning Components for Visualforce 145
Lightning Experience
    add Lightning components 140
Lightning Out
    beta 149
    Connected App 145
    considerations 149
    CORS 145
    events 149
    limitations 149
    OAuth 145
    requirements 145
    SLDS 149
    styling 149
loading data 25
Localization 101
LockerService 205–213, 215–216, 218, 220
Log messages 340

M

Markup 277

N

Namespace
    creating 56
    default 54
    examples 56
    explicit 55
    implicit 54
    organization 55
    prefix 55
Node.js 143

O

OAuth 149
Object-oriented development
    inheritance 310
Online version 6
Open source 3

P

Package 54–56
Packaging 303, 319
Prerequisites 8

Q

Queueing
    queueing server-side actions 288
Quick start, install package 11
quick start, summary 39

R

Reference
    doc app 344
    overview 343
Renderers 258
Rendering lifecycle 192
Rerendering 263

S

Salesforce Lightning Inspector
    Actions tab 332
    Component Tree tab 324
    drop the action 338
    error response 336
    Event Log tab 330
    install 323
    modify action response 335
    override actions 334
    Performance tab 327
    Storage tab 339
    Transactions tab 329
    use 323
Salesforce1
    add Lightning components 139
Security 203
Server-Side Controllers
    action queueing 288
    calling actions 285
    creating 283
    errors 284
    overview 282
SharePoint 143
Static resource 85
Storable actions 290
Storage service
    adapters 315
    initializing 316
    MemoryAdapter 315
    SmartStore 315
    WebSQL 315
Styles 278
Styling
    join 222
    markup 222
    readable 222

T

Ternary operator 78
Themes
    vendor prefixes 226
Tokens
    Communities 246
    design 227–229, 231–233, 246
    force:base 233

U

ui components
    actionMenuItem 130
    aura:component inheritance 106
    button 123
    checkbox 119
    checkboxMenuItem 130
    inputCurrency 113
    inputDate 111
    inputDateTime 111
    inputDefaultError 130
    inputEmail 116
    inputNumber 113
    inputPhone 116
    inputRadio 121
    inputRichText 116, 118
    inputSecret 116
    inputSelect 125
    inputSelect, using Apex 128
    inputText 116
    inputTextArea 116

ui components *(continued)*
    inputURL 116
    menu 130
    menuItemSeparator 130
    menuTrigger 130
    menuTriggerLink 130
    outputCurrency 113
    outputDate 111
    outputDateTime 111
    outputEmail 116
    outputNumber 113
    outputPhone 116
    outputRichText 116, 118
    outputText 116
    outputTextArea 116
    outputURL 116
    radioMenuItem 130
ui components overview 110
ui events 109

V

Value providers
    $Browser 81
    $Label 97
    $Resource 85
versioning 74
Visualforce 141

W

Warnings 342

Notes

Notes

Notes

Notes

Notes

Notes